World of Hockey
Celebrating a Century of the IIHF

Edited by
Szymon Szemberg and Andrew Podnieks

IIHF

WORLD OF HOCKEY
Celebrating a Century of the IIHF

A Fenn Publishing Book / First Published in 2007

Fenn Publishing Company Ltd.
Bolton, Ontario, Canada
www.hbfenn.com

The publisher gratefully acknowledges the support of the Canada Council for the Arts and the Ontario Arts Council for its publishing program. We acknowledge the support of the Government of Ontario through the Ontario Media Development Corporation's Ontario Book Initiative.

We acknowledge the financial support of the Government of Canada through the Book Publishing Industry Development Program (BPIDP) for our publishing activities.

Care has been taken to trace ownership of copyright material in this book and to secure permissions. The publishers will gladly receive any information that will enable them to rectify errors or omissions.

Text design: Laura Brunton

Printed and bound in Canada

Library and Archives Canada Cataloguing in Publication

    World of hockey : celebrating a century of the IIHF / Andrew Podnieks, general editor.

ISBN 978-1-55168-307-2

    1. International Ice Hockey Federation--History. 2. Hockey--Tournaments-- History. I. Podnieks, Andrew
GV846.5.W67 2007   796.962'66   C2007-903071-8

World of Hockey

Celebrating a Century of the IIHF

Edited by

Szymon Szemberg and Andrew Podnieks

Fenn Publishing Company Ltd.

Bolton, Ontario

The McGill University Team at Montreal's Crystal Palace Rink in 1881 — the world's first extant photograph of a hockey team.

CONTENTS

IIHF President René Fasel stands on the exact spot of land in Les Avants, Switzerland where the first LIHG European championships were played, (insert) in 1910.

FROM LES AVANTS TO QUEBEC CITY – A CIRCLE COMPLETED

It's highly improbable that the eight people representing four countries who met at a local sports club at 34 rue de Provence in Paris on May 15, 1908, in even their wildest dreams could have imagined that 65 nations on all five continents would a hundred years later celebrate the centennial of the organization they founded. What initially was named Ligue Internationale de Hockey sur Glace (LIHG) eventually became the International Ice Hockey Federation (IIHF) and ultimately developed into one of the most successful and enduring Olympic team sport federations in the world.

Magnus, a Frenchman, became the organization's first president, and his colleagues from Belgium, Switzerland, and Great Britain worked to internationalize a sport whose structures where vague and whose rules far from uniform. On many occasions in those early years neither the players nor spectators were entirely sure if the game in which they were participating was truly ice hockey or merely a small-ice version of bandy. Today, there is no doubt which is which.

The first international hockey games under the auspices of the LIHG were played in the tiny village of Les Avants, in 1910, in the French-speaking part of Switzerland near Montreux. For the participating players ice hockey was nothing more than a pastime. Today, as we celebrate the first ever IIHF World Championship in Canada, the motherland of the game, hockey boasts the biggest attendance numbers of all sports in the Olympic Winter Games. The IIHF's flagship event, the World Championship, is the biggest annual winter sport championship in the world.

Even though this book is written on the occasion of 100 years of the IIHF, it is not our intention to celebrate ourselves. That is why we devote this book to those who made this game grow to what it is today. The teams, the players, and the great events are what make the IIHF compelling.

By going to Halifax and Quebec City for the 2008 IIHF World Championship, we close a perfect circle. The game developed in eastern Canada in the second half of the nineteenth century and came to Europe in the early 1900s when the LIHG/IIHF was given the mandate by its ever-increasing membership to structure and to develop the sport worldwide. Now, as we celebrate our centennial, we go back to Canada to show the hosts how the international game has developed since the world inherited this beautiful sport from them.

As President of the IIHF, I am immensely proud to present this 100-year publication to our fans in North America, in Europe, and around the world. The book is intended for both devoted fans and for those less acquainted with the sport who may become fans after reading it. Hopefully you will follow us during the most exciting time in international hockey.

René Fasel
IIHF President
Zurich, September 2007

Victoria Skating Rink, Montreal

ORGANIZED HOCKEY STARTED HERE IN 1875

The Victoria Skating Rink in Montreal is not only the birthplace of organized hockey, but it also determined the shape of the modern hockey rink. Built in 1862, it was squeezed into a parcel of land bounded by Drummond and Stanley Streets. The distance between these two streets was just over 200 feet (60 metres), so the ice surface inside measured almost exactly 200 feet by 80 feet, virtually the same measurements of any standard North American hockey rink from that day to this (200 feet by 85 feet).

When Captain Creighton's McGill team and Captain Torrance's Victoria team faced off against each other in an indoor, nine-a-side match on March 3, 1875, the first hockey rules had not yet been written and there was no proscribed rink size. It was the Victoria Skating Rink that established an appropriate shape and size. Creighton's team defeated Torrance's men by a score of two "games" (i.e., goals) to one in a contest that was played with a "circular piece of wood" as the puck. Each team defended a goal that was made by flags spaced eight feet (2.44 metres) apart, and a referee officiated play. The game of hockey was born.

VICTORIA RINK.—A game of Hockey will be played at the Victoria Skating Rink this evening, between two nines chosen from among the members. Good fun may be expected, as some of the players are reputed to be exceedingly expert at the game. Some fears have been expressed on the part of intending spectators that accidents were likely to occur through the ball flying about in too lively a manner, to the imminent danger of lookers-on, but we understand that the game will be played with a flat circular piece of wood, thus preventing all danger of its leaving the surface of the ice. Subscribers will be admitted on presentation of their tickets.

The Montreal Gazette *from March 3, 1875, the first known story announcing the playing of a hockey game.*

The Victoria Skating Rink in the late 1800s as two Montreal teams square off in front of a large and interested crowd. This is more or less how the game looked when Creighton's team defeated Torrance's team 2-1 on March 3, 1875.

The site of the Victoria Skating Rink is today a car rental centre (bottom), just north of the Sheraton hotel (a modern rink has been superimposed over the roof of the photo to illustrate its size and ratio to a standard rink). The entrance to the rink was from Drummond Street (left). The building across Stanley Street (to the right of the rink) is the Windsor Hotel. The Montreal Canadiens, the oldest active professional hockey club in the world, was founded on December 4, 1909, in Room 129 of the hotel, and on November 26, 1917, the National Hockey League was founded in the same hotel. Stanley Street is named after Lord Stanley of Preston who donated the Stanley Cup to the amateur champions of Canada.

DRUMMOND

STANLEY

[ERAS AND EPOCHS]

Chapter 1
1908-1919

Les Avants and the Bohemians

THE BIRTH OF INTERNATIONAL HOCKEY

By Birger Nordmark

In the winter of 1889, Pierre Coubertin of France, the founder of the modern Olympic games, travelled to Canada and the United States. While abroad, he discovered various winter sports and was particularly impressed by the Canadian version of ice hockey. Nonetheless, it was several years before this impression had any influence on bandy, the European big-ice version of hockey.

There were other teams and individuals who paved the way for the development of hockey in Europe. Champion skater George Meagher of Kingston, Ontario, came to Paris in 1894 and discovered that the French and Europeans in general had never heard about the Canadian version of hockey. So, when he returned to Europe in late 1897, he brought hockey equipment. He gathered skaters

The original minutes page from the first day of meetings as the LIHG is formed, ushering in the era of international hockey on May 15, 1908. Great Britain, Belgium, Switzerland, and France were the founding members.

and skating instructors from the Palais de Glace club in Paris to play a series of friendly games against bandy clubs from London and Glasgow.

This Bohemian team won the European championship in 1911. The country, later called Czechoslovakia, also won in 1914 and finished second in 1913. (l to r) Jaroslav Jarkovsky, Otakar Vindys, reporter Josef Laufer, Josef Sroubek, federation president Emil Prochazka, Jan Hamacek, Miroslav Fleischmann, Jan Palous, Jaroslav Fleischmann (seated, l to r) Jaroslav Jirkovsky, Josef Rublic.

The Parisians were newcomers to hockey altogether, while the Scottish players were bandy players. In a report published in *The Scotsman* on January 17, 1933, it was clear from Scottish captain William Pollock-Wylie that, for the first time in Europe, hockey was played using a puck. Beyond that, bandy rules were used. Appropriate for the class of both players and fans, the players were dressed in tennis clothes and flannel trousers.

According to the first issue of the British publication *Ice Hockey* in 1932, the first real ice hockey games were played in England in the winter of 1902-03, at the Princes' Skating Club in Knightsbridge. A London-Canadian team was formed, composed mainly of law and medical students, and captained by Donald Hingston of Montreal who introduced the Canadian-style of play to the Princes' players. Just a few years later, another team with Canadian influence was introduced. The elegant and swift skating Oxford Canadians, formed in 1906, was a team made up of mainly Canadian Rhodes scholars. They toured Europe and displayed their superior skills, skating circles around their European opponents.

In March 1905, two games were played which are now regarded as the first "official" international

The following is part of a letter published in Canada in January 1913 in which Oxford's captain Gustav Lanctôt described European hockey.

HOCKEY GROWING IN POPULARITY

At the present time hockey is winning great popularity every-where in Europe. England has erected two new artificial ice rinks in Manchester and Glasgow. Germany boasts of two rinks in Berlin, one in Munich and is building one in Hamburg. Bohemia ranks first of all, with eleven hockey clubs and Switzerland being second with seven or eight. Hungary is willing to replace bandy — a short stick game unknown in Canada — by the real Canadian game; and Holland, Austria, and Russia are studying the idea of founding hockey clubs.

I must say to the praise of the European players that better hockeyists can really be met with, but certainly no better sportsmen. Coming nearly all from the university trained class they are gentlemen before being players. They play the game for the sake of it, and though always keen in a fight they would never think in order to win to resort to second-class tricks or hardly fair tactics.

Needless to say, rough play is un-known. The expulsion of a player nearly creates a sensation, and the most innocent tripping is spurned and booed down the whole house, though the play begins to show ten-dencies of becoming more strenuous and aggressive.

In Brussels hockey is not only a noble sport, but it might be called with good reasons a 'sport of nobles'. Many a son of Belgian noblemen make it their favourite pastime. We meet on the ice young men whose names figure prominently in the Gotha.

A remarkable feature of the European ice rinks is the way the spectators are accommodated. There are no rows of seats, but the place, which generally possesses a gallery, has its two floors laid up with tables at which you sit and drink and even dine, if you care for, while watching the matches.
—Birger Nordmark

hockey games in European history (although Prince's Club had played games earlier both in Lyon and Paris). The games were advertised as Belgium-France, but in fact they were club matches between FPB Brussels and CP Paris (Belgium won both games, 3-0 and 4-2).

Initially, Louis Magnus was the most important figure in the development of hockey in Paris. Magnus was born to French parents in Jamaica in 1881, and the family moved to Paris eight years later. This small, moustachioed man was the

The Oxford Canadians of 1910-11. They represented Canada on several occasions before Canada officially joined the LIHG in 1920. (standing, l to r) Robert Tait, Christopher Adamson, W.M. Martin, John Higgins, Rupert Price (seated, l to r) Ernest Munro, Gustave Lanctot, Howard Henry

driving force behind CP Paris (officially called Club de Patineurs de Paris) and the development

FOCUS ON **PAUL LOICQ**

Paul Loicq—player, official, LIHG president

Loicq explains the format of play for (probably) the 1936 Olympics.

THE LONGEST–SERVING PRESIDENT

By Szymon Szemberg

In international hockey, one is usually a player, a referee, or a federation president. Belgian Paul Loicq was all three. Born in Clermont, in 1888, Loicq studied at the city's renowned university specializing in law. During World War I, he served with distinction and received a citation for bravery.

Being an accomplished speed skater, Loicq was fascinated by the new game that emerged out of European bandy in the first decade of the 20th century, Canadian ice hockey. He played for Belgium in the first LIHG European Championship in Les Avants, Switzerland, where he captured a bronze medal.

Even as a player he showed an affinity for management by being an energetic supporter of the movement to make ice hockey an official Olympic sport. He was rewarded for his efforts in 1920. Loicq, still an active player, took part in the games playing for the Belgian team.

Loicq retired from the national team four years later, but only after managing his country at the 1924 Olympic Winter Games in Chamonix,

France. Even before calling it a career, Loicq began to officiate games and was assigned to referee several international championships. He worked 65 official matches at the Olympics and the European and World Championships. Loicq demonstrated his dedication to this craft by founding the International College of Referees.

Between 1920 and 1922, Loicq acted as vice president of the LIHG, and from 1922 until 1947 he guided the world governing body of ice hockey as president, becoming the federation's longest serving leader. He skillfully navigated the LIHG ship, taking hockey from a marginal leisure activity for the upper class to a prestigious Olympic winter sport.

Loicq was also a passionate leader in the domestic affairs of Belgium. He was promoted to the rank of colonel during World War II and was an active leader of the resistance during the Nazi occupation. Following the war, Loicq served at the war crimes trial in Nuremberg on behalf of Belgium. He passed away on March 26, 1953.

He was posthumously elected to the Hockey Hall of Fame in 1961 (the first European upon whom the honour was bestowed) and to the IIHF Hall of Fame in 1998, the inaugural year of that institution. Also in 1998, the IIHF introduced an award in his name, to be presented annually to an individual who has made extraordinary contributions to the IIHF and international hockey. ∎

of international ice hockey in the years before World War I. His influence on the game among the elite also provided stark contrast to the development of hockey in Canada in the later part of the 19th century.

While Lord Stanley authenticated the game by introducing the Stanley Cup in 1893, organized

The Prince's Club of London (left) and the Sporting Club de Lyon have their portrait taken prior to their meeting on February 25, 1906. London won, 4-3.

hockey itself dates back much earlier when students from McGill University in Montreal played in 1875. In Canada, much of the growth of the game occurred at the middle and lower classes of society. Hockey was a sport of the people in Canada, but in Europe its earliest influences were aristocratic and high society. This explains the rise of the game in countries such as Belgium and France and equally explains its eventual demise at the expense of more popular waves

of interest in countries such as Sweden and Bohemia/Czechoslovakia.

The Belgium-France games in 1905 highlighted the differences in rules between various European nations. These discrepancies were equally evident in a game in Les Avants, Switzerland, on January 15, 1905, much to the frustration of Magnus. In a column in the *Bulletin du Club des Patineurs de Paris*, he wrote: "It would be wise to find a solution for the unification of the rules of hockey. The question is being studied and we hope to bring a solu-

The Oxford Canadians playing at Chateau d'Oex in Switzerland in 1910.

tion this year." Initially, the proposals were to be presented to the International Ice Skating Union, but that organization was not interested in the issue and no resolution to the problem seemed imminent.

This was, in retrospect, a blessing in disguise because Magnus decided to form an independent federation devoted specifically to ice hockey. La Ligue Internationale de Hockey sur Glace (LIHG), precursor to the IIHF, was born.

The first Congress of the LIHG was organized by Magnus on May 15-16, 1908, at a local sports club located at 34 rue de Provence in Paris. Participating delegates included the executives of the French CPP (Magnus, Robert Planque and Robert van der Hoeven), representatives of Belgium (Eddie De Clercq and Eduard Malaret), Switzerland (Eduard Mellor and Louis Dufour), and Great Britain (represented by E.E. Mavrogodato of the National Skating Association). The LIHG, with Magnus as president and Planque as general secretary, also added Bohemia to its list of members, but not until November 15.

Although the LIHG was formed in the spring of 1908, it had to wait until the following winter before it could organize its first international tournament, which it did, in Berlin, Germany, on November 3-5. Four teams participated (Berliner SC, CP Paris, Prince's Club of London, and Berliner HC) and games were played using a Canadian puck and Canadian sticks. Playing time consisted of two, 20-minute halves. The winning team won a silver trophy. Prince's Skating Club, representing Great Britain, won 3-1 in the final against CP Paris. The winning goal was scored by William Duden before an enthusiastic capacity crowd. He and his brother, Harold, were the stars of the British team while the American dentist Charles Hartley was the best player for Berlin. Hartley stunned the crowd with his quickness and end-to-end rushes.

The second significant international tournament took place in Chamonix, France, on January 23-25, 1909. This was the first time that the Bohemian players played hockey with a puck and a Canadian-style hockey stick. According to *The Times* of London, the Bohemians adjusted quickly and made a favourable impression. The second Congress of the LIHG took place during the tournament. On that occasion, it established its own rules of play.

The first LIHG European Championship took place in the Swiss winter resort of Les Avants, not far from Montreux, on January 10-12, 1910. Players stayed at the hotel on the property, and the rink was set up on the open space in front of it. For several months before this official LIHG tournament, two pressing issues were debated by the participating countries: (a) the playing format; (b) the use of foreign players.

On the first point, the Swiss organizers wanted the tournament to adhere to a round-robin schedule,

Belgium and Great Britain play to a 1-1 tie in
Les Avants in 1910.

An exhibition game in Les Avants in 1907 between
HC Les Avants and SC de Lyon.

B.M. Patton carries the puck for Great Britain in a game in
Les Avants against Switzerland in 1910.

but Magnus was an ardent believer in a system of direct elimination because he wanted a format that would remain unchanged year after year. He believed that as more countries attended the championship, the elimination setup was the only viable option. On the second point, France was opposed to teams using foreign players.

As it turned out, France and Bohemia both withdrew from the tournament only two weeks before the first games were to be played. Meanwhile, the third LIHG Congress was held at the Montreux Casino on January 9, 1910. Some 13 representatives from five nations attended, during which time it was decided to use a round-robin system and not to allow foreign players (but only starting in 1911). These two decisions made Magnus furious and disappointed after all "he had done for European ice hockey."

The four-nation event (Germany, Great Britain, Belgium, Switzerland) started the day after the Congress, a Sunday morning. Ice conditions during the whole tournament were poor because of sunny and mild weather. There were also complaints from the teams because one half of the ice was markedly wider than the other! (Helpers built snowdrifts instead of using sideboards to form the shape of the playing surface.)

The first game featured Great Britain and Belgium, the former represented again by the Prince's Club and the latter by a combination of the best players from the two Brussels clubs Brussels Ice Hockey Club and Féderation des Patineurs de Belgique. The game was rough and ended in a 1-1 tie. The British defender B.M. Patton and the Belgium forward Etienne Coupez, who learned the game in Winnipeg, were the dominant players. There were

about 400 spectators crowded around the ice surface, among them many British ski tourists who gave great support to their team.

The most exciting game of the tournament was the England-Germany match, won 1-0 by the British. Great Britain was hard-pressed to earn the win because it had no substitutes. The Germans passed the puck well, but the brilliant play of Tommy Sopwith in the British goal proved to be the difference. The Brits went on to win the first European championship ahead of Germany.

The Oxford Canadians also played three out-of-competition games in Les Avants, winning each with relative ease. The students were the dominating team on continent before World War I. This was the first hockey team to represent Canada wearing the famous red maple leaf. The Europeans, however, learned the game quickly, and in coming years Oxford had a much tougher time of it. Oxford's heart and soul, and the team's spokesman, Gustave Lanctôt, played both as a defenceman and goaltender during his career. The top scorer on the team was the youngster, John Gillis, a player with exceptional offensive skills.

On March 14, 1911, the LIHG adopted Canadian rules for hockey at all levels of play, an honour bestowed upon the motherland for its quality and skill of play.

According to newspapers and magazines from many of the ice hockey playing countries during the years before World War I, the so-called LIHG-tournaments (LIHG Championat), in which foreign players were allowed to participate, had more prestige than the European Championships. So in the years 1912-1914 the new world governing body of ice hockey organized two major events: the LIHG European Championship and the "open" LIHG Championat. The first LIHG Championat was organized in Brussels in March 1912 at the elegant Palais de Glace Saint Sauveur and was well attended by the nobility of Brussels society.

Germany, France, Switzerland, Oxford (representing Canada), and Belgium participated in this event. LIHG president Louis Magnus asked the Brussels IHC to organize the tournament as a replacement to the European Championship in Prague earlier that year, the results of which were annulled in part because Austria participated without being a member in the LIHG. Further,

when some teams played with imports, the congress decided that the European Championship couldn't be considered an official event.

Nevertheless, Switzerland had problems with injuries and was forced to take three Belgium players on loan just to be able to participate (among them

The CSHB Brussels team for the 1934-35 season.

future LIHG president Paul Loicq). The fifth LIHG Congress accepted membership applications from Austria, Sweden, and Luxembourg. The newly-elected president was the lawyer and chairman of the Brussels IHC, Henri van den Bulcke.

Austria and Germany tried to exclude Bohemia from the LIHG because, in point of fact, Bohemia was part of the Austrian Empire. The president of the Bohemian Federation was Adolf Dusek. He had replaced Emil Prochazka, who resigned after the re-

sults of the European Championship in Prague 1912 were annulled. Dusek was successful in convincing the other delegates to vote for keeping Bohemia as an independent LIHG member.

Germany won all of its games in the 1912 LIHG Championat, including a thrilling 9-8-win against the Oxford Canadians. Franz Lange scored eight of the Germans' goals and 21 of the team's 31 goals in the tournament. The Belgians also scored a surprising 5-5 tie against Oxford, thanks in large measure to two Toronto-born players, Amilius and William Jarvis.

The second LIHG Championat was organized in St. Moritz in 1913, and it was an exciting tournament made possible by excellent ice conditions. The Oxford Canadians didn't participate after experiencing a bad season on the continent. Germany, England, and France each had the same record but Germany was ruled the winner because it had scored the most goals. As usual, Franz Lange and Charles Hartley were the stars of the team.

Great Britain, represented by the Prince's Club, won the last LIHG Championat in January 1914,

in Chamonix. In Berlin, the seventh and last Congress before World War I took place in the elegant Hotel Esplanade, and it was unquestionably the stormiest. Henri van den Bulcke was re-elected LIHG president but not without incident. During a span of a couple of hours there were three different presidents elected — Magnus, B.M. Patton, and, finally, van den Bulcke.

The Brussels Hockey Club, 1908.

Only three teams participated in the 1914 European Championship (Bohemia, Germany, and Belgium). Switzerland arrived in Berlin with only four players and played outside the competition with some players on loan from different Berlin clubs.

The first European champions, in 1910, were the Prince's Club of London representing Great Britain.

The final and deciding game of the tournament pitted Germany against Bohemia at the Berliner Eispalast. Nearly 3,000 fans jammed the elegant rink. The Germans dominated the early going and had several good scoring chances, but Bohemian goalie Karel Wälzer was outstanding. The big German star Franz Lange was well checked by the Prague players. Bohemia's defence was practically impregnable, however. In the last minute of the first period, centreman Jaroslav Jirkovsky scored the opening goal for Bohemia and in the second period teammate Jan Parals made it 2-0. The score stood, and Bohemia won its second European Championship.

The team was praised for its brilliant passing game and the skill of their best player, Jirkovsky, who scored seven of his team's eleven goals in the tournament. Bohemia tried to play a Canadian-style game, and thousands of fans welcomed their heroes when they arrived back home in Prague. That marked the end of the first era of LIHG history. There would be no more international hockey until 1920 as normal life was interrupted by World War I.

Chapter 2
1920-1939

Hockey Goes Global

CANADA SHOWS EUROPE HOW TO PLAY THE GAME

By Patrick Houda

In the years immediately after World War I, the interest in hockey in Europe grew to the point that organizers of the 1920 Summer Olympics in Antwerp, Belgium, declared that if Canada participated, they would put hockey in the program (along with figure skating).

The organizers for this historic event were all Belgians. Count de Lannoy served as president, and the Belgian hockey players Paul Loicq (later LIHG president) and Paul Goemine were members of the committee. The hockey games were played at the Palais de Glace in

Antwerp. It was built in a very short time by the wealthy Sheid family, ship magnates of that city. The ice palace wasn't designed for hockey and the playing surface was much smaller than what most players were used to, measuring only 56m x 18m

Canada's Olympic hockey team for 1920, the mostly Icelandic-Canadians known as the Winnipeg Falcons. (l to r) Gordon Sigurjonsson (trainer), Hebbie Axford (president), Wally Byron, Slim Halderson, Frank Frederickson, Bill Hewitt (CAHA representative), Konnie Johannesson, Mike Goodman, Huck Woodman, Bobby Benson, Chris Fridfinsson, Bill Fridfinnsson (secretary).

(185 feet x 59 feet). Canada, USA, Czechoslovakia, Sweden, Switzerland, France, and Belgium were the participants.

The most controversial issue prior to the tournament was the format. The so called "Bergvall system" (named after Erik Bergvall) was a modified version of Louis Magnus's strict elimination format. The idea was to find the winner through a regular elimination competition (tournament A). Thereafter, a new tournament (tournament B) for second place was played between the teams that had lost to the winner in tournament A. And finally, there was a similar tournament for the bronze medal between the teams that had been beaten in tournaments A and B by the silver medal winner. It was a very complicated system that by today's standards didn't make much sense. France, for example, got to play only one game — a 4-0 loss

Three members of the Czechoslovak team from the early 1930s: (l to r) Oldrich Kucera, Josef Malecek, and Jiri Tozicka. Malecek was inducted into the IIHF Hall of Fame in 2003, the centenary of his birth.

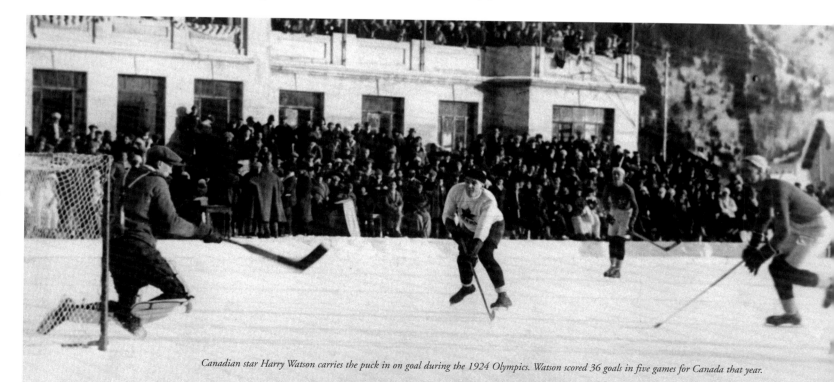

Canadian star Harry Watson carries the puck in on goal during the 1924 Olympics. Watson scored 36 goals in five games for Canada that year.

The cover of the 1930 World Championship program, the first non-Olympic tournament which began the annual competition for hockey supremacy.

The Great Britain team of the 1936 Olympics that upset Canada 2-1 to win gold.

to Sweden — and that was their Olympic experience. Sweden, by contrast, played six games.

The Canadians were represented by the Winnipeg Falcons, a team made up mostly of Canadians of Icelandic origin. The Falcons had qualified as the Canadian representatives after beating the University of Toronto in a two-game series to win the Allan Cup, symbolic of amateur supremacy in the country.

The Canadians adapted quickly to the small ice surface of the Palais de Glace, having learned to skate on small neighborhood outdoor ice rinks in Manitoba. Future NHL star and Hall of Famer Frank Fredrickson tied for the tournament lead in scoring and speed skating champion Mike Goodman was a crowd pleaser. The only players who could keep up with the Canadians were their geographic neighbours, the Americans. They had four Canadian-born players on the team, including captain Joe McCormick who hailed from Buckingham, Quebec. He and teammate Anthony Conroy were the top scorers for the Americans.

The Czechoslovakian team came to the tournament without their two best goalscorers. Jaroslav

Jirkovsky and Jaroslav Jarkovsky had both been stars of the Bohemian national team before World War I and had combined for 33 of the 53 national team goals in the four previous LIHG European Championships. Jirkovsky had been a prisoner of war and wasn't released until late in 1920, after the Olympics. Furthermore, their regular goalie, Karel Wälzer, broke his thumb during training and could not play either. Instead, the Czechs had to dress Jan Peka against the North American teams. Peka, who had been a prisoner of war in Greece and didn't return home until 1919, was victimized 15-0 by Canada and 16-0 by the Americans.

Wälzer was back for the bronze-medal game against Sweden, and he posted a shutout as Czechoslovakia won, 1-0. Despite being outscored 31-1 in three games, Czechoslovakia won the bronze medal.

The Swedes were newcomers to the Canadian version of ice hockey. Everyone on the team was a bandy player. But just as the big-ice game with curved stick was a perfect training ground from which the Soviets launched their ice hockey program more than 30 years later, proficiency in

Members of the Great Britain team confer at ice level while SS soldiers above take in the action from the stands during the 1936 Olympics in Garmisch-Partenkirchen, Germany. War broke out just three years later, bringing a halt to international hockey until 1947.

bandy paid off very well in ice hockey for the Swedes, especially in the 1920s when the hockey played in Europe was so poor that Sweden's bandy players had little problem defeating Belgium (8-0) and France (4-0). This was a surprising development to the losers who prided themselves on playing "real" ice hockey.

The Swedes were reported to play such a physical game in the 8-0 rout of Belgium that Canadian referee William Hewitt (father of legendary radio play-by-play man Foster Hewitt) had to urge them to calm down. In retrospect, the truth was probably that the Swedes didn't play overly physical at all. Albeit "only" bandy players, they were nevertheless capable athletes from various social classes who trained seriously. Ice hockey in countries such as France, Belgium, and, to a certain extent Great

German goalie Walter Leinweber played an heroic game for his country, keeping Canada to a 4-1 win at the 1932 Olympics in Lake Placid despite a serious eye injury.

FOCUS ON HARRY WATSON

THE GREATEST AMATEUR

By Andrew Podnieks

Although he was born on Canada's East Coast, Harry Watson spent the first few years of his life in England. When his family moved back to Canada, Watson learned to skate and play hockey on frozen rivers and ponds, as did many of his neighbourhood friends. When the family moved to Toronto in 1913, Watson signed on to play for the Whitby Athletics of the OHA. He moved on to St. Andrews College in the OHA Jr. and was named a First Team All-Star in 1915. By the 1916-17 season, he was leading the OHA Sr. league in scoring.

Watson joined the Flying Corps and served overseas during World War I before returning to hockey action with the Toronto Dentals of the OHA Sr. league. He made it back in time for one playoff game against the Hamilton Tigers in which he scored a goal in a losing cause. In 1919, the Toronto Granites hockey team was formed by the eponymous curling club and Watson was their star player, leading them to Allan Cup titles in 1921-22 and 1922-23. Individual awards followed Watson as well. He was named to the OHA Sr. Second All-Star Team in 1920 and made the First Team All-Stars in 1922 and 1923. He was also named as the OHA Sr. most valuable player in 1922 and 1923.

As a result of these Allan Cup victories, the Granites went on to represent Canada at the 1924 Olympics and win the gold medal. Watson scored an astounding 37 goals in five games against the competition, notably 13 goals in a single game against Switzerland in a 33-0 win. He also scored eleven times against Czechoslovakia, but his finest performance came in the gold-medal showdown against the Americans.

The great Harry Watson's goal-scoring feats were the stuff of legend, but the proud amateur never turned professional.

There was clearly an air of animosity to the game, created in part by Watson's remarks earlier that Canada would win 10 or 12 to nothing. Less than two minutes after the puck had been faced off, Watson was bleeding from the nose. By the end of the game, the Americans were exhausted and gasping for breath, and the Canadians tired but victorious thanks to the heroic and skilful play of their star forward trio of Watson, Hooley Smith, and Bert McCaffery. Watson scored three of his team's goals in a convincing 6-1 win.

The fame of the Granites and their exploits did not go unnoticed by the National Hockey League. A number of the Granites players, notably Watson, Hooley Smith, and Dunc Munro, were made offers to turn professional. Smith and Munro agreed to turn pro, but Harry Watson clung proudly to his amateur status and never turned pro for the rest of his playing days.

Harry Watson was inducted into the Hockey Hall of Fame in 1962 and into the IIHF Hall of Fame in 1998. ∎

Britain, started and remained through the 1920s mainly as a sport of the aristocracy. This was most certainly the reason why these countries, although having started with the sport very early, were left behind during the post-World War I era. Nobility seldom produced good athletes.

The Swiss team bowed out of the tournament after two losses, against USA and Sweden. The captain of the Swiss team, 38-year-old Max Sillig, had just been named president of the LIHG. Another man of wealth who dedicated his time to hockey, Sillig was one of the driving forces behind Swiss hockey in the early days. When he took over the LIHG presidency, he left his position as the president of the Swiss Ice Hockey Federation.

Canada easily won gold in 1920 and again four years later when the Toronto Granites stole the headlines at the Chamonix Olympics. The Granites were considered by many to be the finest pre-World War II team. They won all five games and outscored their opponents by a margin of 110-3. Their lineup included future Hall of Famer Harry Watson who dazzled spectators and opponents alike with his blistering shot. His 37 goals still stand as an Olympic record. Watson took

plenty of punishment from his opponents but this seemed only to make him better.

Another slick player was the young Reginald "Hooley" Smith who went on to have a stellar 17-year NHL career. He had Gretzky-like vision and was a superb passer. Captain Dunc Munro and his offensive rushes from the blueline won many accolades as well. The Toronto Varsity Grads who represented Canada in the 1928 Olympics in St. Moritz may not have been as good as the Granites, but it was still a very capable team that had no difficulties in winning the gold. The stars of the team were Dave Trottier and Hugh Plaxton, both future NHLers. They accounted for 24 of the 38 goals that the Canadians scored.

The only European teams that could afford to send squads over to Lake Placid for the 1932 Olympics were Germany and Poland. Germany eventually edged Poland to win the bronze. The catalyst of the German team was the quick and tiny Rudi Ball who had three goals and two assists in six games. Prior to the tournament, Poland trained together with the New York Rangers of the NHL and relied heavily on their goaltender, Jozef Stogowski. Canada defeated USA for the gold medal, but it

needed two overtime periods against the Americans to do so. The leading scorers were Canada's Wally "Pop" Monson and USA's Winthrop "Ding" Palmer. All twelve games in Lake Placid were

officiated by the same pair of referees: Don Sands (USA) and Lou Marsh (Canada).

The pre-World War II version of "Miracle on Ice"

INTERNATIONAL HOCKEY'S WAR VICTIMS

Compiled by Birger Nordmark and Patrick Houda

LAST NAME	FIRST NAME	DATE AND PLACE OF BIRTH	DATE AND PLACE OF DEATH	NAT.	WC/OG/EC/LIHG*
Barbanson	Jean	19-12-1915 - Paris, FRA	10-05-1940 - Goetsenhoven, BEL	BEL	1934.35
Bliesener	Willi	unknown - Berlin, GER	31-10-1917 - Flandres, BEL	GER	1910.11
Blom	Lars	25-01-1920 - Helsinki, FIN	19-03-1944 - Ontajärvi, FIN	FIN	1939
Boak	George Albert	31-03-1888 - York County, CAN	28-09-1918 - Raillencourt, FRA	CAN	1913,14 (Germany)
Buchanan	Buck	1918 - North Battleford, CAN	06-01-1942 - unknown	CAN	1939
Bureau	Roger	01-02-1905 - Antwerp, BEL	04-1945 - Germany	BEL	1926,27,28,36,39
Cohen-Tervaert	Thijs	11-02-1915 - unknown	01-01-1945 - Buchenwald, GER	NED	1939
Czaplicki	Edmund	19-10-1898 - Warszawa, POL	1940 - Warszawa, POL	POL	1926,27,28,29
Fullerton	Billy	23-11-1913 - Eastwood, GBR	17-01-1941- Oxford, GBR (Plane crash)	GBR	1939
Granström	Holger	25-12-1917 - Ruokolahti, FIN	22-07-1941 - Miessaari, FIN	FIN	1939
Grauel	Bruno	24-08-1882 - Berlin, GER	08-02-1945 - unknown	GER	1910,11,12
Jarvis	William	31-03-1892 - Toronto, CAN	14-04-1915 - Ypres, BEL	CAN	1912 (Belgium)
Kelch	Günther	unknown - unknown	31-07-1943 - unknown	GER	1937.39
Kelly	Jimmy	1910 - Glasgow, GBR	07-07-1945 - Holten, NED	GBR	1937,38,39
Kowalski	Aleksander	07-10-1902 - Warszawa, POL	03-04-1940 - Katyn, POL	POL	1926,27,28,30,31,32
Kulig	Józef	1913 - unknown	1940 - Lyon, FRA	POL	1937
Maas	Hans	10-07-1912 - unknown	11-1941 - unknown	NED	1935
Maesciuc	Emil	unknown - Czernowitz, AUT	1944/45 - unknown, URS	ROM	1935,37,38
Nyholm	Olof	14-01-1918 - Helsinki, FIN	20-02-1940 - Sotas, FIN	FIN	1939
Pálfalvy	Béla	1917 - unknown	1944 - Budapest, HUN	HUN	1938.39
Polizu	Nicolae	02-07-1904 - Harlau, ROM	02-05-1943 - unknown, ROM	ROM	1931,32,33,34
Putnins	Ludvigs	1920 - unknown	1945 - unknown	LAT	1938.39
Rabinovici	Iuliu	unknown - unknown	1944 - Bucharest, ROM	ROM	1933,34,35
Reinbahs	Indriks	09-08-1904 - unknown	1944/45 - unknown, URS	LAT	1933
Rintala	Erkki	10-04-1918 - Tampere, FIN	25-12-1941 - Poventsa, FIN	FIN	1939
Sachs	Tadeusz	12-06-1899 - Pinsk, POL	03-08-1942 - Auschwitz (Oswiecim), POL	POL	1930,31,32
Smalhout	Hans	31-12-1920 - Velsen, NED	31-10-1942 - unknown	NED	1939
Stertin	Hans	16-02-1909 - Villach, AUT	08-12-1942 - Don & Wolga, URS	AUT	1934.38
Suck	Wilhelm	12-12-1915 - Czernowitz, AUT	07-01-1943 - Stalingrad, URS	ROM	1935,37,38
Sutinen	Kalevi	29-01-1915 - Tampere, FIN	1945/46 as result of war injuries	FIN	1939
Tarlowski	Kazimierz	25-02-1915 - Kraków, POL	1941-44 - Oswiecim, POL	POL	1938
Tobien	Rudolf	04-02-1915 - Berlin, GER	28-02-1942 - Leshajkina, URS	GER	1938.39
Zebrowski	Kazimierz	04-03-1891 - Warszawa, POL	unknown - WW II, unknown	POL	1926,27,28
Zilpauss	Karlis	unknown - unknown	1944 - unknown, URS	LAT	1938.39

This list honours the hockey players whose lives were ended by World War I and World War II.
WC=World Championship; OG=Olympic Games; EC=European Championship; LIHG=LIHG Championat

occurred in the 1936 Olympics in Garmisch-Partenkirchen, the German winter sport resort. Great Britain upset Canada by winning the gold medal, beating the Canadians, 2-1, in what proved to be the decisive matchup during the early round robin series of games. Eleven of the Brits were born in England, one in Scotland, and one in Canada. More telling is that eleven were raised in Canada, where they got their hockey schooling. Only two were homegrown Brits — captain Carl Erhardt and Bob Wyman. The most valuable player of the tournament was the Scottish-born goaltender Jimmy Foster. The Winnipeg-raised netminder was outstanding, leading Great Britain to victory with four shutouts.

The first LIHG World Championship tournament independent of the Olympics was held in Chamonix and Berlin in 1930. Canada was represented by Toronto C.C.M., a team sponsored by the sporting goods company. As in Antwerp in 1920, the playing format was odd. The Canadian team was seeded directly to the final game, where it defeated Germany, 6-1.

The teams that represented Canada in the World Championships and Olympics, 1930-39, played a total of 330 games in Europe (most of them exhibitions), winning 293 and losing only 16. The only blemishes on their record were the silver in the 1936 Olympics and a second-place finish to USA at the 1933 World Championship in Prague. It was there that another goaltender emerged as the hero. American Gerry Cosby, who later opened an eponymous sporting goods store inside New York's Madison Square Garden, was inducted to the IIHF Hall of Fame posthumously in 1997. He allowed just one goal in five games.

The 1930s produced a more dramatic globalization of the sport. Asia, Africa, and Oceania all had active hockey leagues. Asia entered the European hockey scene in 1930 when a group of medical students from the University of Mukden in Manchuria toured Europe and participated in the first World Championship representing Japan. They were cheered by European fans who admired their fighting spirit and energy in the only game they got to play, a 5-0-loss to Poland.

Although Africa had to wait until 1961 before entering the World Championships (South Africa sent a team to Lausanne for the C pool competition), that continent's international hockey-playing

A formal portrait of the members of the LIHG's Congress that met in 1924 during the Olympics for their annual meeting. Sitting, third from left, is Bethune Patton. Beside him are Paul Loicq, Louis Magnus, and Max Sillig. All four served as IIHF president during their careers.

days started in September 1936 when British university teams from Oxford and Cambridge travelled to Johannesburg to play nine exhibition games. The first South African team was made up of eight Canadians, two Germans, and one Austrian. Although the South African league featured several homegrown players, the national team consisted of foreigners. The captain, Canadian Jimmy Britton, was the team's leading player.

In June and July 1937, the Austrian team Wiener EV played nine games in Johannesburg. This time

South Africa had Canadian Rolland "Johnny" Desilets, brother of NHLer Joffre Desilets, in its lineup. Desilets was the shining star in South African hockey during the 1930s and '40s.

Australia has a longer ice hockey tradition than most fans of the game generally believe. The first games were played in 1906 (bandy style), and the first international game was staged in 1907 when a team from Melbourne played against sailors from the warship "Baltimore." In 1909, the first set of Canadian rules and equipment was used. This was

also the year that the first interstate game took place. Much of the credit for the development of the sport in Australia goes to Newman Reid and his two sons, Andy and Hal. Reid built and managed the first artificial ice rinks in Australia, the Ice Palace in Adelaide and the Glaciarium in Melbourne. In 1938, Sydney formed a team (Bears) with six Canadian players and the following year ex-NHLer Tom Coulter (brother of the better known NHLer, Art Coulter) represented the Sydney-based team St. George.

Although World War II effectively stopped Olympic and World Championship competition until 1947-1948, it didn't entirely stop club and national teams from competing. Nonetheless, most teams were considerably weakened as many hockey players were called into duty. As a result, many players emerged from the war as heroes for their actions on the battlefield. One such player was the Dutchman Bram (Bob) van der Stok, a member of the Netherlands' 1935 World Championship team. The Sumatra-born van der Stok was the country's ace pilot. He was eventually captured and became a prisoner of war. Van der Stok was sent to Stalag Luft III camp in lower Silesia. He was part of the "Great Escape," the most spectacular breakout during the war.

Initially, there were 220 prisoners who planned to escape, but only 75 managed to get out. Stok was one of only three prisoners who was not re-captured. He took part in many battles during the war and received war honours from five different countries.

Another pilot and war hero was the Romanian prince Constantin "Bazu" Cantacuzino. He was one of the best Romanian tennis players in the late 1920s and early '30s and was the driving force behind the Romanian national team in hockey. He captained Romania in five LIHG World Championships (1931, '33, '34, '35, '37). Beyond that, he was also an accomplished sports car driver and pilot. Cantacuzino became the highest decorated war pilot in Romania with 608 combat missions and 56 confirmed kills.

Strangely enough, there were many international games during the war. One significant tournament was the international winter sports week in Garmisch-Partenkirchen in 1940 and 1941. Indulging in international sport competitions amidst war activities was an important home-front strategy by the Nazis. As soldiers and civilians were killed in nearby fields or in camps of mass destruction, turning to international sport exchange and

Berlin's Sportpalast is left a shell of its formal self after allied bombs damaged the roof and much of the structure in late 1943.

inviting national teams from invaded, annexed, and war-neutral countries averted the people's attention from atrocities and grim war bulletins.

Bohemia/Moravia won the 1940 tournament after beating Hungary in the final. One year later, Germany edged Sweden for the win. Neither in hockey nor in other team sports did Swedish or Swiss sports authorities in those days have any moral qualms about traveling to Germany to play friendly games.

Between December 1940 and November 1943, there were 35 international hockey games played in the magnificent Berlin Sportpalast. A 36th, against HC Davos, had to be cancelled because of allied bombings on November 22, 1943, when the Sportpalast was virtually destroyed. But the darkest days of mankind were soon to be over as the world would start to recover and eventually get back to normal after six years of destruction throughout Europe. So also in international ice hockey.

Chapter 3
1947-1953

Last Days of Canada's World Dominance

THE WORLD STARTS TO CATCH UP TO THE MOTHERLAND

By Andrew Podnieks

By all outward appearances, not much had changed in the hockey world during the war.

Canada won the gold medal at the 1948 Olympics in St. Moritz, Switzerland, compiling a near-perfect record of seven wins and a tie, scoring 69 goals and giving up just five. Yet, those numbers were misleading for several reasons.

On the one hand, Canada's march to the gold medal was as impressive as ever. The RCAF Flyers,

Canada's RCAF Flyers celebrate their gold medal at the 1948 Olympics in St. Moritz, Switzerland. Although they went undefeated in eight games, they claimed top spot only by virtue of goal differential with Czechoslovakia.

the team which represented Canada that year, was not assembled until only a few weeks prior to the first game. Canada had such talent that pretty much any group of skilled players could go to Europe and win. That being said, Canada did not win by scores that it had compiled even in the late 1930s. Most significantly, Canada and Czechoslovakia played to a scoreless tie in St. Moritz, a shocking result, really. It was only the second time since 1920 that Canada had failed to score a goal in a game (the other came at the 1931 World Championship against Sweden). Also, it gave an indication of the vast improvement of the Czechoslovaks who last played Canada in 1936 and lost, 7-0.

Although Canada scored easy wins against Italy (21-1) and Poland (15-0) at the 1948 Olympics, it had a much tougher time defeating Switzerland (3-0) and Great Britain (also 3-0). In short, the end result was the same — gold medal — but the means of achieving that result had been diminished substantially.

The progression to a more global game took a dramatic turn the next year at the World Championship in Stockholm, Sweden, where the Canadians were represented by the Sudbury Wolves. From the minute the team arrived in Europe early in the new year to start its exhibition series, things just weren't right for the Canadians. Headlines which before the war shouted, "Canada routs local team 13-0," now featured news that, "Sudbury team loses, 4-2" or "Streatham Team Hands Sudbury Sound Walloping." Indeed, the team had trouble scoring goals, had trouble preventing goals, and, as a result, had trouble winning games.

Things got so bad that coach Max Silverman cabled the CAHA back home pleading for reinforcements. Late arrivals included Don Stanley, who had been playing in Edmonton, and Tommy Russell of the North Sydney Vics. The small infusion of talent helped, but not that much. To make matters worse, the players started playing more physically and complaining about the refereeing, drawing the ire of local fans, damaging their reputations, and driving down confidence in their own play even further.

Although the Wolves scored a record 47-0 victory over Denmark to begin the 1949 tournament — a record for the top level of world championship play that continues to stand — they won only two

CZECHOSLOVAKS' FIRST DYNASTY PUT IN JAIL

Czechoslovakia was the best national team in the world in the immediate post-World War II years. It won the 1947 and 1949 World Championships and lost the 1948 Olympic gold on goal differential to Canada. But it was their own people, driven by conspiracy theories in Stalinist Czechoslovakia, who prevented the great team from defending its title at the 1950 World Championship in London, England. Just before the team was about to board the plane for London on March 11, 1950, the players were handcuffed by the national state security police and taken to jail. Seven months later, on October 7, the players appeared in court accused of treason and attempting to defect. The players, of course, pleaded not guilty. Their fate, however, was pre-determined.

Goaltender Bohumil Modry was sentenced to 15 years in prison, forward Gustav Bubnik to 14 years, forward Stanislav Konopasek to 12, Vaclav Rozinak and Vladimir Kobranov each got ten years and Josef Jirka got six years. Six other players were given sentences ranging from eight months to three years. Modry, the best goaltender in Europe of that era, died in 1963, at the age of 47, from prison-related health complications. Most of the players were released after five years, but their lives and families were shattered. So was a great hockey team.

Czechoslovakia had to wait 23 years, until 1972, before it won another World Championship. —Szymon Szemberg

of five games in the final round robin and finished second to the Czechs. Indeed, Canada beat Austria and USA easily, but fell 3-2 to Czechoslovakia and managed unimpressive ties against both Sweden and Switzerland. What was becoming clear was that (a) Canada's senior club teams could no longer count on waltzing over to Europe to win gold and (b) the gap between Canada and some of the European nations was closing rapidly.

Canadian journalist Jack Sullivan noted in one column that, "European countries may be Johnny-come-latelies in this hockey business, but they've advanced at a fast clip since the war."

Canada's reputation was restored at the 1950 and 1951 World Championships. In '50, the Edmonton

Twenty years after his Olympic debut, Swiss star Bibi Torriani was back in St. Moritz in 1948. Here he takes a shot during his team's 3-0 loss to Canada on the final day. Torriani, at age 36, had five goals.

FOCUS ON JAROSLAV DROBNY

DROBNY WAS WORLD CLASS — ON ICE, CLAY, AND GRASS

By Andrew Podnieks

That Canada won gold at the 1948 Olympics was no surprise. But, the RCAF Flyers claimed that gold by the slimmest of margins, needing goal differential to earn a superior placing to Czechoslovakia. That year, teams played a simple round-robin series of games, and the Canada-Czechoslovakia game ended in a scoreless tie, an amazing result for the Czechs who had won gold at the World Championship the previous year. This was the first European nation to develop enough talent to compete with Canada since the birth of international hockey in 1920.

One of the stars of that team was forward Jaroslav Drobny who played only two major international hockey tournaments. He had won gold with the Czechs in 1947 (Canada did not compete that year), scoring a hat trick in the decisive victory over USA.

Incredibly, Drobny was also a world-class tennis player. In fact, just a few weeks after the Olympics he lost the French Open finals, one of tennis's grand slam events, going down to Frank Parker in four sets. Imagine Saku Koivu claiming silver in Turin and then losing to Rafael Nadal at Roland Garros for the championship. That puts Drobny's achievements in perspective. Drobny made up for this defeat to Parker by winning the doubles and mixed doubles championships that same year. In fact, Drobny had made it to the French Open finals two years previous, but his tennis career was hardly limited to this brief success. His started in 1938 when he played Wimbledon for the first time at age 16.

During the war years, the Communist Czechoslovak government prevented Drobny from traveling, thus putting a seeming end to his tennis career. He turned his skills to hockey, where he proved equally adept. After the war, the Czech government allowed him to travel and play tennis again, and he picked up the racquet as if time had stood still.

His success culminated in the late 1940s after he and Davis Cup teammate Vladimir Cernik defected while playing at a tournament in Switzerland. For the next decade, Drobny toured the tennis circuit as an Egyptian citizen. Even more amazing, Drobny had suffered an eye injury playing hockey and was forced to wear dark, protective glasses for the rest of his tennis days.

In 1949, Drobny went to the finals at Wimbledon, losing 6-4 in the fifth set to Ted Schroeder. "Drob" made it to the French Open finals in 1950, and

Jaroslav Drobny won a gold medal at the World Championships and also won the men's singles title at both Wimbledon and the French Open, an unmatchable accomplishment.

then won the grand slam event in both 1951 and 1952 on the clay of Roland Garros. In 1954, he defeated the legendary Ken Rosewall at grassy Centre Court to win the hallowed Wimbledon championship, the first left-handed player to win the greatest tennis title. It was a final that needed 58 games to decide the winner, the longest match to date in the history of Wimbledon. Again, imagine Borje Salming beating Bjorn Borg at the Wimbledon finals, and one starts to see how amazing was Drobny's achievement.

In all, Drobny played Wimbledon 17 times and won five Grand Slam titles. He was later inducted into the International Tennis Hall of Fame. After his playing days, he settled in England in 1959 with his British wife, running a sports shop in London. Drobny died in that city in 2001, a world champion in both hockey and tennis. ■

The victorious 1947 Czechoslovakian team. The third player from the left, in the back row, is Vladimir Zabrodsky. On May 15, 1948, Zabrodsky and Jaroslav Drobny (back row, first on left) won a Davis Cup doubles match against Brazil in three sets. Zabrodsky had 158 goals for the Czechs in 93 international games.

Bibi Torriani tries to move the puck in front of Murray Dowey's goal in this Switzerland-Canada game at the 1948 Olympics.

Canada defeated Great Britain 3-0 in St. Moritz in 1948 to exact a measure of revenge for the 2-1 loss in 1936 that cost the Canadians a gold medal.

Mercurys were a perfect 8-0-0, scoring 88 goals and allowing just five en route to an easy gold medal. The next year, the Lethbridge Maple Leafs had similar success, going undefeated and allowing just six goals in as many games.

What was most impressive about these wins was that neither the Mercurys nor the Maple Leafs had been Allan Cup champions, em-

To the surprise of no one, the Edmonton Mercurys won gold for Canada at the 1952 Olympics in Oslo. What was stunning was that Canada would wait fully 50 years before claiming another Olympic gold.

blematic of senior hockey (i.e., amateur) supremacy in Canada. Most years since 1920, it was the Allan Cup winners who had been nominated by the CAHA to represent Canada, but later it was decided to alternate the honour between teams from the west and east. For half a century or more, the Allan Cup was as important in Canada as the Stanley Cup, and winning teams were feted in much the same way — parades, banquets, honours, everlasting fame.

Both Edmonton and Lethbridge were from the west because the CAHA had a tough time finding a high-calibre team with all amateur players during an era when many leagues were moving from amateur to professional status. Nonetheless, the depth

of skilled hockey teams in Canada was so impressive that even non-Allan Cup winners of this era could return overseas victorious.

The 1950 victory was not without intrigue. Every year that the Canadians came to Europe for the World Championship, they played a series of exhibition games before and after the tournament itself, much to the delight of fans across the continent. In the weeks leading up to the 1950 event in London, a Czechoslovakian contingent followed Canada, compiling a scouting report on the players. These scouting reports proved useless. The authorities in communist Czechoslovakia accused several players of planning to defect while in Great Britain, and

shortly before the championship the government withdrew its team from competition. Twelve players were sentenced to prison for treason.

Unquestionably, one aspect of the improved play of the Europeans was due to those nations hiring Canadians to coach the national teams. In fact, Mike Buckna was perhaps the leading figure in the development of hockey across Europe, taking the game away from bandy and 33-0 losses and turning it into a well-coached, disciplined sport. A native of Trail, British Columbia, he played for Czechoslovakia before the war and coached its national team after it. Indeed, he was behind the bench when the Czechoslovaks won gold at the 1947 World Championship (which Canada did not attend) and silver at the 1948 Olympics.

Similarly, legendary Canadian Frank Trottier coached Sweden at the 1950 World Championship, and countryman Bud McEachern led Norway in 1951. Even before the war, Bobby Bell had coached Germany in 1937; John Dewar led Hungary in 1934; and, that same season, Howie Grant coached Czechoslovakia. Of course, since Buckna many more Canadians have been recruited to coach European national teams, giving them firsthand insight into the practices and techniques of the mother country's top players.

An ancillary aspect of European improvement came thanks to the recruitment of Canadian players to play in leagues throughout the continent. Before the war, teams in England were full of Canadians who were looking for a different experience other than minor-league or senior hockey in Canada and gladly played for Harringay, London, or other top clubs. After the war, teams in France, Sweden, Switzerland, and elsewhere offered Canadians the chance to play.

Canada seemed to restore its pride fully at the 1951 World Championship as it dominated the exhibition season, won the gold medal, and even captured the newly-minted Winston Churchill Cup in a tournament after the World Championship before going home. Yet the win came with one startling asterisk. The Lethbrige Maple Leafs won almost every game it played leading up to the world tournament in Paris, yet just days before their first official game they recruited three forwards from the senior Kitchener-Waterloo Dutchmen, a Senior A team in southern Ontario. The three — Billy Flick, Den Flanagan, and Mickey Roth — were the Dutchmen's top line,

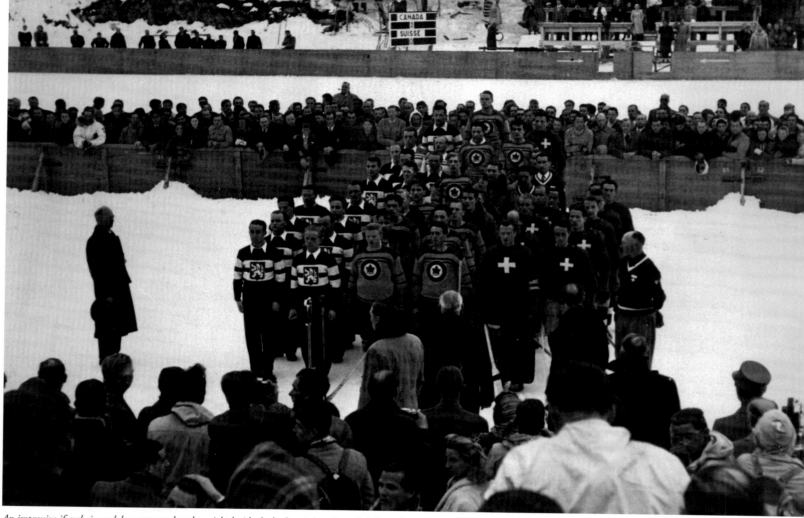

An impressive if archaic medal ceremony takes place right beside the hockey rink at the end of the 1948 Olympics in St. Moritz as Canada (middle) receives gold while the Czechs (left) take silver and the Swiss (right) claim bronze.

and Canada's coach Dick Gray gave them like status in Paris. It was the first time that real "recruitments" had been used by Canada to augment its World Championship lineup and foreshadowed Father Bauer's National Team of the 1960s.

A turning point in hockey's history came at the 1952 Olympics in Oslo, Norway, though. The Edmonton Mercurys again represented Canada, and that in itself was worrisome because the Mercs were only an intermediate team, not a senior level team. Furthermore, in the exhibition games they played in

Canada prior to their December '51 departure for a tour of Europe, many critics slammed the CAHA for making such a poor selection to represent Canada at the Olympics.

Nevertheless, the Edmonton team did, in fact, win the gold medal, but there were even clearer warning signs that all was not well with the apparent Canadian dominance of the hockey world. The team had a tough time with the Czechoslovakians again (4-1 victory), and a goal in the final minute gave the Mercs a 3-2 win over

The opening day of the 1948 Olympics saw Canada defeat Sweden, 3-1. Here, Swedish goalie Arne Johansson keeps his eye on play. Sweden took an early 1-0 lead on a goal by Claes Lindstrom before the Canadians rallied for the win.

Opening ceremonies from the 1952 Olympics in Oslo, Norway, at Bislet Stadium.

Sweden. These were the two teams making the most headway in hockey in Europe. In fact, CAHA president Doug Grimston said afterward that, "European teams have improved considerably the last few years and, with some proper coaching, could be mighty troublesome to Canada."

Indeed, 1952 was the last time Canada would have a relatively easy time of it in international competition. The Canadians boycotted the 1953 World Championship because the CAHA had become frustrated by complaints and attacks in the media

throughout Europe of the Canadian style of play, notably in the use of body-checking. As W.B. George, CAHA president after Grimston, noted, "Every year we spend $10,000 to send a Canadian hockey team to Europe to play forty exhibition games. All of these games are played to packed houses that only enrich European coffers. In return, we are subjected to constant, unnecessary abuse over our Canadian style of play."

What was at the heart of the controversy surrounding body-checking, however, was a mon-

umental difference in rules. Even though the IIHF and Europe whole-heartedly adopted the Canadian rules of the CAHA in 1920 after the remarkable display by the Canadians at those Olympics, the rule for body-checking remained night-and-day different for decades. It wasn't until 1969 that body-checking was permitted in the offensive end of the ice in international hockey, a rule that had handicapped Canada severely both because of style of play and because of having to make the necessary adjustment at the World Championship and Olympics. As a result, what Europeans thought as dirty play Canadians thought as clean, aggressive, and perfectly acceptable play.

The 1953 World Championship was a major letdown for several reasons. Canada did not attend, and the Czechs withdrew after the death of their president, Klement Gottwald. Only three teams competed, and all, of course, won medals. By the time the 1954 World Championship arrived, the Czechoslovaks had played precious little international hockey in recent times, having missed 1950 and '51 and leaving '53 early. They had won gold in 1947,

silver in '48, gold again in '49, and finished fourth in '52. They returned in 1954 with a new, domestic head coach, two new goalies, and only two players from that '49 gold-medal team.

More significant, the Soviet Union entered a team for the first time, introducing the world to names such as Puchkov, Bobrov, and Kuzin, and changing the balance of power forever. Canada's last days of supremacy took place at the 1952 Olympics, and although the country would still win many medals

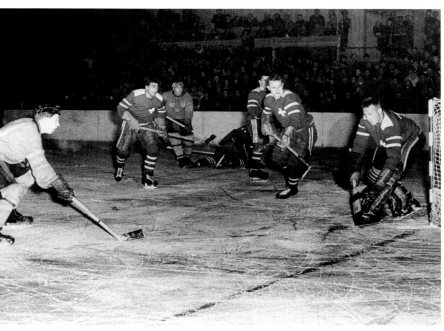

Sweden and Switzerland play during the 1952 Olympics. The Swedes won the game, 5-2, although Swiss goalie Paul Wyss makes the save on this play.

and championships in the coming years and decades, it would do so by narrow scores against better teams using a mixture of top players from across the country.

Chapter 4
1954-1962

The Fall of the Maple Leaf and Rise of the Star

THE SOVIETS BLAZE ONTO THE INTERNATIONAL SCENE

By Igor Kuperman

It was a major turning point for the Soviets, who had started to play hockey just 14 months earlier.

"When we first saw their equipment, we couldn't stop laughing," Gustav Bubnik, the legendary Czechoslovak player recalled. "They had soccer

The 1950s began with Canada clearly on top of the hockey world, but the decade did not close with equal dominance for the proud maple leaf nation. The Czechoslovaks became Canada's rivals in the late 1940s, and in February 1948, the club team LTC Prague visited Moscow just 18 days after the Czechoslovaks earned a silver medal at the Olympics. Twelve players on the LTC club had been members of that Czechoslovak national team.

An outdoor practice of the Soviet national team in Sokolniki Park in the mid-1950s. Coach Anatoli Tarasov (left) puts the players through a workout while curious spectators look on.

uniforms, leather bicycle helmets, and very long sticks." However, it didn't stop the Soviet players

(called the Moscow Selects) from surprising their guests. In the three-game series, the Selects won 6-3, lost 5-3, and tied 2-2. After the series, Vladimir Zabrodsky, the Czechoslovak team captain, predicted that the Soviets would come to dominate the hockey world.

How did the Soviets learn to play hockey in such a short time? The answer: it took longer than most people realize.

Despite the stereotype of being weak and agrarian, the Russian Empire was one of the strongest coun-tries economically in Europe. Russian athletes were among the best on the continent, and bandy was popular throughout the land. In fact, a form of hockey was played in Russia from the 17th century using sticks with hooked blades and a wood ball made from oak tree roots. The first official Russian hockey game took place in 1890 in St. Petersburg — not with the ball, but with a cast-iron nut.

Although the official date of starting hockey in Russia is 1946, the first attempt to play occurred in 1911. At the fourth IIHF congress in Berlin, Germany, in February 1911, Russia was admitted

The Penticton Vees represented Canada at the 1955 World Championship, defeating the Soviets 5-0 to reclaim the gold they had lost a year earlier.

Connie Broden (left) and George Samolenko of the 1958 Whitby Dunlops. Broden joined the Montreal Canadiens after helping Canada win gold, and added the Stanley Cup to his trophy case. To this day, he remains the only player to win both titles in the same year.

The 1954 World Championship team from the Soviet Union stunned Canada and the world, winning gold in its first major international tournament. Superstar Vsevolod Bobrov holds the championship trophy (standing, second from left).

Canada and USA battled hard during the 1960 Olympics, but the Americans prevailed by a score of 2-1. Rodney Paavola (#9) looks on as a scrum develops behind the goal.

Goalie hero Jack McCartan at the 1960 Olympics.

as a seventh member of the LIHG. However, the membership didn't last long — on September 25 of the same year, Russia was expelled from the IIHF for "inactivity."

American Tommy Williams (#12) leaps for joy and teammate Rodney Paavola (#9) raises his arms as Roger Christian (far left) scores the winning goal in a 3-2 win over the Soviet Union at the 1960 Olympics. Christian beat goalie Nikolai Puchkov in the key game en route to the first ever Olympic gold for USA.

Any interest in the game was virtually non-existent in the Soviet Union after the revolution in 1917. A few enthusiasts tried to learn the game by reading the few Canadian books which occasionally found their way into the Soviet Union. Citizens read these books in secret, because such activities — "idolizing the west" — could lead to

THE UNHERALDED MIRACLE OF 1960

Twenty years before the American "Miracle on Ice" in Lake Placid in 1980, an earlier generation Team USA shocked the hockey world at the 1960 Olympics in Squaw Valley, California. Coming into the tournament, the U.S. had never beaten the Soviet Union and always struggled against Canada, and this year the two hockey powerhouses were once again huge favourites for the gold while the Americans were considered a middle-of-the-pack team.

Just as goalie Jim Craig was the hero in 1980, however, the 1960 hero was goalie Jack McCartan, who was superb in the 2-1-win over Canada and the 3-2-victory against the Soviet Union. But that was not enough. The Americans had to beat Czechoslovakia in the final game to win gold. Yet, after two periods, they trailed the Czechoslovaks, 4-3.

Soviet captain Nikolai Sologubov — who wanted the U.S. to win gold more than Canada — entered the U.S. dressing room during the second intermission and used charade-like hand gestures to tell the Americans they needed to take oxygen to given them an edge. Some did. But Roger Christian did not, and he scored three of the team's six goals in the third period to lead the USA to a 9-4-win and give the country its first Olympic hockey gold.

There were no invitations to the White House, no *Sports Illustrated* covers, no fame or fortune that lasted beyond a week or so. One of the best U.S. players, Bill Cleary, had made the decision not to pursue a pro career prior to the Olympics. Proud that he was paid $15 a month to play with the Olympic team, he lamented at a reunion in 1995 that modern Olympics are dominated by high-paid athletes.

"I wouldn't trade my chance to march in the Olympic opening ceremony for 100 Stanley Cup championships," said Cleary. "When it was over, we all went back to our lives. That's the way we wanted it."
—Szymon Szemberg

severe punishment. The ideologists of the new regime couldn't even imagine that a non-Russian game could make an impact on national sports. In 1928, the magazine *Fizkultura i Sport* ("Physical Culture and Sports") published an article in which hockey was heavily criticized despite the fact that nobody had ever seen the game. "Games in hot indoor arenas on artificial ice are harmful

sisting of factory workers from Berlin, visited Moscow. The Soviet bandy players, who had never heard of this new game, and who were supplied with hockey sticks by the visitors, won all three exhibition games and didn't even allow a single goal. The games, however, were panned by the press which called hockey an "individual and typically capitalistic sport."

Team USA 1960, the original "miracle-makers" prior to the Olympics. Herb Brooks is in the front row, second from the left. He was the final cut from the roster but later coached the more famous "Miracle" team of 1980.

to the sportsmen and the spectators," the magazine reported.

The first more or less close encounter with ice hockey, or "Canadian hockey," took place in 1932, when Fichte, a German amateur team con-

After World War II, the game received a sudden jolt. The Soviet government realized that the entire population, tired of the hardships of war, needed something extraordinary to lift its collective spirit. The summer months were already taken up by soccer, but people needed something to do in the winter. So, in 1946, the government insisted that all sports clubs in the Soviet Union had to create a hockey team. On December 22, 1946, the first games of the first official Soviet championship were played.

The Soviets clearly were on the route to international success, yet it still took seven years to make

their debut at the 1954 IIHF World and European Championship in Stockholm, Sweden. Two events caused this delay.

General Vasili Stalin, the son of Josef Stalin, loved sports and decided to create his own teams in many sports. They supposedly represented the Military Air Forces of the Moscow Region and were known as VVS MVO, or just VVS (Voenno-Vozdushnye Sily). His hockey team quickly became the best in the country, but when it was time to play internationally, catastrophe struck. On January 7, 1950, a plane carrying the entire hockey team crashed near Sverdlovsk, in the Ural Mountains, killing the best players in the country.

Finally, the 1954 World Championship in Stockholm became the first, historic showdown of the two hockey superpowers, Canada and the Soviet Union. Of course, nobody gave the Soviet newcomers much of a chance. Swedish newspapers praised the Canadians (represented by the Toronto Lyndhursts) and even published a comic drawing depicting the big teacher in a Canadian uniform

The Soviets' Vsevolod Bobrov (left) congratulates adversary George McAvoy, captain of the Pentincton Vees, after Canada defeated the Soviets 5-0 to win gold at the 1955 World Championship in Krefeld, Germany. Bobrov holds the 1954 edition of the championship trophy.

lecturing the small Russian player, who was sitting behind the school desk. The player's face resembled the Soviet captain, Vsevelod Bobrov.

The setting at the championship was altogether unfamiliar to the Soviet players who had never seen the Canadians play. Still, leading up to the final game against Canada, the Soviets won five out of six games and tied the other, 1-1, against Sweden. The historic day of the last game, March 7, 1954, began with a surprise — tickets went on sale for a second game between the Soviet Union and Sweden. The logic was simple: If Canada were to beat the Soviets (which practically everyone expected), an additional game would have to be staged to decide the European champion because the Soviets and Swedes would be tied for second place at that point. The European champion had always been the top-ranked European team at the World Championships, which prior to 1954 usually meant second place to Canada's first place.

A crowd of 16,000 watched this first unforgettable USSR-Canada game, including Gunther Sabetzki, a correspondent for the German news agency Sport-Informations Dienst and the future president of the IIHF. The Soviets took their opponent by surprise. The team had developed its own style of hockey based on fast skating and passing. The Canadians were beaten 7-2 and the Soviets won their first title. It was the first time that the IIHF awarded prizes to the best players of the tournament. The brilliant Bobrov was named the best forward.

The loss shocked all of Canada, and the Toronto Lyndhursts, in fact only a Senior B team (well below NHL calibre), were severely criticized by media and fans back home for the poor showing. Next year, in 1955, the country expected revenge. The Penticton Vees, the amateur team from a town of 14,000 in British Columbia, was chosen to restore Canadian national pride. A "tough crowd" of reinstated professionals and hard-hitting amateurs, the Vees were led by the Warwick brothers — Grant, Bill, and Dick. Canada won all eight games and — most importantly — settled accounts with the Soviets, beating them by a resounding score, 5-0. Following the game, the Penticton players received congratulations from the governor-general and the prime minister of Canada.

The much anticipated Canada–Soviet game to decide gold at the 1956 Olympics took place on a

cold Saturday evening, February 4, 1956. The Soviets used warm blankets while sitting on the bench, and the Canadians felt comfortable in their wool sweaters. The game began with the Canadians storming the net of Nikolai Puchkov, and they continued unabated for 60 minutes as Jim Logan, Paul Knox, Jack MacKenzie, and others attacked the Soviet goal. Nonetheless, Puchkov held his ground and the Soviets won 2-0, giving them their first Olympic gold medal.

The tournament was a celebration of hockey. "In my humble opinion, the hockey tournament at the Seventh Olympic Winter Games of Cortina d'Ampezzo was the finest in history," said IIHF president Walter Brown. Most importantly, the tournament solidified the Canada-Soviet Union rivalry.

The decision to hold the 1957 World Championship in Moscow was made by the IIHF in recognition of the instant success of Soviet

Soviet goalie Nikolai Puchkov makes the save against the USA during the team's 4-0 win during the 1956 Olympics.

hockey. When it was learned that neither the Canadians nor the Americans were coming to the Soviet Union, the hosts were unanimously considered the tournament favourites. However, two outstanding national teams from Sweden and Czechoslovakia shone in the shadow of the Canada-Soviet Union rivalry.

Most of the games in 1957 were held in the newly-built Luzhniki Sports Palace. Due to the impact of the last game, Soviet Union against Sweden, the tournament directorate decided to play it on the

INTERVIEW WITH HARRY SINDEN

ONE OF THE FEW WHO KNEW BEFORE '72

By Andrew Podnieks

Long before Harry Sinden coached Canada at the 1972 Summit Series he was a player, and a pretty good one, too. In fact, he was one of the few people involved in '72 who had firsthand experience with the Soviet Union, having twice played for Canada internationally — at the 1958 World Championship and the 1960 Olympics.

"I lived in Toronto in the shadow of Casa Loma as a kid and then moved to York Township and went to York Memorial Collegiate," Sinden related of his start in hockey. "I played for a variety of teams in the Toronto Hockey League, and in 1949 I started playing junior hockey in Oshawa."

Once his junior career was over, there were very few choices. "After three years, you had a decision to make," he explained. "I was 20 and could either play in a league like the American league or Western league, or I could get a job. In those days, very few players — and I mean very few — went straight from junior to the NHL, maybe one a year and that was always a superstar player. So, given all of this, I didn't see a career in the NHL for myself, so I stayed at home and played senior hockey."

"In those days, senior hockey was a very good brand of hockey and there were a lot of people playing who were in my position. There were only six teams in the NHL, so senior had a lot of players who maybe weren't good enough for the NHL but who were very talented all the same."

That being said, however, not many players went from senior hockey to the NHL, either, so once Sinden decided not to play in the AHL or a league directly affiliated with the NHL, he had more or less given up on playing for the Stanley Cup. "I started senior hockey in 1953 with Oshawa, but the arena burned down so we moved to Bowmanville and then Whitby where we became the Dunlops. I was also working in Oshawa pursuing a career at General Motors. I was training to become a stationery engineer at the power plant. I only played hockey because I loved the game, and at the senior level I felt I could also supplement my income a little bit as well."

And so began a career that would take him overseas to represent his country. "My first international game was in 1957 when the Soviets toured Canada" he recalled from his Boston Bruins office. "We played them at Maple Leaf Gardens, which was packed. They scored two quick goals and we settled down and won 7-2. The thing I remember the most was how horrible their equipment was! They used one-piece sticks that weighed a ton. Their skates were old. When I think about what they had to play in, they did very well." ∎

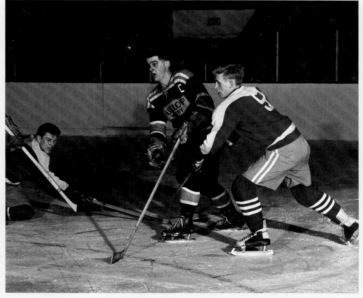

Defenceman Harry Sinden captained the Whitby Dunlops at the 1958 World Championship.

Sinden holds his sweater from nearly half a century ago during a visit to the Hockey Hall of Fame in Toronto in 2006.

Three members of the Soviets' 1956 Olympic team: (l to r) Nikolai Sologubov, Dmitri Ukolov, and Gennadi Sidorenkov.

Sweden's Lars-Eric Lundvall races for the puck against Alfred Kuchevsky of the Soviet Union during an exhibition game in Moscow in 1959.

nearby Luzhniki soccer stadium where some 50,000 spectators were in attendance to watch a World Championship game played on a natural ice-rink set up on a soccer pitch. To this day, no other world championship game has attracted a larger audience. The tie (4-4) brought gold medals to the Swedes, led by a brilliant group of players including Sven "Tumba" Johansson, Lasse Bjorn, Roland Stoltz, Nils Nilsson, and Ronald Pettersson.

The Canadians continued their dominance in 1958, 1959, and 1961, winning 26 of 29 games and beating the Soviets in all four head-to-head clashes. Different teams represented Canada in these tournaments, and it surely looked like that the "good old days" were back. In 1958, in Norway, Canada was represented by the Whitby Dunlops. The tournament generated two memorable moments. Connie Broden, Canada's forward, became the first player to win the world championship title and the Stanley Cup (with the Montreal Canadiens) in the same year. While the Dunlops went on a European tour after the tournament, Broden was flown to Montreal where he immediately joined the Canadiens and became part of their 1958 Stanley Cup-winning team. Another member of the team, Dunlops captain

and defenceman Harry Sinden, became a Stanley Cup-winning coach with the Boston Bruins and coached Team Canada during the 1972 Summit Series.

In 1960, the Americans won their first Olympic title (in Squaw Valley, California) after a game which is still shrouded by controversy. Trailing the Czechoslovaks 4-3 after the second period, the Americans got unexpected help from none other than the Soviet team. Once they had been eliminated from gold-medal contention — and in consideration of their Iron Curtain rivalry with the Czechoslovaks — the Soviets actually offered the Americans oxygen tanks which they had used themselves during the games. The result of this benevolence was astonishing. The Americans scored six unanswered goals in the third period and won the Olympic champion title, a less-heralded but equally astonishing "miracle" that was replicated more famously 20 years later in Lake Placid.

The 1961 World Championship was the last time that the games were played outdoors. A swimming pool was used for this purpose in Lausanne, Switzerland, where powerful freezers turned the water into ice. Oddly, the diving platforms at one

end remained in place. The indoor skating rink in Geneva was also unusual because the "boards" were transparent and made of plastic. The world champion title went to Canada's Trail Smoke Eaters, led by a brilliant goaltender, Seth Martin. However, the dawn of a new era was already in the making. The Soviet squad, which finished third, had 12 future would-be world champions on its roster.

Calling themselves "amateurs," the Soviets now entered a professional era, fully supported by the socialist state which realized the enormous publicity provided by international hockey. The next time they won the World Championship, in 1963, they started a dynasty that lasted nine consecutive years. When Seth Martin, Darryl Sly, Don Fletcher, Addie Tambellini and the other Smoke Eaters jubilantly skated off the ice in Geneva following their convincing 5-1-win over the Soviets to claim gold in 1961, no one could have imagined that it would take Canada another 33 years to capture its next world championship gold.

Anatoli Tarasov performs the double duty of coaching the national team and filming the game during a tour of Canada in the early 1960s. Seated in front of him are (l to r) Stanislav Petukhov, Viktor Yaroslavtsev (with helmet), Vitali Davydov, and Valentin Kozin.

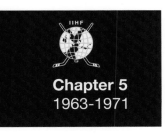

Tarasov's Unstoppable Dynasty

THE "BIG RED MACHINE" WINS NINE CONSECUTIVE GOLD MEDALS

By Igor Kuperman

The 1960s were a magnificent decade for hockey in the Soviet Union. The national team was winning one World Championship and Olympic title after another. Almost all young boys in the country were dreaming of becoming either a cosmonaut or a hockey player (Yuri Gagarin's first flight around the Earth was in 1961). To get a ticket for a hockey game in Moscow was almost impossible.

Hockey became a sport of which the Soviet government was proud. However, in the early 1960s, when Soviet teams began to travel periodically to North America, they became aware of something called "professional hockey." During receptions at the Kremlin, where government officials had an opportunity to rub shoulders with players and coaches, Soviet leaders Nikita Khruschev and later Leonid Brezhnev, sometimes asked the question, "Could we beat the NHL?" Legendary coach Anatoli Tarasov, one of the creators of Soviet hockey, cautiously avoided a straight answer. And why wouldn't he? The Soviet teams were considered the best in the world. Canadians? We beat them regularly at the World Championships! The National Hockey League? Hardly heard of it! In international hockey, we are the best.

Who could criticize this position, especially as the IIHF and IOC strictly prohibited amateurs playing against professionals? Instead, the battles were fought on paper. Tarasov methodically and thoroughly compared the elements of the game — skill, skating, passing, toughness. In his mind, the Soviets were superior. How could he suggest to his hockey-crazed government that the national team, their beloved "sbornaya," was not the best in the world?

The NHL didn't want to deal with that question,

The dominating troika of the 1970s—(l to r) Boris Mikhailov, Vladimir Petrov, and Valeri Kharlamov

either. The Stanley Cup champions were often proclaimed "World Champions," and a challenge from Soviet "amateurs" wasn't all that enticing. There was nothing to prove for the NHL, presumably the best league with the best players in the world.

But the Soviet Ice Hockey Federation first had to solve one big problem before it could consider the NHL question — how to make the national team the best in the world. Coach Arkadi Chernyshev, who led the team in the glorious mid-1950s, had been replaced by his most vocal opponent, Tarasov, in the late '50s. Later, Tarasov was in turn replaced by Chernyshev. Finally, an unexpected

consensus was arrived at by the Soviet Ice Hockey Federation — let them work together.

It was almost impossible to imagine how two such different personalities would work side-by-side. Chernyshev, the "hockey professor," always retained composure and elegance. He loved his stars and knew how to deal with the most talented players. Tarasov was the volcano of passion, sometimes angry, sometimes sarcastic, but always trying to bring out the best from his players.

Chernyshev and Tarasov were not only the coaches who led the Soviet national team to nine unprece-

Anatoli Tarasov (centre) talks to Frank Orr of the Toronto Star *(right) and an unidentified reporter during the Soviets' tour of Canada in the late 1960s.*

Coach Anatoli Tarasov (left) talks to an official as one of Tarasov's players, Viktor Kushtanov, hops onto the ice.

dented consecutive world titles and three Olympic gold medals from 1963 to 1972. They also are the men responsible for polishng the marvelous style of Soviet hockey to perfection. "The speed at which the Soviet team plays is fantastic," Sven "Tumba" Johansson, the Swedish superstar, stated after the 1965 World Championship. "The skills of the world champions are almost beyond the possible," the Austrian newspapers wrote during

summarized the Soviet style of play: "They demonstrated the unique way of playing the game, very different from everything which has been known before. They succeeded and showed the world how to win using this fascinating style."

The incredible run of victories began in 1963, in Stockholm. This championship, which was the first to be shown on Soviet TV, has gone down as one of the most dramatic in the history of international hockey. The day of March 16, 1963, marked the first day of a golden era of the "new wave" of Soviet players. They defeated Canada 4-2 and clinched the gold. This was the first time that the Canadians didn't win a medal in the world event. The championship showed that amateur clubs from Canada (this time it was the Trail Smoke Eaters), even with reinforcements, were clearly no longer able to compete against the best European national teams.

Alexander Yakushev goes through the rigors of a typical Soviet practice in the early 1970s, demonstrating why the team was renowned for its superior conditioning.

the 1967 tournament in Vienna. Many years later, Ken Dryden, one of the greatest goalies of all time,

Players from the Soviet league team Dynamo Riga endure intense dryland training during the early 1970s.

The Soviet national team of 1964 won its third straight gold medal the the 1964 Olympics in Innsbruck.

Father David Bauer poses with the National Team that represented Canada at the 1964 Olympics. This was the first year the country failed to win a medal.

Next year, in their pursuit of an Olympic hockey program, the Canadians brought a National Team to the games in Innsbruck, but even this squad left without an Olympic medal for the first time.

The Soviets continued their march in 1965, when, for the second straight year, the "Big Red Machine" won every game it played. They became

Soviet players hold the World Championship trophy in 1967 in Vienna: (l to r) Viktor Yakushev, Alexander Almetov, and Veniamin Alexandrov.

The Soviets traveled to Montreal to play the Junior Canadiens during the 1964-65 season. Here, Jacques Lemaire (left) challenges Alexander Ragulin as goalie Viktor Konovalenko makes a save.

Juhani Wahlsten celebrates one of his two goals against the Czechs during a 3-1 win at the 1967 World Championship, the first time ever the Finns had defeated Czechoslovakia. He is greeted by teammate Matti Keinonen.

the first European team to capture the World Championship trophy three years in a row, and they got to keep it. The Soviet dominance continued in 1966 and 1967 and at the 1968 Winter Olympics, where after winning its sixth world championship title in a row, the Soviet Union matched Canada's record achievement of 1920-1932. Three years later, in 1971, the Soviet Union national team won its ninth straight title, a record that will surely stand the test of time. The names of Viktor Konovalenko, Alexander Ragulin, Anatoli Firsov, Vyacheslav Starshinov, Boris Mayorov, Veniamin Alexandrov, among others will be forever linked to these years of dominance.

However, the events of the previous year cast a pall over international hockey. The 1970 World Championship was originally allocated to Canada. But Canadians were becoming more and more convinced that their amateur players, even reinforced by ex-pros, were unable to compete against the best European national teams. Having played at six World Championships since 1964, Canada managed to win the bronze only three times.

Canada's representatives at the IIHF Congress in March 1969 in Stockholm opened a discussion about the joint participation of amateurs and professionals. The summer congress in July 1969 in Crans-sur-Sierre, Switzerland, was attended by an unusually large Canadian delegation headed by NHL president Clarence Campbell. A documentary film about professional hockey was also shown and Canada's Prime Minister addressed the delegates with a proposal to make the World Championships open to all players, amateur and pro.

Canada's emissaries succeeded to a great degree. The congress made the rules of the international game virtually identical to those of the NHL. Most significant, the rule forbidding body-checking in the defensive end was abolished.

The vote on the "open" concept, however, was divided — 20 delegates were in favor and 30 against. The congress, however, decided to allow nine professionals on national teams as an experiment for one year, provided that the players were not from the NHL but from minor–league clubs. Furthermore, it was decided that amateur status would be given to players who had left professional hockey six weeks prior to the championships as opposed to six months as had been the practice previously.

Czechoslovak forward Jiri Holik expresses disbelief as his teammates celebrate their second win over the Soviets at the 1969 World Championship, 4-3, in Stockholm. They had earlier won, 2-0. The games were played just months after the Soviet invasion of Czechoslovakia. Despite the two emotional wins, the Czechoslovaks settled for a bronze medal.

Jiri Holik (#20) and Jaroslav Holik (#5) celebrate Czechoslovaks' teammate Jan Suchy's opening goal in the team's 2-0 win over the Soviets in the 1969 World Championship.

Vladimir Dzurilla's crease is full as his Czechoslovak teammates keep the Soviets at bay during the 1968 Olympics.

Goalie Viktor Konovalenko is fooled by Jaroslav Jirik's deflection in front during the Czechoslovaks' 5-4 win in 1968 that ended the Soviets' six-year unbeaten streak in international play.

Using the new rules, Canada went to Moscow in December 1969 to participate in the Izvestia tournament with the allowable number of professionals. The Canadians finished a surprising second after defeating Sweden 5-2 and Finland 10-1 and, most important of all, they posted an impressive 2-2-tie against the Soviet Union. It was the first point a Canadian team had managed against the Soviets on European ice in eight years. The USSR still won the tournament, but Canada's inspired showing with nine more or less mediocre professionals was bad news for the "amateur" establishment.

TWO GAMES CZECHOSLOVAKIA SIMPLY COULDN'T LOSE

There is absolutely no doubt that the most emotionally charged games in the history of international hockey were the two between Czechoslovakia and the Soviet Union in the 1969 World Championship in Stockholm. The tournament was originally allocated to Czechoslovakia, but the country declined to organize the event following the Soviet-led Warsaw Pact invasion of the country in August 1968.

It was, of course, the occupation that put its mark on and totally overshadowed the two clashes between Czechoslovakia and the Soviet Union at the Johanneshov arena in Stockholm on March 21 and 28. The Soviets came to Sweden having won the last six World Championships and three out of the last four Olympics, and they were unquestionably the better team. But these were the games the Czechoslovaks simply could not lose. Playing with unprecedented national fervor, Team CSSR outhustled the Soviets, 2-0 and 4-3.

It was the first time since 1961 that the Soviet Union lost two games in one championship, and it was the first time ever that the USSR lost two games against the same opponent in one IIHF event. Amazingly, Czechoslovakia did not win the gold medal. In fact, it didn't even win silver. After each of the draining encounters with the Soviet Union, the Czechoslovaks could not generate the same sentiments against Sweden. They lost both games against the home team, 2-0 and 1-0, and because of a tie in the standings with the Swedes dropped to third place on goal differential. But perhaps in a larger context, that wasn't so important. Their primary mission had been accomplished.
—Szymon Szemberg

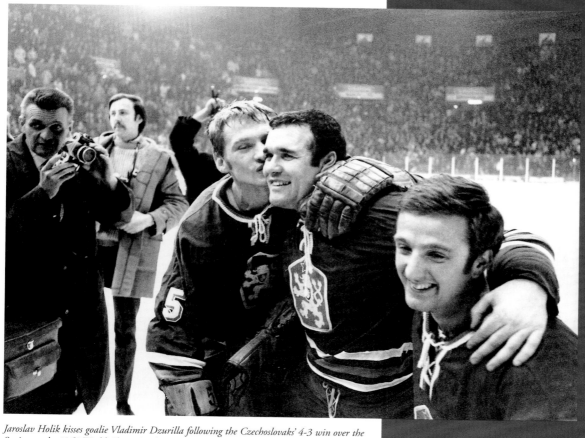

Jaroslav Holik kisses goalie Vladimir Dzurilla following the Czechoslovaks' 4-3 win over the Soviets at the 1969 World Championship.

Meetings that were held in Geneva, Switzerland, in January 1970 produced new tensions between the IIHF and the Canadians when it was decided to prohibit the 1970 hosts from using professional players altogether. The Canadians reacted by withdrawing from the championship and all international hockey. They didn't return until 1977.

In many respects, this was the darkest period of the game. The country that introduced hockey to the world and that had won 19 World Championships and six Olympic hockey gold medals would miss the next seven of the former events and two of the latter in the coming years.

During Canada's seven-year absence, European teams were making it tough for the Soviets. Often, just goal differential or a single point was the difference between the gold and the silver medals. The Czechoslovakians, who had a national hockey system similar to the Soviets, had many brilliant players of their own — Vladimir Dzurilla, Jan Suchy, Frantisek Pospisil, Vaclav Nedomansky, Jozef Golonka, Jiri Holik, and Josef Cerny. The Swedes also had their own heroes — Leif Holmqvist, Roland Stoltz, Sven "Tumba" Johansson, Lars-Eric Lundvall, Ulf Sterner, and Lars-Goran Nilsson. The

INTERVIEW WITH VIKTOR TIKHONOV

Coach Viktor Tikhonov was respected by some players, not so well-liked by others, but his near-perfect record in international play speaks for itself.

CANADA CUP 1987 WAS "PERFECT HOCKEY"

By Vsevolod Kukushkin

Q: Tell us about your playing career.
A: I was quite active in sports, but at the beginning my sport was soccer. It was after the war and as young kids we played soccer in the summer and bandy hockey in winter. Winters were pretty cold and there was no problem with natural ice. I played defence and once Vsevolod Bobrov, who came to Burevestnik stadium, mentioned me to his assistant coach and I got an invitation to play Canadian-style hockey with the VVS (Air Force) team. Bobrov was my godfather in hockey. After VVS, I played with Moscow Dynamo under Arkadi Chernyshov.

Q: When we you aware that you wanted to spend your life in hockey?
A: There was no particular date. When our coach in Dynamo, Arkadi Chernyshov, went to the national team he asked me to run practices and I enjoyed doing that. Soon after, he told me I was going to be his assistant coach. Actually, I wanted to play a little longer, but he insisted. Now I understand that he was right.

Q: What do you remember about the first game you ever coached?
A: When I was working with Chernyshov, I wrote down everything about our practices, so I knew I was ready to coach. But even with Chernyshov in Dynamo we had discussions about my ideas, and when I was coaching in Riga, I had the chance to prove that I was right. Actually, at that time the Dynamo juniors were stronger than Riga's senior team. But I had no choice. We were playing in the third division and I worked about 18 hours a day. We had to improve tactics, physical conditioning, and discipline. Once, a high-

ranked Latvian official stopped me on the street and said that he had heard that I had high demands for the players. "Our Latvian people are not accustomed to work so hard," he said. I answered that it was my job to get the Latvian team to the first division of the Soviet Union league. Several years later we met again and he just smiled when he recalled that meeting. He was big fan and never missed a game in Riga.

Q: Who was your coaching mentor?
A: My coaching mentor was Chernyshov. He was great understanding tactics, very clever. As for Anatoli Tarasov, he was an outstanding club coach, but I later realized that there is big difference between a club coach and a national team coach.

Q: What was the reason why you were named as head coach of the 1976 Soviet Canada Cup team, considering it was two years before you took over as national team coach?
A: In 1976, when our team went to the first Canada Cup, head coach Boris Kulagin had lost the gold medal at the world championship earlier in the year. So, he did not want to go. Maybe he feared the consequences if he were to lose again, I don't know. There was a meeting headed by Valentin Sych. I had been coaching the B team and was one of the coaches interviewed for the job. Everyone was asked how the team would perform if we sent a new group of players, as an experiment. One coach predicted fifth place, another said fourth. I said third, but only if Tretiak was the goalie. I got the job. After the Canada Cup, Kulagin was national team coach again, but then he lost the gold again in 1977, and I was doing well with my team, so I was invited to coach CSKA and the national team.

Q: As a result of the 10-3 exhibition win over the U.S. in New York prior to the Lake Placid Olympics in 1980, do you feel your team took the U.S. team too lightly when you played them in Lake Placid.
A: Yes, I think this is true, to a degree.

Q: Even in the first period of that game in Lake Placid, things weren't right. Can you pinpoint or describe what it was?
A: Actually I had the flu and was not physically at my best. I understand now that even a coach must be in good shape for an event like the Olympics.

Q: Was your decision to remove Tretiak the result of the 2-2-goal or had you been thinking he wasn't playing well for several minutes?
A: It was my mistake. As I said I was not at my best because of flu and all of a sudden I remembered how Vladimir Myshkin played at the Challenge Cup.

Q: Who was the player that you were most proud of developing?
A: With the Moscow Dynamo it was Mikhail Titov and with Riga Dynamo it was Helmut Balderis. When I first saw him, I asked why he wasn't on the national senior team, and they told me it was because of his character. I insisted

that he be on the team, and I started to work with him. He was not an easy guy, but we worked and he wanted to be a champion. He was one the best of those who are "my" players.

Q: Which was the most perfect game by the Soviet national team under your leadership — the 8-1-win 1981 in Montreal, or the 6-0-win in 1979 in New York, or another game?
A: In 1981, we were lucky. The same can be said for 1979. To me, the most perfect hockey was played at the 1987 Canada Cup. Three games with 6-5 scores. I'm not sure which was better between game one and game three.

Q: You were very demanding on your players. Some responded well and some didn't. Looking back, would you have handled some players differently?
A: Each era of hockey presents its own circumstances. At that time, our team was together for eleven months a year and we won almost every game we played. There were many advantages of that system. We had proper nutrition, a careful system of diet, excellent medical services. Also, we had the opportunity to work with the junior players. Today is another world. It is impossible to say whether I would handle Balderis today in the same way as 30 years ago. It wouldn't be the same Helmut, not the same Tikhonov, not the same team, not the same stick and skates.

Q: Did you ever have any ambitions to coach in the NHL?
A: No.

Q: Which of all your wins do you treasure the most?
A: My first world championship in 1978 was the most important for me personally. Nobody thought we would win in Prague at a time when the Czechoslovakians were very difficult to beat at home. I also treasure the Olympic wins in 1984, 1988, and 1992.

Q: How would you compare Ovechkin to Kharlamov?
A: I would put Kharlamov above Alexander Ovechkin. Both of them are great players, but the advantage with Kharlamov is that he could play any style of hockey and play any position.

Q: Before the breakup of the Soviet Union, the country won 28 World and Olympic Gold medals (22+6) and only one after 1990. What reasons can you give for the lack of success since 1990?
A: There are several reasons. In 1992 and 1993 we were playing by inertia. We still had talented young players who were able to play at the highest level. But even then players were starting to go to the NHL. But one year, I had 14 players leave CSKA, and the economy was also in a bad way. Things were changing. Coaches were not thinking about the game but how to feed their families. Now the situation had changed again and we are producing a new generation of talented players. Still, we must work on tactics and skills if they are to be truly great. ■

Finns made remarkable progress in the early 1970s and were led by Urpo Ylonen, Seppo Lindstrom, Pekka Marjamaki, Matti Keinonen, Lasse Oksanen, and Jorma Peltonen.

The Soviet players, though, paid a heavy price for their victories. They endured grueling practices eleven months of the year and lived by rigid rules typical of a totalitarian society. While a Canadian, a Swede, or a Finn went home to his family and friends after a game, the Soviet players went back to the "baza," the training camp.

Soviet national defenceman Alexander Ragulin stands in front of a portrait of himself.

Many of the brilliant Soviet hockey players of the 1960s succumbed to injuries they suffered during their playing days or from the effects of alcoholism. They were largely forgotten after they retired, and they were no longer supported by the government after having passed their prime. Several Soviet hockey heroes passed away long before they reached old age, notably Viktor Konovalenko (age 57), Alexander Ragulin (63), Alexander Almetov (52), Konstantin Loktev (65), Anatoli Firsov (59), Veniamin Alexandrov (54), Gennadi Tsygankov (59), and Yevgeni Mishakov (66).

How would Soviet hockey have fared, if it were played in a free society? Would it have reached the same heights under a democratic system? It is very doubtful. Soviet citizens were accustomed to this simple formula: They say and you do. Sport was not an exception. Talented athletes didn't consider dictatorship in sports as something extraordinary. They were used to it from daily life.

Despite ten World Championships and four Olympic gold medals from 1956 to 1972, there was one lingering question left unanswered: How would the undisputed masters of "amateur" international ice hockey fare in a direct confrontation with Canada's best NHL professionals?

Chapter 6
1972-1979

Old Hockey, New Hockey

EIGHT GAMES THAT CHANGED THE SPORT FOREVER

By Szymon Szemberg

When Team Canada and the Soviet national team skated onto the Montreal Forum ice on the balmy Saturday evening of September 2, 1972, none of the 18,818 fans could have imagined that they were about to witness the start of an eight-game series that would eventually change hockey forever. And why would the fans on this Labour Day weekend anticipate something extraordinary, more than an emphatic confirmation of the Canadian professionals' superiority over the "amateurs" from the Soviet Union?

The 1972 Summit Series between the two traditional powers of the hockey world was not just about hockey, despite this being the first time in history that the best Canada could assemble would meet the team that had dominated the international scene for a decade. It was more "our society against theirs" — the free world against communism — because from a purely hockey perspective the Canadian team was superior, at least according to the pundits.

More or less every reporter and expert who covered the NHL on a daily basis predicted that Team Canada would sweep the series, eight games to zero. Perhaps the Soviets would win one game during a weak Canadian moment. Those who didn't agree with this view were considered eccentric, unpatriotic, soft on communism — or they simply didn't know their hockey. One dissenting view came from former NHLer Billy Harris, who a few months earlier had coached the Swedish national team at both the 1972 Olympics and the IIHF World Championship in Prague. Harris knew, if nothing else, how well conditioned were the Soviets.

There was legendary Canadian national team coach,

J.P. Parise swings his stick toward referee Josef Kompalla during the heat of action in game eight of the 1972 Summit Series. Although he didn't make contact, Parise was given a game misconduct. His actions, however, crystallize the unparalleled emotional intensity of the series. (inset) Kompalla, at home many years later, holds a print of that infamous moment.

Pete Mahovlich's short-handed goal in game two of the Summit Series is regarded as one of the greatest goals ever scored in international hockey. The goal, against Vladislav Tretiak, gave Canada a 3-1 lead at Maple Leaf Gardens and helped Canada tie the series, 1-1.

Father David Bauer, who had taken his amateur Canadian National Team to the world tournaments and Olympics every year between 1964 and 1968. He also knew that the Soviets could skate like the wind, how hard they practiced, and what a sound team concept they had developed.

There were a few other naysayers, but their warnings, as well as the ones from Harris and Bauer, were drowned amidst ignorance and arrogance. As the Forum's public announcer Claude Mouton introduced the Soviet players one by one, the names

Tretiak, Kharlamov, Mikhailov, and Petrov gave the fans no reference. They represented a group of unknowns who were about to be slaughtered. But two hours later, the expected parade of goals had turned into a national trauma: Soviet Union 7, Canada 3. This was without doubt the biggest upset in the history of the game, far, far bigger than the East York Lyndhursts' loss to the upstart Soviets in 1954.

But the bombshell was related to the expectations, not reality. If the term professional stands for the amount of time one devotes to the occupation,

Jubilant players from Team Canada celebrate their dramatic win at Luzhniki Arena in Moscow after game eight as they prepare to shake their adversaries' hands. This rare photo sheds light on what happened in the moments immediately after the 6-5 win.

then the Soviets were, indeed, more professional than the NHL pros themselves. Even in those secretive days, everyone who had any kind of knowledge about the Soviet hockey system knew how seriously they trained. Yet, Canadian officials who negotiated the terms of the series believed Soviet assurances that players were soldiers first, hockey players second. While the NHLers did virtually no exercise between May and September, arrived at training camp in autumn, and worked them themselves into playing condition, the Soviets stayed together for eleven months at their "baza," or, training ground and trained every day. In truth, calling them "amateurs" was as hypocritical as the players' military grades were phony.

Considering the Soviets' superior preparation and their long-standing belief in the team concept, it was no wonder that Team Canada ran out of gas despite an early 2-0-lead in this historic opening game. The Summit Series ended seven games and 26 days later in Moscow in a way that will forever remain as the defining moment in Canadian history. The score was 5-5 with time running out.

The teams were even at three wins each and one tie. When the terms of the series were negotiated

Goalie Tony Esposito makes a great pad save off a shot from Valeri Kharlamov during game two of the 1972 Summit Series at Maple Leaf Gardens in Toronto.

several months earlier, nobody considered the need to discuss any potential tie-breaking procedure. One Soviet official told the Canadian bench in the dying minutes that the Soviet Union would claim victory on goal difference if the last game ended with a tie: they had scored 32 goals to Canada's 30.

With about 40 seconds left in the game, the puck went into the Soviet end and both defencemen — Valeri Vasiliev and Yuri Liapkin — seemed to have full control of the situation. Astonishingly, they mishandled the puck and an exhausted Phil Esposito was able to take a swing at it. Goaltender Vladislav Tretiak made an easy save but allowed a rebound.

Paul Henderson, who just seconds earlier had fallen behind the Soviet goal, scrambled to his feet and suddenly found himself all alone in front of the goalie. Henderson jumped on the rebound. Tretiak made the first save, but he fell on his back as the puck again came out to Henderson. The Canadian forward shot again and this time the puck went through the narrow space between Tretiak's body and the goalie's left post.

The most intriguing match-up in the history of the game was decided with 34 seconds left on the Luzhniki Arena's scoreclock.

More than ten commemorative books were produced about the series, many published several years after the series. There were the television documentaries, video and DVD editions of the games, with interviews, and as late as 2006 a staged documentary (produced by the CBC), a two-part mini-series, re-setting the 1972 drama with actors. The players have gone through several anniversaries and reunions, and in 1999 they were named "Canada's Team of the Century" by the news

The Goal, as it is known in Canada, shows a jubilant Paul Henderson hugging Yvan Cournoyer after his last-minute goal in game eight gave his country the series win over the Soviets. Goalie Vladislav Tretiak lies on the ice while his teammates Vladimir Shadrin (#19) and Yuri Lyapkin react with dismay and anguish.

agency Canadian Press. Paul Henderson has often said that there has not been a day since September 28, 1972, that he has not been reminded of the goal. It was not only a defining sports moment for an entire nation; it was a defining moment of a generation. Ask any Canadian who is old enough to remember, and he can tell you where he was when Henderson scored.

It must be remembered that this series held no "official" importance. There was no trophy, and the players were awarded no medals, not even the smallest commemorative token. There was no prize money. But what it boiled down to was the most essential incentive and basic instinct — national pride and the desire to be the best. Today, Canadians realize that hockey is a global game and that many teams can win any title on any given day. Such was not the case in 1972. Reporters who didn't cover the Olympics and the IIHF World Championship assumed, regardless of how much players from other countries practiced and how the international game evolved, that as soon a player made it to the NHL, he was among the best.

Because the series didn't go the way it was expected, Canadians felt that the game — "our game" — was being taken away from them.

Czechoslovak team captain Frantisek Pospisil holds the World Championship trophy in 1972, the team's first win in 23 years.

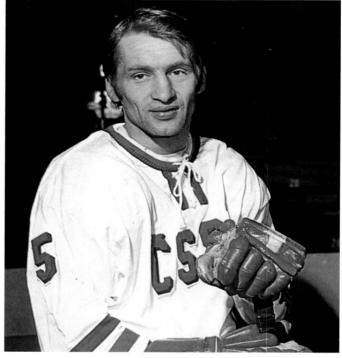

Jaroslav Holik scored the winning goal in the decisive game against the Soviets in 1972 in Prague.

Hockey, the one point of identification that the entire nation from Newfoundland to British Columbia could share, was played more efficiently and more aesthetically by a team from a Communist power that only started to compete internationally 18 years earlier. When Henderson scored, the world order, according to Canadians, was re-established, if only briefly.

The fact is that the Summit Series of 1972 changed international hockey profoundly. Officials who ran the Canadian hockey program and the entire NHL establishment found out the hard way there was another way of playing the game than the dump-and-chase method of generating offense.

The Soviets introduced a style based on criss-cross skating, positional changes, and puck control. In the offensive end, they didn't look for the quick release but rather for another pass to set up the perfect scoring chance. Storming down one side and shooting from the wings — a trademark of many NHL-forwards — was to the Soviets a waste of possession. Team Canada was also frustrated at the Soviet tactic of skating back, regrouping, and staging a new attack when the lane for an adequate outlet pass wasn't available on the first

attempt. This style was in direct contradiction to the traditional NHL approach where players more or less skated up and down in straight lines and where shooting at the net from all angles was encouraged.

However, to say that it was only the Canadians who learned from the Summit Series would be inaccurate. Although not eager to admit it, the Soviets adjusted parts of their game after playing the Canadians. They had lost, after all. Before the Summit, the Soviets treated the boards almost exclusively as a confinement of the rink. They learned from Team Canada to use the boards as an "extra player." Other aspects of the game such as defensive positioning, organization in short-handed situations, protecting the goalie, faceoffs, and storming the net for rebounds were elements the Soviets learned to incorporate into their game.

Just as sports observers consider the 1958 World Cup as the start of modern soccer for Brazil's revolutionary system of using four attackers instead of five, so too was the Summit Series '72 the beginning of modern, international hockey for its clash of styles. The series also generated an atmosphere and flow of emotions never before experienced by

Bobby Hull shakes hands with Czechoslovakian goalie Vladimir Dzurilla after Canada won the inaugural Canada Cup in 1976 with a dramatic 5-4 win in overtime of game two of the best-of-three finals.

Steve Shutt falls awkwardly to the side of Jiri Holecek's crease in a battle with Czechoslovak defenceman Milan Chalupa during game one of the 1976 Canada Cup finals won 6-0 by Canada. Pete Mahovlich looks on in the background.

Bobby Clarke (arm covering face) scores a goal to give Canada a 3-2 lead over the Czechs in game two of the 1976 Canada Cup finals. Bill Barber celebrates for Canada in the background while goalie Vladimir Dzurilla slumps his shoulders in dismay.

either players or fans. In a commemorative book from 2001, Team Canada's goaltender Ken Dryden summarized his memories of the Summit Series: "I've been fortunate to have played on six Stanley Cup winning teams in Montreal. But nothing in hockey ever brought me so low or took me so high [as 1972]. And nothing meant so much."

Few observations describe the sentiments better than the comment made several years later by Phil Esposito, Canada's best player and spiritual leader in the series: "It scares the hell out of me when I think about it now, but I was prepared to kill to win that series."

There were no killings, of course, but at least one

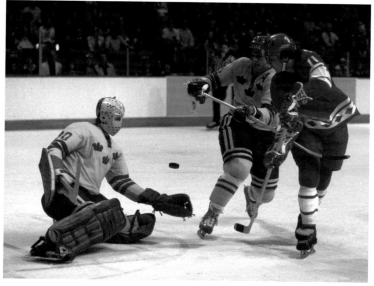

Goalie Hardy Astrom makes a routine save as his defenceman Thommie Bergman takes Boris Alexandrov out of the play during the Sweden-Soviet Union 3-3 tie at the Montreal Forum during the 1976 Canada Cup.

premeditated attack with clear intent to injure. In game six, the second in Moscow, Team Canada's assistant coach John Ferguson gave instructions to Bobby Clarke to take care of Valeri Kharlamov, the Soviet star who the Canadians simply couldn't contain. Clarke whacked the brilliant winger with a vicious slash, cracking his ankle. The Soviets were quick to learn and respond. Boris Mikhailov kicked Canadian defenceman Gary Bergman so hard he bloodied Bergman's leg — through the shin pads.

How Team Canada turned this series around and finally won remains one of the great physiological mysteries in sports history. Despite being painfully ill-prepared and overconfident, and playing an opponent with outstanding skills and stamina, Team Canada somehow pulled out victory. Canada, and only Canada, could have managed to come back from such a seemingly impossible situation. In Moscow, the Canadians had to win the last three games — and they did, 4-3, 3-2, and 6-5. During the 37 years that Soviet ice hockey existed, this was the only time the "Big Red Machine" lost three straight games at home. And all three game-winners were scored by Henderson — a star NHLer but hardly the best of the best — whose speed was a perfect fit for the international game.

The games also had an immediate impact on how the NHL started to view European players. Soviet authorities refused to release any of their stars to the capitalist West, but NHL teams started to look to Sweden and Finland, the best of the free world in Europe, for young players. Swedish defenceman Thommie Bergman became the first European to play a full season as a regular, for the Detroit Red Wings, in the 1972-1973 season. The next year, the Toronto Maple Leafs signed defenceman Borje Salming and forward Inge Hammarstrom. Salming became the first European to become an NHL star,

The medal ceremony at the 1976 Olympics. The Soviets won gold, the Czechs silver, and the West Germans, surprisingly, the bronze.

putting a stop to the pre-conceived notion that Europeans weren't able to deal with the physical strain of the North American game.

The 1972 Summit Series also triggered future exhibition games in North America. Top Soviet club teams began to play exhibition games against NHL teams during the 1975-76 season, and the so-called Super Series, which continued well into the 1990s, produced some memorable hockey.

The 1975 New Year's Eve game between the Montreal Canadiens and CSKA Moscow (labeled "Red Army" to further incite cold war tensions) was probably the best hockey game on a club level ever played. This time, three years after the Summit Series opener in the same arena, the Montreal Forum crowd knew all the players, as CSKA was more or less equivalent to the Soviet national team. The 3-3-tie remains a classic of pure hockey.

The inaugural Canada Cup was staged in 1976, an "open" tournament in which the top six countries in the world were invited to use their best players, amateur or pro. The host nation, now so much more enlightened and better prepared than four years earlier, defeated Czechoslovakia 6-0 and 5-4 in the best-of-three finals and positioned the Canada Cup in the international calendar as the most important tournament alongside the Olympics and World Championships. The Soviets, not wanting to risk too much of their prestige as an "amateur" world power, sent what they called an "experimental team" in

1976, one which managed to defeat only USA and Finland.

As the IIHF abandoned its long-standing amateur rules, Canada returned to the World Championship in the spring of 1977 after a seven-year absence. It

Wieslaw Jobczyk celebrates his team's final goal at 19:40 of the third period during Poland's astonishing 6-4 victory over the Soviets (and goalie Vladislav Tretiak) during the 1976 World Championship.

was not a glorious comeback. Father David Bauer's amateur program had been replaced by the best available NHLers who were not involved in the

THE MOTHER OF ALL HOCKEY UPSETS

On February 8, 1976, the Soviet Union demolished Poland 16-1 in the first game of the Innsbruck Olympics. The Soviets were superior throughout the tournament and didn't lose a game, capturing their fourth straight Olympic gold medal. Exactly two months after the slaughter at Innsbruck, the same teams met again on April 8 in the first game of the World Championship at Katowice, Poland.

In the last seven World Championships prior to the 1976 event, the Soviets had defeated Poland by scores of 9-3, 20-0, 8-3, 17-0, 13-2, 15-1, and 16-1. But in Katowice, in front of 10,000 raucous Polish fans, the Soviets committed the biggest mistake in sports — underestimating their opponents. A virtually unknown forward by the name of Wieslaw Jobczyk, 22, scored three goals and led Poland to a 6-4 victory. Soviet coach Boris Kulagin started seldom used backup goalie Alexander Sidelnikov in goal, but he was forced to insert star Vladislav Tretiak with Poland 4-1 up in the second period.

This was arguably the biggest single-game upset in international hockey history, even bigger than the American "Miracle on Ice" victory against the USSR in Lake Placid 1980.

But the difference was that the Polish win was just a one-off miracle and had no further implications (other than that the Soviet team never recovered from the embarrassment and eventually lost the 1976 World Championship to the Czechoslovaks). Poland never recovered either. The next day, the Poles lost to Czechoslovakia 12-0 and were later relegated to the B pool of the World Championships for 1977.
—Szymon Szemberg

Vladislav Tretiak (left) and Ken Dryden (right) hold hands high during the retirement of Dryden's number 29 sweater at the Bell Centre, Montreal, on January 29, 2007. The moment is in stark contrast to their adversarial roles 35 years earlier during the Summit Series.

Stanley Cup playoffs, but the tournament showed that the years with very limited international competition affected Canada negatively. The Soviets pounded Canada 11-1 and 8-1 in two games, and Canada's showing was a sportive and public relations disaster. Led by the undisciplined play of Wilf Paiement, Canada, which finished fourth, regressed to violence and came home shamed and scorned, so much so that its performance was mentioned in the Canadian parliament.

The 1970s was the most important decade in hockey history. It saw the re-establishment of relations between the old continent and Europe. It showed that competition by the best against the best is fundamental to a sport's health, while isolation is destructive. The Cold War was not good for mankind, but it generated a phenomenal hockey rivalry — Canada and the Soviet Union — and it gave the world games with such heated atmosphere which only a clash with social and political undertones could produce.

Starting with the 1972 Summit Series, the rivalry lasted fifteen years. The 1987 Canada Cup would be the last major tournament that would generate such strong sentiments. After that, games would be just about hockey.

EUROPE'S FIRST NHL SUPERSTAR

By Andrew Podnieks

For a European player to be drafted into the NHL, play junior hockey in Canada, and have a nice, steady place in the NHL for a decade is nothing new at all in the 21st century. But in 1973, there were no Europeans who had made an impact in the NHL. Only Thommie Bergman had lasted a season, in Detroit in 1972-73, but he was a 26-year-old stay-at-home defenceman, not a player to build a team around.

In the summer of 1973, the Toronto Maple Leafs signed two Swedish players, forward Inge Hammarstrom and defenceman Borje Salming. Hammarstrom had a tough time adjusting to the physical NHL game, the long road trips, and the grind of a season that had nearly 100 games to it (exhibition, regular season, playoffs). Salming, who was billed as a smooth-skating blueliner in the style of Bobby Orr, had greater pressures to face, and he dealt with them head on.

"I knew what was going to happen when I came over here," he said the day his number was raised to the rafters of Air Canada Centre in Toronto on October 6, 2006. "I knew it would be tough hockey. I talked to Thommie Bergman, who played for Detroit, and we talked about how much fighting there would be."

Salming, indeed, had to fight to earn the respect of his teammates and opponents alike. He took punishment other players didn't have to, and he dropped his gloves against the true brawlers of the game such as Dave Schultz in Philadelphia. Salming did it all to survive, and he combined this brawn with the skill he had founded his reputation on, leading the attack from the blueline, guiding the power play, and playing solid defence in his own end. It was clear very quickly he was going to stay in the NHL a long time.

"I think in training camp, when we first came over, we realized we were doing pretty well," Salming suggested. "At that time, a lot of the players didn't arrive in good shape, but we came in in really, really good shape because we had been on the ice already for two months and had trained hard all summer long. When we came on the ice, me and Inge Hammarstrom, we were

flying. That gave us a lot of confidence and everybody else saw that we had come over to play hockey."

Of course, it didn't take long for the Leafs to figure out he was a special player, and as such they did whatever they could to keep him on the ice and out of the penalty box and trainer's room. "After a couple of years, the Leafs didn't want me to fight, so they said don't drop the gloves," he explained. "You can help us more this way. But sometimes you had to fight and sometimes there were brawls."

The true nature of Salming's success, and the start of the European influence in the NHL, wasn't fully understood until the 1976 Canada Cup. Several of the games took place at Maple Leaf Gardens, including Sweden's game against the U.S. Prior to the opening faceoff, Salming received a standing ovation that to this day goes down as one of the greatest moment's in that arena's long and storied history.

"That was a special game for me," he said. "It was sort of different because I didn't realize what was going on and people watching back home in Sweden didn't realize what was going on because the fans were cheering me. I thought if anything the fans would go the other way because they had Team Canada and I was playing for another country, Sweden. It was incredible."

Some 17 NHL years later (16 with the Leafs), Salming, the all-time points leader for Toronto defencemen, returned home, played at the 1992 Olympics, and then retired from international hockey. He was inducted into the Hockey Hall of Fame in 1996, the first European so honoured for his NHL career. ■

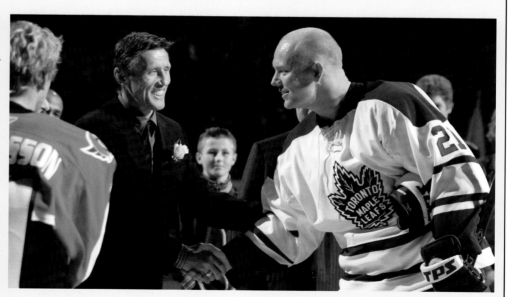

Borje Salming shakes hands with countrymen Mats Sundin of Toronto and Ottawa's Daniel Alfredsson. The pre-game ceremony was part of the Maple Leafs' honouring of Salming's #21 sweater at the Air Canada Centre.

The Miracle—Team USA celebrates its historic 4-3 defeat of the Soviets at the 1980 Olympics in Lake Placid. While the Americans rejoice, Soviet goalie Vladislav Tretiak, pulled late in the first period, looks away (foreground, bottom left).

The Americans fall to the ice in disbelief after their historic conquest.

XIII OLYMPIC WINTER GAMES LAKE PLACID 1980

```
DATE:  02.22.80          OFFICIAL HOCKEY GAME REPORT              PAGE
TIME:  19.37.38               OLYMPIC FIELDHOUSE       GAME 32  FINAL RESULT
                           GAME TIME:  S17.06  E19.26
   TEAM A:  USA      DRESS:  WHITE     TEAM B:  URS      DRESS:  RED
-------------------------------------------------------------------------
    1  G    JANASZAK Steve              1  G    MYSHKIN Vladimir
   30  G  * CRAIG James               20  G  * TRETJAK Vladislav
    3  D  * MORROW Kenneth             2  D  * FETISOV Viacheslav
    5  D  * RAMSEY Michael             5  D    PERVUKHIN Vasili
    6  D  A BAKER William             6  D  A VASILIEV Valeri
   17  D    O'CALLAHAN John            7  D  * KASATONOV Aleksei
   20  D    SUTER Bob                 12  D    STARIKOV Sergei
    8  F  * SILK David                14  D    BILJALETDINOV Zinetulla
    9  F    BROTEN Neal                9  F    KRUTOV Vladimir
   10  F  * JOHNSON Mark              10  F    MALTSEV Alexandre
    1  F    CHRISTOFF Steven          11  F    LEBEDEV Juri
   15  F    WELLS Mark                13  F C* MIKHAILOV Boris
   16  F    PAVELICH Mark             16  F  * PETROV Vladimir
   19  F    STROBEL Eric              17  F  * KHARLAMOV Valeri
   21  F  C ERUZIONE Michael          19  F    BALDERIS Helmut
   23  F    CHRISTIAN David           22  F    ZHLUKTOV Victor
   24  F  * McCLANAHAN Robert         23  F    GOLIKOV Aleksandre
   25  F    SCHNEIDER William         24  F    MAKAROV Sergei
   27  F    VERCHOTA Philip           25  F    GOLIKOV Vladimir
   28  F    HARRINGTON John           26  F    SKVORTSOV Aleksandre
-------------------------------------------------------------------------
SCORING TIME    GOAL                    ASSISTS

09:12   9 URS  KRUTOV          7  KASATONOV
14:03  25 USA  SCHNEIDER      16  PAVELICH
17:34  24 URS  MAKAROV        23  GOLIKOV
19:59  10 USA  JOHNSON        23  CHRISTIAN        8  SILK
22:18  10 URS  MALTSEV         9  KRUTOV
46  9 10 USA  JOHNSON         8  SILK
50:00  21 USA  ERUZIONE       16  PAVELICH        28  HARRINGTON


-------------------------------------------------------------------------
PENALTY TIME                  MIN OFFENSE  !STATISTICS 1/3 2/3 3/3   F
-------------------------------------------------------------------------
03:25  13 URS  MIKHAILOV       2  HOOKING   !
20:58  28 USA  HARRINGTON      2  HOLDING   !  SHOTS ON GOAL
29:50  30 USA  CRAIG           2  DELAY     !     USA     8   2   6  16
37:08  11 URS  LEBEDEV         2  UNSPORT   !     URS    18  12   9  39
37:08   3 USA  MORROW          2  X-CHECK   !  PEN MIN
46:47   9 URS  KRUTOV          2  HI-STICK  !     USA     0   6   0   6
                                          !     URS     2   2   2   6
                                          !  GOALS
                                          !     USA     2   0   2   4
                                          !     URS     2   1   0   3
                                          !
                                          !  REFEREE:   KAISLA
                                          !  LINESMEN:  LAROCHELLE
                                          !             TOEMAN
```

The official scoresheet provides statistical proof that the game really was 4-3 for USA!

Chapter 7
1980-1985

The Miracle and the Revenge

PURE AMATEURS MAKE HOCKEY HISTORY

By John Sanful

By 1978, the Soviet Union had won six of nine IIHF World Championships over the decade. But after consecutive gold losses to Czechoslovakia at the 1976 and 1977 World Championships, there were changes behind the bench when Boris Kulagin was replaced by Viktor Tikhonov under whom the Soviets recaptured the world title in 1978.

A new test in a series of Soviet versus North American confrontations came with the 1979 Challenge Cup. This was the first time the NHL devoted its all-star break to an international challenge. Held at Madison Square Garden in New York City, the newly–introduced cup would be given to the winner of a best-of-three series between the NHL All-Stars the Soviet national team.

NHL President John Ziegler (left) and NHLPA executive director Alan Eagleson (right) look on as Soviet captain Boris Mikhailov holds the Challenge Cup after the devastating 6-0 win over the NHL All-Stars at Madison Square Garden.

Despite winning game one, 4-2, the NHL All-Stars could not contain a Soviet team that roared back to win the final two games. As the series progressed,

the USSR grew stronger and more confident, holding the All-Stars scoreless over the final 94:54 of the series. In game three, the Soviets won 6-0 with backup Vladimir Myshkin in goal. In truth, Tikhonov and the Soviet hockey authorities valued

Not only did the Soviets solidly defeat the best that the NHL had to offer, they did so in mid-season when the NHLers where at their peak. And, the win was accomplished in the "capitalist capital of the world." To suggest the win was merely a step to

Led by Mike Eruzione holding the torch, members of the 1980 Miracle on Ice team light the cauldron at the opening ceremonies to the 2002 Olympics in Salt Lake City, Utah.

Team USA players celebrate after receiving their gold medals in 1980.

this lop-sided win over the NHL as much as any World Championship or Olympic victory. Publicly, however, their words were more forward-looking and less congratulatory.

"Actually, the two best teams of the world have confronted each other and the result indicated that ours was the best team," said Vyacheslav Koloskov, the deputy minister in charge of hockey. "We said before this series that it was merely an important stage in our preparation for the world championship. This was our opinion before the victory, and we hold the same opinion after the victory."

something bigger added insult to injury for the North American hockey establishment.

That April, the Soviet Union triumphed again at the World Championships in Moscow, defeating Czechoslovakia, 6-1, in the decisive game. Team Canada, loaded with NHL players, was humbled 9-2 and 5-2 by the Soviets in the process. With the Olympics ten months away, the Soviets were better than ever.

One week before the start of the 1980 Olympics in Lake Placid, New York, the Soviet nationals re-

USA goalie Jim Craig, one of the heroes of the 1980 victory.

turned to Madison Square Garden for an exhibition game against the USA Olympic team. It was a route of embarrassing proportions. Exactly one year to the date after the USSR blanked the best pros 6-0 in the same arena, they trounced the collegian Americans, 10-3. The wide-eyed Americans were in awe of their rivals, but head coach Herb Brooks had a different take on things.

"I hurt these kids by being too conservative," Brooks said after the game. "I should have turned

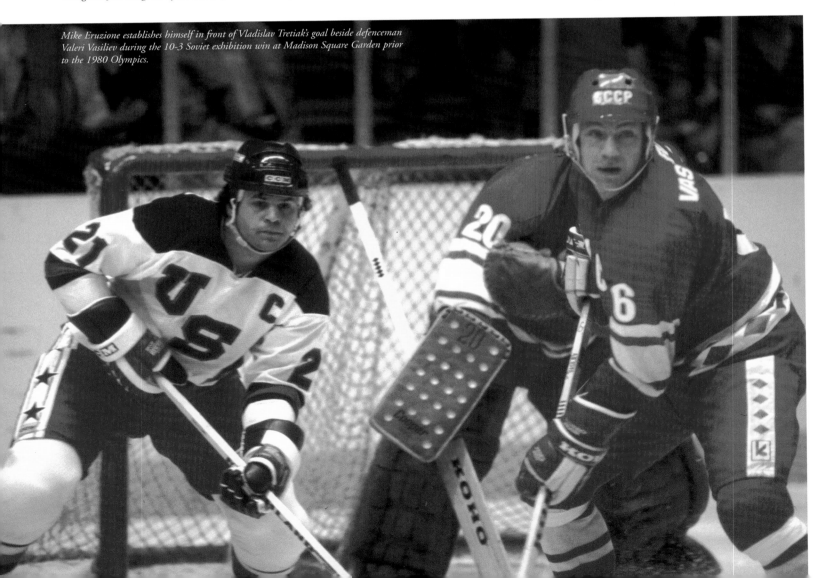

Mike Eruzione establishes himself in front of Vladislav Tretiak's goal beside defenceman Valeri Vasiliev during the 10-3 Soviet exhibition win at Madison Square Garden prior to the 1980 Olympics.

them loose. I helped make them nervous, but even so, we learned about speed of execution and that you can't chase those guys."

Brooks was an inspired choice as head coach. He was not afraid to incorporate European styles into his system. But Brooks' team was young, and, on paper, no match for the competition they would face in Lake Placid. If the 10-3 result was a sign of things to come, surely the Soviet team would not be stopped from winning their third consecutive Olympic gold medal.

1980 USA head coach Herb Brooks.

On February 12, 1980, the Soviet Union manhandled Japan 16-0 to win its opening game of the round robin preliminary round while the Americans struggled to a 2-2 tie with Sweden. Defenceman Bill Baker's booming slapshot goal with just 27 seconds left in the game salvaged the tie. At that point, the biggest surprise of the tournament was Poland's 5-4 victory over Finland. Two days later, while the Soviets easily dispatched the Netherlands, USA shocked Czechoslovakia, 7-4. Czechoslovakia was the only other nation to win

gold during the 1970s, winning the 1972, 1976, and 1977 World Championships.

The USSR won Group A with a perfect 5-0-0 record. In Group B, Sweden and the Americans both finished with four wins and a loss. In the first games of the final round of four teams, Sweden faced Finland and the Americans took on the Soviet Union.

"For the U.S. team, it will be discovery time; it is one thing to be young and promising but quite another to be good," said recently retired Canadian goaltender Ken Dryden during the pre-game show on American television. "They will be playing against a very good team, a team that is better than they are… and after it is all over this team will find out an awful lot about themselves."

As if the game required further subplot, the United States and Soviet Union were immersed in Cold War tensions ranging from the nuclear arms race to the Soviet invasion of Afghanistan. But for one afternoon, political considerations between

Kurt Russell (middle, arms raised) played coach Herb Brooks in the movie "Miracle," shot in Vancouver in 2003.

both nations would be played out on Olympic-sized ice. That afternoon, the winner would have bragging rights no matter what were the larger foreign policy issues. There was an electric feeling in the air as the upstart Americans took on the "Big Red Machine."

The Soviets took play to the Americans from the opening faceoff. But when the Soviets scored, Team USA answered back. Vladimir Krutov's opening goal at 9:12 was offset by Buzz Schneider's long shot that sailed over Vladislav Tretiak's glove. A late goal by Sergei Makarov gave his team a 2-1 lead, but Mark Johnson weaved through defenders in front of Tretiak to collect a rebound off a long shot from centre ice by Dave Christian to tie the game at 19:59 of the first period. It was a shocking goal that provided the Americans with a spark and led to a coaching decision that had ramifications beyond the game.

With the lone second remaining on the scoreclock, coach Tikhonov had already sent their players to the dressing room thinking the period was over. But the referee called the team back to the ice, and when they returned for the faceoff, backup goalie Vladimir Myshkin had replaced Tretiak.

"Tikhonov later said 'it was the biggest mistake of my life'," said Tretiak 26 years after the game. "I was very mad about being replaced, and after the Olympics it was the first time that I thought maybe I did not want to play hockey anymore."

In the middle period, Alexander Maltsev scored to give his team a one-goal lead for the third time, but the Americans replied in the third when Johnson scored his second of the afternoon. The game remained deadlocked until Mike Eruzione scored an unassisted goal midway through the final period. Tretiak could do nothing but watch helplessly as Eruzione's shot went past Myshkin, who threw his arms up in the air to disavow any fault on his part. American goalie Jim Craig played the best ten minutes of his career for the remainder of the game. The Americans defeated the Soviet Union, 4-3.

Those who watched the game understood the sig-nificance of the moment. The American under-dogs shocked the Soviet national team and the millions of its hockey-loving fans in the USSR. At home, the miracle inspired young American boys who watched the game to pick up a stick and play hockey. The American victory over the Soviets was without equal — a group of true amateurs defeated a team that was amateur by name only, a team that was, in fact, the most professionally-trained group of hockey players ever.

Tikhonov did not take the loss well, telling his players, "this is your loss," specifically identifying Tretiak, Petrov, Mikhailov, and Kharlamov. Things grew murkier after the team returned to Moscow. At one point, defenceman Vladimir Vasiliev grabbed Tikhonov menacingly before he was pulled away.

After Lake Placid, the Soviet national side was a team more focused, one that played with remark-able intensity. Not only did the Soviets recover, they struck back harder then ever. They won every World Championship tournament leading up to the 1984 Olympics in Sarajevo, winning 28 straight games. At the 1981 World Championship in Goteborg, Sweden, they dismantled host

The Soviet "Fab Five" of the 1980s—(back, l to r) defencemen Alexei Kasatonov and Vyacheslav Fetisov; (front, l to r) forwards Sergei Makarov, Igor Larionov, and Vladmir Krutov.

Viktor Tikhonov coached the Soviets to eight World Championships and three Olympic gold medals.

could put on skates were thrashed to the tune of 8-1 by the Soviets, handing Canada its worst loss at a senior competition.

If one ranked the different periods of Soviet hockey superiority during their 38-years of international existence, this would probably be the peak day. The very best players in Canada were soundly taken apart, piece by piece. Just like on the opening night of the Summit Series nine years earlier, the fans at the Forum could not grasp what was happening.

Heading into the 1984 Olympics in Sarajevo, the Soviets were more guarded in their confidence, but the subplot centred around whether the Americans could recapture the magic to win gold again. Only two players remained from the 1980 team — Phil Verchota and John Harrington. Moreover, the team was even younger that its predecessor. Herb Brooks, who was coaching the New York Rangers, was replaced by Lou Vairo.

Tre Kronor 13-1 in the game that decided the gold medal.

The apex of Soviet hockey superiority occurred on September 13, 1981, the finals of the 1981 Canada Cup. That night, the very best players Canada

The Soviets were far different than the team from Lake Placid and only ten players remained. The top forwards — Mikhailov, Petrov, and Kharlamov — were replaced by new stars. Kharlamov, the

heart and soul of the team going back to the 1972 Summit Series, had suffered injuries that slowed him down. Sadly, he perished in an automobile accident on August, 28, 1981, after being cut from the roster for the upcoming Canada Cup. Vyacheslav Fetisov, Alexei Kasatonov, Sergei Makarov, and Krutov were members of the 1980 team. Now, they were confirmed stars. Igor Larionov was added to the forward line with Makarov and Krutov.

At the 1983 World Championship in West Germany, the Soviet Union went undefeated in winning gold. All the six championship all-stars were Soviets — Tretiak in goal and the five-man

KRALIK AND SEJBA — CZECHOSLOVAK HEROES IN '85

Following the devastating Olympic loss to the United States in Lake Placid on February 22, 1980, the Soviet national team went on a five-year rampage during which time it didn't lose a single World Championship or Olympic game until it was stopped by Czechoslovakia in the 1985 World Championship.

Prior to the game on April 29, 1985, in Prague, the Soviets had accumulated a streak of 43 games without a loss (39 wins, 4 ties). In the playoff game before 13,908 fans at the Sportovni Hala in 1985, goaltender Jiri Kralik was the hero as the Czechoslovaks ended the Soviet parade with a 2-1-win.

The Soviet team was so shaken by the defeat that it also lost the next game, against Canada, when a 19-year old Mario Lemieux scored two goals inflicting the Soviet Union with a 3-1-loss. The gold medal game featured Czechoslovakia and Canada, and this time another Czechoslovak hero emerged in the 5-3 win. Little known Jiri Sejba scored a hat trick to give the country its sixth World Championship gold medal. The next time the nation celebrated a World Championship gold medal, in 1996, it was known as the Czech Republic.
—Szymon Szemberg

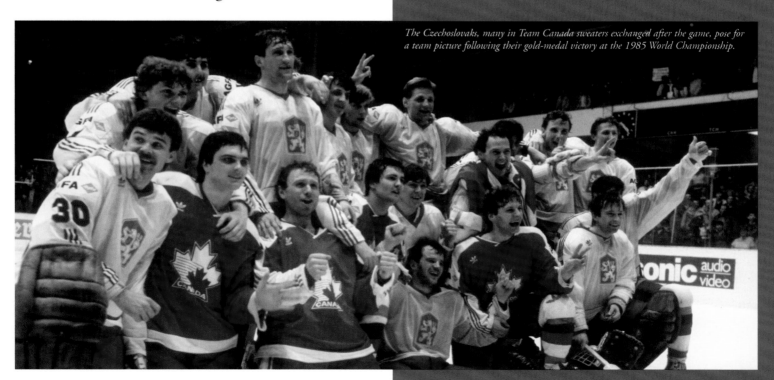

The Czechoslovaks, many in Team Canada sweaters exchanged after the game, pose for a team picture following their gold-medal victory at the 1985 World Championship.

The most accomplished goalie in international hockey history, Vladislav Tretiak poses in a dressing room at the Riga Arena during the 2006 World Championship in Latvia.

THE ESSENTIAL TRETIAK

By Andrew Podnieks
and John Sanful

Now the president of the Russian Ice Hockey Federation, Vladislav Tretiak looks back on a career of unparalleled success in international hockey.

CHILDHOOD

I was born in Moscow, in a sports family. My mother played hockey — bandy, actually. When I was two or three years old, I played with my mother's bandy stick every day. When I was a kid, hockey was the number-one sport in the Soviet Union. I watched the World Championship every year on TV and the Olympics, and we always had a strong team. I wanted to play like them.

I was always very disciplined. My father was an army pilot in the air force,

and he pushed my brother [Valeri] and I to be disciplined in school, in sports, everything. He pushed me to play soccer, to ski, to swim, play hockey. I tried everything.

I went to Red Army training camp because I liked their uniforms — red sticks, gloves, helmet, sweater. Each professional club had small teams for kids. I started with Red Army when I was eleven, and I was with them my whole career. The first time I went, there must have been 200 kids trying out. They needed four. I was the third player chosen because I skated very well, and I was strong. I was a forward. I was eleven years old. I played forward for about five months, but I didn't have any equipment, so whenever the puck hit me, it bruised me. One day, my father asked me why I had so many bruises. I told him, and he said I had to quit hockey if they didn't give me the proper equipment. The next day, I went to the coach and told him I needed equipment to play. He said the only equipment the team could give me was for a goalie. I didn't care. I just wanted to play for the Red Army. So, that's how I started to play goal!

In my first year, I played against boys who were two years older. For the first

INTERVIEW WITH VLADISLAV TRETIAK

half of the season, I was the backup, but I played better and better and then I became the starting goalie. I was lucky because all my teammates went to school in the morning and I went to school in the afternoon, so I never practiced with them. So, the coach always had a lot of time for me and we worked on technique every day. Tarasov taught me my own style. I was the first goalie in Europe to play the full butterfly. After me, every goalie in Europe played the full butterfly.

My father never liked hockey, but then I told him I was a professional and the government paid me. He said, "Oh, well, then, that's okay!" Then when friends of his in the army said the new goalie is also named Tretiak, he said, "Yes, that's my son!"

When I was 17 and playing for the Red Army, a professional team, every newspaper was writing about this new goalie who was playing for the best team in the Soviet Union! It was unbelievable.

CAREER DECISION

I played four years at the World Junior Championship. Back then it was only Sweden, Finland, Czech, Russia. I won three gold medals. I played at 15,16,17, 18. The first time I played for the national team, I was 17. Mr. Tarasov gave me the chance. He said come to practice tomorrow. I said I can't — I have school. He said, hockey or school. Choose. So I went to practice the next day. He said if I kept playing, I will be the best goalie in the world one day. He said it was good experience for me to play for Red Army. I was the backup for Viktor Konovalenko for two years. He was my hero growing up. I liked goalies. He looked like a mushroom — small, stocky, tough.

I loved hockey, but I never thought about playing as a professional or on the national team. I liked beating the other team. I like seeing Konovalenko. I like being a goalie. But I never thought about anything else.

My favourite way to practice was with tennis balls. It's very good for your concentration. I would stand in front of a wall and play catch with two balls, one for each hand.

ON THE 1972 SUMMIT SERIES

We had heard for quite a while about the possibility of playing Team Canada, but we didn't know anything about the players. I stood in my crease before the first game, and they introduced Bobby Clarke. He got a three-minute ovation. Jean Ratelle — three-minute ovation. Then Kharlamov — three claps. It was a little bit scary. Fans in the Soviet Union were quiet in those days, but in Canada, I wanted to talk to my defencemen during whistles but I couldn't because they played loud music. The arena was so big.

The first three or four minutes of game one was very fast hockey. They scored two goals, and Phil Esposito came up to me and said, "Don't worry — there'll be more and more!" For me, it was good because I like lots of shots. I don't think; I just play. It helps me.

LOSING IT ON HOME ICE

We went home and believed that since we beat Canada in Canada the games in Moscow would be the easy part — we'll win for sure. Then, we won the first game and we were sure we'd win, but Canada was different. They came to Russia and were focused, and everything changed. We practiced every day, but we didn't concentrate. And then, in the last game, we had some bad luck.

After two periods, we were leading 5-3 and we thought we'd won, but we made some mistakes and Canada played unbelievably well. On the winning goal, my defenceman, Vasiliev, had the puck but he waited and waited, and then Paul Henderson had the puck. He shot once, twice, and third time he scored. I don't know where my defencemen were! I think it's God who made Team Canada beat us. But I don't think anybody lost. Everybody won because Team Canada and Team Russia played the best. And here we are 34 years later, and everyone remembers 1972. That was the best hockey.

BEST AND WORST OF TIMES

New Year's Eve, 1975, in Montreal. That was my best game. The worst game was at the 1980 Olympics against USA because my coach, Tikhonov, pulled me after the first period with the score 2-2. I went to the dressing room and I wanted to play, but the coach said, "Tretiak, you made a mistake. You don't play anymore." I never go to the bench after allowing two goals! If the score was 5-0, okay. I could understand. That was the first time in my life I had been pulled in a 2-2 game. Tikhonov later said it was the biggest mistake of his life. I think so, too. I was very mad. After the Olympics, I thought about retiring. Then, I thought I could play better and better, so I didn't retire.

PLAYING IN THE NHL

I remember we beat the Czechs in the 1984 Olympic finals, and I thought that was my last game. I wanted to play for the Montreal Canadiens, but the government said no. They told me I had to stay in Moscow, that I'd never play in North America. I played 15, 16 years with the same team. Today I have ten gold medals. If I had eleven, it wouldn't matter. If I had ten gold medals and one Stanley Cup, that's different. Because I was a professional goalie, I wanted to play in the NHL, the best league in the world. If I played in the NHL, I would have played four, six years more because the desire was there. There was no more motivation to play with Red Army in Russia. I was tired. ■

unit of the KLM line (Krutov, Larionov, Makarov) and defencemen Fetisov and Kasatonov. This had never happened before — or since.

In Sarajevo, the Soviets advanced to the playoff round with ease. They won all five games and outscored their opponents by 42-5. In the playoff round, they blanked Canada 4-0 and Czechoslovakia, in what became the gold medal game, 2-0. Tretiak was virtually unbeatable, not allowing a goal in the medal round. On the decisive day, January 19, 1984, only the 32-year old Vladislav Tretiak knew that this would be his last major tournament game.

"I feel extremely happy," Tikhonov said through an interpreter at the press conference. "In the last few years, we've had a number of wins… and the only thing we've been missing is the Olympic gold medal. And now we've achieved it."

The USA, defending Olympic champions from Lake Placid, finished seventh.

As the Soviet team regained its status atop the international hockey community, there was internal dissention the seeds of which were sown from the

first period of the game against the Americans at Lake Placid. Perhaps stung by the loss in 1980, Tikhonov became more relentless as a coach. In only a few short years, however, his tactics had exacted a toll on the players.

The biggest blow to the national team was Tretiak's retirement. When the Montreal Canadiens drafted Tretiak in the sixth round of the 1983 NHL Entry Draft, he was excited by the possibility of playing in the NHL. During the Sarajevo Olympics, the Canadiens negotiated with Soviet authorities for his release. At only 32, Tretiak seemed the perfect choice to become the first Soviet-trained player to come to the NHL with permission of authorities. Further discussions proved fruitless, however, and his participation in the NHL was not permitted. As a result, he saw no reason to continue playing; the greatest goaltender in the history of Soviet/Russian hockey retired two months after Sarajevo, following an insignificant exhibition tournament in the spring of 1984 in Sweden.

"I had ten gold medals at the World Championships; an eleventh (in 1985) would not have made a difference," said Tretiak. "But

to compete for a Stanley Cup is different. I wanted to play in the NHL because it is the best league in the world."

The spectacular play of Tretiak over 15 years was not something that could be easily replaced. In fact, one might argue from that day to this, he has never adequately been replaced.

In the fall of 1984, the Canada Cup saw the Soviet Union lose the one-game semi-final to Canada in Calgary on Mike Bossy's overtime goal. The following spring, the USSR saw its World Championship streak of five consecutive titles come to an end when it was unseated by Czechoslovakia in Prague and finished third, the worst finish since 1977. No one can say that the Soviet streak would have continued had Tretiak — and not Vladimir Myshkin — been in nets for the 1984 and 1985 losses, but even Myshkin agreed that he was no Tretiak.

Indeed, the golden age of Soviet hockey was coming to an end; the once secretive makeup of the "Big Red Machine" would soon be revealed. And the changing world would, with the fall of the Berlin Wall, also have a profound effect on the Soviet hockey system.

The great Gretzky, from behind, during his one and only trip to the World Championship, in 1982. He Led the tournament in scoring with 14 points in ten games.

IIHF
Chapter 8
1986-1997

New World Order

THE END OF HOCKEY'S OLD POWER BALANCE

By Klaus Zaugg

Several years before U.S. author Francis Fukuyama published his famous "The End of History and the Last Man" in 1992, international hockey had started changing in much the same way Fukuyama was to describe in his book. It was a change that brought about the end of a divided world of clear opposites and simple structure; it marked the globalization of markets and the transformation of the world into a global village. In the wake of the fall of communism and the collapse of the Soviet Union, the sport of hockey echoed Fukuyama.

In retrospect, 1986 marks the single most significant year in the history of international hockey. It all began that April when Moscow hosted the IIHF World Championship for the fourth time (after 1957, 1973, and 1979).

The Soviet national team, the fabled "Big Red Machine," had ruled the world since its arrival at the 1954 World Championship. The 1986 edition was easily among the best in history, and, at the time, it looked like the USSR would rule international hockey forever. In those April days, people could have imagined that they were about to witness the swan song of a sports dynasty.

On ice, the Soviets won every game they played and claimed their 20th world championship title unchallenged. The tournament's all-star team featured the team's top five-man unit in its entirety, as it had in 1983: the famed KLM line of Vladimir Krutov, Igor Larionov, and Sergei Makarov, plus Vyacheslav Fetisov and Alexei Kasatonov on defence. It was inconceivable that this would be the third-last World Championship gold won under the Soviet banner and the last tango at a World Championship behind the iron curtain.

When the World Championship returned to Russia

Yevgeni Davydov celebrates a most unusual gold medal at the 1992 Olympics. He and his Soviet teammates played under the name Commonwealth of Independent States (CIS) after the breakup of the Soviet Union prior to the start of the Olympics. Because the team had no time to produce new sweaters, it simply removed "CCCP" from the old ones. After receiving their medals, they heard no national anthem, and the IIHF later credited the win to the new incarnation, Russia.

14 years later, Leningrad had changed its name back to St. Petersburg; the Soviet Union had been dissolved; and, the governing body of hockey in the USSR had split into nine different independent national federations. Five of these (Russia, Latvia, Ukraine, Belarus, and Kazakhstan) went on to establish themselves as regulars at the highest-level of international competition. On the other hand, the millennium event in St. Petersburg saw the home team finish in 11th place, losing 3-0 to the USA, 3-2 to both Switzerland and Latvia, and 1-0 to Belarus. It was the lowest point in the history of Russian hockey. The power balance in the sport had clearly shifted, and it is no coincidence that Russia would later turn to an icon of the glory years of the "Big Red Machine" when it named Fetisov its new Minister of Sports in the hope of reapplying some polish to a once-bright reputation.

No one could have imagined the collapse of the Soviet nationals watching that team in Moscow in April 1986. No one could have predicted the consequences when, in that very same year, a former referee from Switzerland by the name of René Fasel

A gold medal goal for Sweden! Tomas Sandstrom scored at 18:39 of the third period to give Sweden a 2-2 tie with the Soviet Union at the 1987 World Championship in Vienna. The tie kept Sweden atop the standings and the Soviets in second place, ensuring gold for Tre Kronor and silver for CCCP.

was elected to the IIHF Council. Few people took notice of his appointment, but this election also led to dramatic changes in the world of hockey. Only 12 years later, Fasel had established himself as the most powerful president in the history of the IIHF. He was on the verge of becoming a member of the IOC, and he managed to bring the NHL and women's hockey to the Olympics. Fasel turned the IIHF into the most influential winter sports federation in the world. He also moved the IIHF's

head office from Vienna to Zurich, and the number of its independent members more than doubled from that day to this, from 31 to 65.

In 1989, the political change in the Soviet Union brought about by Mikhail Gorbachev and his "perestroika" policy had deeply altered the country. The new climate also encouraged Soviet national team players to rebel against their authoritarian coach, Viktor Tikhonov. Larionov was the first to

Wayne Gretzky during the Canada Cup 1987.

The Soviet team that participated in the 1987 Canada Cup, the last great Canada-Soviet hockey showdown.

speak up. In *Ogonyok* magazine, he attacked his coach broadly, calling him a dictator. Team captain Fetisov concurred, dubbing the tough Tikhonov a tyrant and declaring that he — Fetisov — was no longer prepared to play for him. The most dominant defenceman in international hockey wanted to leave Russia for the NHL, but Tikhonov refused to grant him release and kicked him off the team instead.

This led to fellow "Sbornaya" mainstays Makarov, Larionov, Vyacheslav Bykov, and Andrei Khomutov threatening to withdraw if Fetisov was not back on the team for the 1989 World Championship in Stockholm. Tikhonov caved in, Fetisov returned, and the team ended up with another gold medal.

Yet the rift was undeniable and Stockholm marked the last time the "Big Red Machine" iced all the best Soviet players. One year later, all 1986 all-stars had moved on to the NHL, and only Makarov (Calgary Flames) and Fetisov (New Jersey Devils) returned from their new North American homes to play for their country ever again. Immediately following the 1989 World Championship, Alexander Mogilny, the young shining star of the Soviet team, became the first Soviet player to defect to North America to play in the NHL.

The first wave of Soviet defectors to North America soon turned into a flood, and authorities in the crumbling state had no way of stemming the tide. They tried to regulate transfers by imposing a

minimum age limit, but that only led to more talented youngsters such as Sergei Fedorov and Pavel Bure leaving the country without permission and their Soviet clubs without compensation. The change was permanent. For over 30 years, virtually all the best players of the Soviet Union had played and practiced together on one team — CSKA Moscow, the Red Army team, which was nearly identical to the Soviet national team. Superficially, its members were officially soldiers and officers of the Red Army, but the reality was that they played hockey together year round to prepare for the Olympics and World Championships.

Russians became free-market hockey players, able to play wherever they wanted or were able. Of course, their services were much in demand. Sergei Makarov was named the NHL's rookie of the year in his inaugural season with the Calgary Flames in 1990. The migration of the Soviets started ten years after players from other east European countries started to defect. The Stastny brothers — Peter, Anton, Marian — left Czechoslovakia under dramatic circumstances in 1980 and gained hero status in Quebec City, where they played on the same line for the Nordiques. And the Finnish flavour was an important ingredient of the famous Edmonton

INTERVIEW WITH JARI KURRI

FINLAND'S GREATEST HERO

By Szymon Szemberg

Ask any hockey expert to name the three best Europeans to have played in the NHL and one of the names will invariably be Jari Kurri. No wonder. Try to compete with these numbers: 17 NHL seasons, 1,251 games, 601 goals and 797 assists, 1,398 points. If this is not impressive enough, how about Kurri's playoff statistics: 200 games, 106 goals and 127 assists for 233 points. And, to save the best last, Kurri also won five Stanley Cups.

"These are numbers I am very proud of," said Kurri who was the first Finn inducted into the Hockey Hall of Fame in 2001, a year after his induction into the IIHF Hall of Fame. "I want to be remembered as a complete player who could do a little bit of everything," he said, perhaps wanting to deflect the general perception that he was a pure scorer who mainly benefited from Wayne Gretzky's passing brilliance. His 797 career assists further attest to his value as more than just a scorer.

For North American hockey fans, the Jari Kurri story begins in 1980 when he arrived in Edmonton as a shy 20-year-old to start a telepathic relationship with Gretzky. But one of Kurri's career highlights occurred two years earlier when Finland won the European Junior Championship. It was the first Finnish championship in international hockey, a win that triggered Finland's ascendance as a hockey power, and Jari Kurri was the main man in the final game against the Soviet Union in front of 9,500 home fans in the old Helsinki ice rink.

"It was a crazy game," he remembered. "It was 3-3 at the end of regulation and when they scored the 4-3-goal in overtime, they thought they'd won it and jumped to the ice to celebrate. But the rules said that the first overtime period would be a full 20 minutes, and only if it went to a fifth period would it be sudden death."

So the game continued and the Finns forced a second OT-period with an equalizer with eleven seconds left in the fourth period. That's when Karri entered the books of Finnish hockey lore.

"I recall that defenceman Timo Blomqvist shot from the point and I was the first to reach the rebound, and I just lifted the puck over the line," he said of his championship goal at 1:42 of the fifth period.

A great career had just started, and two years later, a 19-year-old Kurri was named to the Finnish Olympic team for Lake Placid 1980, a team that could have spoiled the American "Miracle on Ice." Some hockey fans might not

But the young Americans went on to score three third-period goals, and the rest is hockey history.

It would take another 18 years before Kurri could take part in another Olympic tournament — and that's were he finally got his medal. "It was a big moment for me. I was already 38 and my career was basically over. I think our achievement is still underappreciated. It was the first Olympic hockey tournament where all teams could select their best NHL players. And to win an Olympic medal in that competition was really tough. And to beat Canada with Wayne Gretzky in the bronze game was extra sweet for me."

Kurri lists Nagano 1998 as his biggest international moment and Milan in 1994 as his low point. It was Finland against Canada in the gold medal game of the World Championship and the Finns were vying for their first men's senior gold in the country's history.

"We were leading 1-0 with some minutes left and killing a power-play when Rod Brind'Amour tripped me at centre ice. It was a clear penalty, but the ref didn't call it and Brind'Amour walked in and scored the tying goal."

Despite scoring a goal in the shootout that followed the 1-1-game, Kurri could only watch when his Los Angeles Kings teammate Luc Robitaille gave Canada its first World Championship gold in 34 years by scoring the shootout winner.

The next season was bittersweet for Kurri. His NHL club, Los Angeles, missed the playoffs, but that was the year the schedule had to be extended because of the lockout that reduced the season to just 48 games. As a result, there were no NHLers at the World Championship that year, so when Finland defeated archrival Sweden for its first-ever World Championship gold, Jari Kurri, arguably the best Finnish player of all time, was idle.

The eight years that Kurri played with Gretzky in Edmonton (1980-88) produced incomparable numbers of goals for the two. They won four Stanley Cups together, and just as Kurri was instrumental in assisting Gretzky in setting many of number 99's records, Kurri is aware of that he probably wouldn't have had a total of 707 NHL and Stanley Cup goals had not "The Great One" been his linemate.

Jari Kurri stands at the very spot at the Helsingin jaahalli where his international career took off in 1978 at the European Junior Championship.

"I have seen that stat somewhere," says Kurri when asked about their phenomenal cooperation. "I think that Wayne may have assisted on more than 450 of those goals. We read each other so well and we simply reacted. We never drafted any plays on paper. It just happened."

As for those who believed that Kurri could not win without Gretzky, they got a great surprise in 1990. When Kurri helped the Oilers to the Stanley Cup that year, and scored 25 points in 22 playoff games in the process, Gretzky had already been a member of the Los Angeles Kings for two years. ■

remember that Team USA had to defeat Finland in the last game of the round robin to win the gold medal. The famous U.S. victory against the Soviet Union came two days earlier.

"We were leading 2-1 after two periods, but spoiling the American party was not on our minds. We were playing for a bronze medal and we could have won an historic Olympic medal for Finland had we won or tied the game," said Kurri.

Oilers teams, as Jari Kurri and Esa Tikkanen manned Wayne Gretzky's wings on the Stanley Cup winners of 1985, 1987, and 1988.

In spite of European trailblazers such as Börje Salming, Matti Hagman, Vaclav Nedomansky, Kent Nilsson, and Pelle Lindbergh, North Americans fully realized the extent of hockey's globalization only when the Russians made the NHL. And without all the players from the former Eastern Bloc, NHL expansion from 21 teams in 1980 to 30 teams in 2000 would not have been practical.

Heading into the 1986-87 season, 45 Europeans (25 Swedes, eleven Finns, eight Czechs, plus West German defenceman Uli Hiemer) played in the NHL. The Europeans did not really present a challenge to the Canadians yet. There were still enough jobs in the big league, and the NHL was about to expand soon, creating even more opportunities.

As the 1972 Summit Series was the first best-on-best cold-war confrontation between Canada and the Soviet Union, the 1987 Canada Cup and its amazing three-game final series was to become the

last. The three games, which all ended by the same 6-5 score (two of them in overtime), left fans in awe of the two nations' skill, and many observers called this the best hockey series ever played. Just as nobody could have imagined that the 1986 World Championship in Moscow was going to be the last behind the iron curtain, few could have envisioned in 1987 that they had just witnessed the final clash of the world's reigning hockey cultures. There would be no more magical East-meets-West encounters and battles of skill, will, politics, and national pride. It all ended when the 22-year-old Mario Lemieux scored the winning goal in magical fashion with 1:26 left to play in game three.

On March 29, 1989, the Calgary Flames held a press conference to announce that they had signed Sergei Priakhin — with the permission of the Russian Hockey Federation. Pryakhin, a right winger of marginal talent, had been the captain of Krylya Sovetov. He earned $1,200 per month, but he became a role player on the Flames and went on to win the Stanley Cup that spring. It was a humble beginning, but some 15 years later, Alexei Yashin was captain of the New York Islanders and earning $630,000 a month.

The Priakhin signing did not cause much of a stir, but it marked the dawning of a new era. Eight years later, the Russians no longer ruled the world of international hockey, but they were threatening to rule the NHL. In 1997, after a 42-year drought, the Detroit Red Wings finally brought the Stanley Cup back to Motown — and they did it with an all-Russian unit as the centerpiece of an impressive roster. Coach Scotty Bowman iced the first Russian five-man unit in NHL history: Vyacheslav Fetisov and Vladimir Konstantinov on defence, Sergei Fedorov on right wing, Igor Larionov at centre, and Vyacheslav Kozlov on the left

side. The demanding Bowman got along very well with the group. After playing under Viktor Tikhonov, the notoriously tough

Vyacheslav Fetisov's 1988 sweater, the last time "CCCP" appeared at the Olympics.

The start of the famous Igor Larionov column that appeared in Ogonyok, a Soviet maga- zine, in 1988. Larionov became the first Soviet athlete to speak openly against the system and his coach, Viktor Tikhonov.

Bowman seemed more like a benevolent father to Fetisov and company than an authoritarian of the same ilk as his Russian equivalent.

The new arrivals from the former Eastern Bloc meant that Europeans were finally becoming a factor in the NHL. Since the dawn of the 21st century, they have been holding about a third of all NHL jobs. In the 1999-2000-season, 236 out of 923 NHL players (25.6 percent) were born in Europe. In 2003-2004, the European share was 29.5 percent. Two Europeans led the league in scoring during this time — Jaromir Jagr (in 1995, 1998, 1999, 2000, 2001) and Peter Forsberg (in 2003).

Prior to the salary-cap system implemented for the 2005-06 season, nine of the NHL's top 20

Twenty-year-old Mats Sundin shows off his gold medal after he scored one of the greatest goals in World Championship history, giving Tre Kronor the gold medal in 1991.

Sundin finishes off a masterful play. After skating around Vyacheslav Fetisov (left), he beat goalie Andrei Trefilov with a great deke to give Sweden a 2-1 lead midway through the third period at the 1991 World Championship in Turku, Finland.

salaries were paid to players from Europe, including the top three: Jaromir Jagr ($8.3 million), Niklas Lidstrom ($7.6 million), and Alexei Yashin ($7.6 million).

But salaries were not the only way to judge. Another indicator was the annual Entry Draft, where, in 1989, Mats Sundin became the first European taken first overall. Roman Hamrlik (1992), Ilya Kovalchuk (2001), and Alexander Ovechkin (2004) followed suit in later years. On ice, a German defencemen (Uwe Krupp)

Ville Peltonen (middle, #16) makes it 3-0 for Finland four seconds before the end of the second period of the 1995 World Championship final against archrival Sweden. Peltonen had three goals in Finland's 4-1 gold-medal game win, their biggest hockey success so far.

scored the Cup-winning goal for the Colorado Avalanche in 1996, and in 2001 and 2006 Swiss goaltenders got their names on the Stanley Cup (David Aebischer with the Colorado Avalanche and Martin Gerber with the Carolina Hurricanes).

But the globalization of hockey also affected league play in Europe as well as international competition, and it radically altered the organization of the IIHF. In earlier times, Europe's top hockey countries strictly limited the numbers of foreigners allowed on a team. Switzerland, for instance, even adopted a zero-tolerance policy and banned all foreigners from its top league between 1959 and 1970.

In the Soviet Union, of course, foreigners were not allowed to play, either. But the economic globalization and the laws of the European Union forced countries to open their frontiers to foreign labour, and that included hockey players. Today some

Peter Forsberg's brave and ingenious goal on Corey Hirsch during the shootout in the 1994 Olympic finals gave Sweden a 3-2 win over Canada. It was Sweden's first Olympic gold.

The stamp celebrating The Goal. It was produced for the 1995 World Championship held in Stockholm.

FORSBERG HAD THE NERVE — AND GOT IT STAMPED

The 1994 gold medal game at the Olympics in Lillehammer came down to a shootout between Canada and Sweden. Canada had been to the final game two years earlier, at the 1992 Olympics, only to lose 3-1 to the Unified Team, and it was seeking its first gold medal since 1952. Sweden had not had chance for gold since 1964.

After 60 minutes, the game stood at 2-2, and another ten minutes of overtime failed to break the tie. In the shootout, both teams scored twice on their first four of five shots, leaving the last shooter for each side to determine who would win Olympic gold. First up was Peter Forsberg, who skated in on goalie Corey Hirsch, moved left to his forehand and then slid the puck to his backhand. With one hand on the stick and the goalie sliding toward Forsberg, the player calmly slid the puck into the open side of the net. It was the most daring, exciting shootout goal in Olympic history, and after Tommy Salo made a great save on Paul Kariya at the other end, Sweden had claimed its first ever Olympic gold.

Two photographers caught the goal from directly above Hirsch. Gary Hershorn clicked his shutter just as "Foppa" released the puck, and Al Behrman did the same a split second later, after the puck had slid under Hirsch's arm and was just inches from crossing the goal line. The image was so famous that Swedish Post made a stamp of the goal, but fans of the game will notice a slight difference in the philatelic representation of the play. Corey Hirsch is wearing number 11, not 1, and his sweater is blue, not red. When he was asked permission for his likeness to be used, Hirsch was so embarrassed by the goal that he declined, a decision he regretted a short time later. Forsberg, of course, had no trouble agreeing.
—Andrew Podnieks

leagues do not put any limit on the number of foreign players, while others have found legal ways to protect homegrown talent by limiting the number of so-called "imports."

For a short time, European clubs were able to compete with the NHL for the signing of world-class players from the Eastern Bloc. Two major cogs of the "Big Red Machine," Vyacheslav Bykov

After Forsberg's goal, Canada still had a chance to tie the shootout but Tommy Salo stoned Paul Kariya (above) to give the Swedes their gold medal.

and Andrei Khomutov, turned down offers from the Quebec Nordiques in 1990 and signed with Swiss team HC Fribourg-Gotteron. But now, with NHL salaries in a class of their own, the general

(l to r) Hakan Loob, Mats Naslund, and Tomas Jonsson show off their Olympic gold medals after winning in 1994. The win was doubly important because these three men became the first members of the Triple Gold Club (World Championship gold, Stanley Cup, Olympic gold).

managers of teams in Sweden, Germany, Finland, and Switzerland are happy if they are able to attract interest from the top scorer of the American Hockey League's Calder Cup playoffs.

Money has changed the geography of hockey, and naturally it has also changed the IIHF. In 1986, at the dawn of change, the IIHF employed two people full-time, General Secretary Jan-Ake Edvinsson and his assistant, Edith Nzekwo. The advertising revenue from the annual IIHF World Championship tournament was modest, and just eight countries participated in the IIHF's showcase event.

Beginning in 1992, the World Championship expanded gradually from eight to 16 nations and began to generate more than $10 million in TV and advertising rights.

From 1920 through 1991, the year the USSR ceased to exist, just six different nations had won the combined 57 World Championship and Olympic tournaments: the Soviet Union, Great Britain,

Peter Forsberg holds a copy of The Hockey News *touting him as the NHL's most valuable player. The photo was taken on April 21, 2003. On June 12, he was, indeed, named winner of the Hart Trophy as the NHL's most valuable player, the first Swede so honoured.*

Slovaks, but also Ukrainians, Belarusians, Germans, Swiss, Latvians, Kazakhs, Austrians, Lithuanians, Poles, and Norwegians.

So the globalization of hockey and the fall of the Soviets enabled other countries to grow and become contributing members to hockey's global community. The Finns finally won their first Olympic medal (1988) and their first World Championship title (1995); Switzerland (1998 World Championships) and Belarus (2002 Olympics) reached the semi-finals of a big competition; and, with the Czech Republic (1998), Canada (2002), and Sweden (2006), the first three Olympic tournaments featuring the cream of the NHL crop saw three different winners.

USA, Canada, Sweden, and Czechoslovakia. But in the 15 years following 1991, the same number of countries has won the two big tournaments: Russia, Canada, Czech Republic, Slovakia, Finland, and Sweden. Entering the 21st century, the NHL featured players from 15 different European countries — not only Czechs, Russians, Swedes, Finns, and

In the spring of 2006, hockey's most storied franchise, the Montreal Canadiens, traded hometown goalie Jose Theodore to Denver for David Aebischer of Switzerland. Aebischer and Cristobal Huet of France were to defend the Canadiens' goal. The cradle of hockey stood in amazement. "A Swiss and a French goalie in Montreal — the end of the world is near," is how one prominent columnist put it. Or, in the words of Francis Fukuyama, "The End of History."

Luc Robitaille lost the puck midway through his shootout shot against Jarmo Myllys at the 1994 World Championship in Milano, Italy. He recovered, made a great move, and scored. Canadian goalie Bill Ranford then stopped Mika Nieminen, and Canada won gold for the first time in 33 years.

The Czech Republic celebrates a gold-medal finish, defeating Canada 4-2 at the 1996 World Championship in Vienna. It was the nation's first victory as the Czech Republic.

**Chapter 9
1990-2008**

Women's Hockey Goes Global

HAYLEY AND CAMMI LEAVE THE PINK PANTS BEHIND

By Lucas Aykroyd

Geraldine Heaney (pictured here in 1992) played for Canada at seven World Women's Championships and two Olympics during her 12-year career (1990-2002). She won gold at every tournament except the 1998 Olympics, and by the time she retired after the Salt Lake City Olympics she had scored 44 points in 46 career games.

Before the 1990s, who could have imagined that millions of TV viewers worldwide would end up watching women's hockey at the Olympic Games? Ever since women started to play the game in Ontario in the late 1800s, the sport has battled to earn respect.

In Canada, the game's prime growth in the 1920s and '30s first occurred at the university level, waned after World War II, and revived in the 1960s. But by 1990, there were just 8,000 registered women players in the country. In the United States, the National Collegiate Athletic Association (NCAA) didn't officially recognize women's hockey until 1993. Female European players depended on the varying resources of their local sports clubs to compete at all.

An unofficial, invitational world tournament took place in Toronto in 1987, the moderate success of

which sparked interest from journalists and hockey executives alike. In 1989, IIHF president Gunther Sabetzki attended the inaugural European Women's Championship in West Germany, and

only World Women's Championship in which bodychecking was permitted.

Wearing flamboyant pink uniforms, Canada dominated the inaugural event, winning every game and accruing a 61-6 goal differential. The tournament highlight was a spectacular goal by Geraldine Heaney in the gold-medal game. But the USA asserted itself as the sport's number-two nation, and the Americans claimed the top three places in tournament scoring. Cindy Curley was first with 23

Hayley Wickenheiser celebrates a Team Canada goal against USA in the 1997 World Women's Championship finals. Canada won 4-3 on an overtime goal by Nancy Drôlet.

subsequently the IIHF Congress awarded Canada the right to host the first-ever official World Women's Championship, in 1990.

The host nation triumphed in this eight-nation tournament in Ottawa, defeating the USA 5-2 in the gold-medal game. Finland claimed the bronze with a 6-3 win over Sweden. Notably, this was the

points, and her eleven goals tied for the lead with Canada's Angela James. Third with 14 points was 19-year-old Cammi Granato, who went on to become the leading scorer in World Women's Championship history.

"It was amazing in front of 10,000 people in Ottawa," Granato said. "We were losing to

Jayna Hefford scored the winning goal of the 2002 Olympics with just one second left in the second period. She beat American goalie Sara DeCosta at 19:59 to make it 3-1 Canada. The game ended 3-2 to give the Canadians their first Olympic gold in women's hockey.

Canada, but honestly, I couldn't have cared less at that point. The crowd was singing 'Na Na, Hey Hey, Goodbye,' and I sat on the bench with a smile on my face, saying: 'This is unbelievable that women's hockey could be here!'"

In 1991, the Finns made an impressive showing by defeating Sweden to win their second of four straight European Championships, and they earned a bronze medal at the second World Women's Championship in 1992 in Tampere. The sensational Riikka Nieminen joined Granato and James among the tournament all-star forwards. China finished an impressive fifth in its debut thanks to Hong Guo's strong goaltending.

Canadian goalie Manon Rheaume recorded a shutout in the 1992 final, an 8-0 whitewashing of the USA. The 20-year-old sensation had already made headlines for playing against men in the Quebec Major Junior Hockey League. In the fall, Rheaume received further publicity when she played one period for the Tampa Bay Lightning in an NHL exhibition game and two games for the NHL team's farm club during its regular season.

But the year's biggest news came on November 17,

when the International Olympic Committee announced the inclusion of women's hockey as a medal sport for the 1998 Games in Nagano, Japan. "Having the Olympics to aspire to is basically our Stanley Cup [for women]," said Hayley Wickenheiser, the future Canadian superstar who was 14 when she heard the news. "It's the best that it gets." Young hockey-playing girls around the world echoed those sentiments as they began dreaming of participating in an Olympic gold-medal game.

By 1994, the USA had high hopes of ending Canada's reign as world champion. That year, the IIHF staged the World Championship in Lake Placid, site of the men's "Miracle on Ice" in 1980. Mike Eruzione, captain of the '80 USA men's team, phoned the American women before their gold-medal final against Canada. As part of his message of support, he implored the players to stay out of the penalty box. His advice went unheeded, as the Canadians scored three power-play goals in a 6-3 victory.

Despite the significant fan support for the tournament, particularly in North America, the World Women's Championship was not yet an

annual event. Canada and the USA finished first and second, respectively, at both the 1995 and 1996 Women's Pacific Championships, and they maintained the status quo at the inaugural Three Nations Cup, in 1996, where Finland came third. But the scores were getting closer. Canada beat the Americans 1-0 in that first final. Meanwhile, Sweden went undefeated to capture

Nancy Drôlet is the only female player to score two overtime, gold-medal winning goals, the first in 1997, the second in 2000.

its first gold medal at the 1996 European Women's Championship, and Russia, which had

THE "SUDDEN DEATH" QUEEN

Since women's hockey became part of the IIHF's annual program in 1990 and the IOC's program eight years later, there have been only nine playoff games that have gone to overtime or a shootout. Five went to game-winning shots and four were decided in the fourth period. Two of those games involved Canada, and the hero each time was Nancy Drôlet.

Drôlet was a member of Team Canada for a decade (1992-2001) during which time she averaged better than a point a game (44 career points in 36 World Championship/Olympic games). None of her goals was bigger than the one on April 6, 1997, in Kitchener, Ontario, when she gave Canada a gold medal at the expense of USA.

Canada got to the final game with a perfect record, but USA had to overcome a 3-3 tie with Finland during the round robin to earn a place in the finals. That game saw the Americans jump into a lead only to have Canada tie the game 3-3 in the third period. At 12:59 of OT, Drôlet scored the winner to keep Canada perfect in World Championship competition.

Three years later, Drôlet struck again. The 2000 World Women's Championships took place in Mississauga, Ontario; the gold-medal game was another Canada-USA affair; and, the score was tied 2-2 after 60 minutes. Again, though, Drolet scored, this time at 6:50, and again Canada claimed gold and relegated USA to silver.

Just as the Canadian men have proved particularly adroit in overtime over the years, so, too, have the women — thanks in large part to Nancy Drôlet.
—Andrew Podnieks

(l to r) Canadians Stacy Wilson, Therese Brisson, and Danielle Goyette shed a tear after losing to USA 3-1 in the finals of the 1998 Olympics.

Team USA celebrates its gold at the first women's Olympic hockey tournament, in Nagano.

formed a national team only in 1994, made its first international impression by winning the silver medal.

The 1997 World Championship in Kitchener, Ontario, was important for several reasons. First, the IIHF mandated the use of female officials, which helped to establish the sport's independence. A 3-3 tie between Finland and the USA marked the first time a European team had won

Colleen Sostorics (#5) and Cheryl Pounder cry with joy after winning gold at the 2002 Olympics in Salt Lake City, erasing memories of the loss in Nagano four years earlier.

a point in the standings from a North American team. Russia debuted with a respectable sixth-place finish, despite arriving in Kitchener without enough sticks and skates. And, when Nancy Drôlet scored in overtime to complete her hat trick to give Canada a 4-3 gold-medal win over the Americans, it was the first game in which over-time was required to settle a World Women's Championship. This tournament also set a new attendance record of 60,418.

As the Olympics approached, the Canada-USA rivalry heated up. American coach Ben Smith was determined to outdo his nemesis, Shannon Miller. When Canada rallied from a 4-1 deficit to beat his team 5-4 in round-robin play at the 1997 Three Nations Cup, Smith made his players listen to the Canadian celebration in the adjacent dressing room. The point was taken, and the Americans responded with an impressive 3-0 win in the finals, defeating Canada in a championship game for the first time.

Expectations for gold in Nagano weighed heavily on the Canadians, and Miller's decision to cut star forward Angela James from the Olympic roster created unwanted friction. The mood in the

Kelly Bechard gives her 2002 Olympic gold medal a kiss.

American dressing room was better. "Going into that first Olympics, there was pressure," Cammi Granato admitted. "The Canadians might have been more talented from a depth standpoint, but for that tournament, we really decided that we needed to go with a team attitude."

That attitude paid off. Canada and the USA each won their first four games of the five-game round-robin series preceding their meeting on February 14. In that contest, Canada had a 4-1 lead early in the third period but lost 7-4 after a stunning rally by the USA. Three days later, the teams met again

for the gold medal, and USA netminder Sarah Tueting outdueled Manon Rheaume in a 3-1 American triumph. Given Canada's perfect record at the four previous World Championships, the result was shocking. Canadian captain Stacy Wilson said: "When they put that silver medal around my neck, I broke down [in tears] because it was not what I'd visualized."

After Nagano, the World Women's Championship became an annual event (except for Olympic years), and in 1999 the IIHF added a B Pool for the first time. The only serious opposition either North American team faced in the A Pool that year came from the host Finns, which lost close games to Canada (1-0) and the USA (3-1). As usual, Canada beat the USA in the final, 3-1.

The founding of the National Women's Hockey League later in 1999 reflected Canada's seriousness about developing the women's game, a seriousness not matched by other nations in the A Pool. Even though "National" was a slight misnomer — all nine franchises were in Ontario and Quebec — the league provided strong club competition for Canadian national team members. (Two years later, Western Canadian cities

(l to r) Americans Angela Ruggiero, Cammi Granato, and Jenny Potter hold the World Championship trophy high after winning it for the first time in 2005 with a 1-0 shootout win over Canada. It was USA's first win in nine tries and prevented Canada from tying the Soviets' record (1963-71) for consecutive victories.

joined the NWHL.) Tellingly, in an exhibition game before the 2000 World Championship in Mississauga, Ontario, the champion Beatrice Aeros defeated Team Finland, 8-2.

At that 2000 tournament, the Canadians and Americans overwhelmed their opponents once again, and only Finland provided a real test, as other nations failed to keep pace. The USA trailed the Finns 3-1 in a round-robin game but roared back for a 4-3 win. In the semi-finals, Canada needed two Danielle Goyette goals to beat Finland, 3-2. The Americans skated to a 2-0 lead in the gold-medal game, but Jayna Hefford scored twice in the third period, and Nancy Drolet reprised her 1997 heroics with another overtime winner for Canada.

Finland dispatched Sweden, 7-1, in the bronze-medal game thanks to Katja Riipi, who was named the tournament's best forward by the IIHF directorate. She shared the spotlight with the USA's Angela Ruggiero (best defenceman) and Sami Jo Small (best goalie).

At the 2001 World Women's Championship in Minnesota, Russia caused the greatest sensation by

edging Finland, 2-1, in the bronze-medal game, the first time Finland had failed to finish third. Canada beat the USA, 3-2, for gold.

The year 2001 was a challenging one for Sweden. Forward Maria Rooth's MVP performance for the victorious University of Minnesota-Duluth at the inaugural women's NCAA championship in March brought pride to the Swedish national team. But the following month, the Swedes collapsed at the World Championship, finishing seventh. They also fared poorly in their exhibition games with Canada, the USA, and Finland leading up to the 2002 Olympics.

"There was a discussion about [pulling out] in our Olympic Committee," admitted Lars Karlsson, head of the Swedish women's program. "Naturally, they wanted to send successful athletes." In the end, Sweden decided to take part in the Salt Lake City Olympics, a wise decision in retrospect.

This time, it was the Americans on home ice who faced pressure to repeat as Olympic champions. Also, the USA had defeated Canada eight straight times in exhibition games leading up to Salt Lake. Ben Smith's team powered its way to the Olympic

final with four straight victories, allowing just one goal en route (a bouncing shot from centre ice against China). Under coach Daniele Sauvageau, Canada was nearly as dominant, but her team experienced a semi-final scare versus Finland. The Finns led 3-2 heading into the third period before Canada exploded for five unanswered goals, setting up a gold-medal rematch with the USA.

Penalties played a vital role in the final game. The Americans received eleven power-play chances and converted only twice, and Canada proved tougher in a 3-2 victory. Jayna Hefford scored the winning goal on a breakaway with one second left in the second period. Teary-eyed Canadian captain Cassie Campbell said: "It's been four long years of thinking of that disappointment in '98, and finally bringing the gold medal home to the country where it belongs, we deserve it."

Meanwhile, the Swedes upset Finland for bronze with a 2-1 victory. Goalie Kim Martin, just 15 years old, made 32 saves, and Evelina Samuelsson scored both of Damkronor's goals. It was Sweden's first-ever medal at either the Olympics or World Women's Championships, and it truly marked Damkronor's emergence alongside Finland as one

of the second-tier nations in women's hockey.

The 2004 World Championship in Halifax and Dartmouth, Nova Scotia, was a huge success. Canada's 37-game winning streak at this tournament ended on April 3 with a 3-1 loss to the

Goalie Kim St. Pierre leaps high in the air as Canada beats USA 2-0 in the gold medal game of the 2004 World Women's Championship in Halifax.

Americans in the second round. But, when the teams met again for gold, the Canadians wouldn't be denied their eighth straight championship. Hayley Wickenheiser scored the winning goal and Kim St. Pierre earned the shutout in a 2-0 decision. A tournament attendance record of 89,461 was established. Finland earned bronze with a 3-2

win over Sweden.

In 2005, the World Women's Championship reached a new level of drama. "All the pressure was on the Canadians, because they were trying to tie the record of the Russian men's team for most consecutive World Championships," recalled Cammi Granato, alluding to the USSR's 1963-71 streak of gold-medal performances.

Canada's quest fell short, even though it didn't allow a single goal in regulation time. The only blemish came during the shootout in the gold-medal game. Angela Ruggiero scored the only shootout goal for a 1-0 victory. The result ended 15 years of frustration for the USA, which finally emerged as world champion.

Sweden was energized by hosting the World Championship for the first time and defeated Finland 5-2 in the bronze-medal game. And while women's hockey remained a more popular spectator sport in Canada than anywhere else (the

Swedish players mob Maria Rooth after her winning goal during the semi-final shootout in Turin in 2006 which allowed the Swedes to advance to the gold-medal game for the first time.

2004 World Championship gold medal game drew 745,000 viewers on TSN), an impressive 412,000 Swedes watched their nation's tournament opener on television via Eurosport.

Heading into the 2006 Olympics, North American dominance of women's hockey was in-

Sixteen-year-old Pernilla Winberg gets high-fives from teammates after scoring in the shootout in Turin 2006. She beat USA goalie Chanda Gunn who skates disconsolately to the bench.

disputable, but this dominance, while impressive, also created some concerns about the sport's international viability. Ruggiero's 2005 autobiography, *Breaking the Ice*, included a prophetic concluding sentence: "Hopefully I retire before a Finland or Sweden beats the U.S., but I would eventually like to see it for the good of the game." The Canadians brought to Turin what Cassie

Campbell dubbed "probably the best hockey team ever assembled by the national program." They obliterated their opponents, recording a 42-1 goal differential leading up to the gold-medal game. The Americans went undefeated through the preliminary round, but not with the same dominance. In one game, they trailed Finland 3-1 and had to rally for a 7-3 win. The two most common explanations for the USA's mediocre showing centred on Ben Smith's decision to cut Cammi Granato from the team in August 2005 and questionable preparation before the Olympics.

Facing Sweden in the semi-finals was supposed to be a formality for the USA, but the Americans looked nervous. Goalie Kim Martin made 37 saves in regulation time and Maria Rooth added two goals plus the shootout clincher as Damkronor won, 3-2. It was the biggest upset in women's hockey history. "I can't believe it," said Martin. "We've watched the movie "Miracle" many times, and I always imagine that I am Jim Craig."

INTERVIEW WITH HAYLEY WICKENHEISER

Hayley Wickenheiser stands in front of a display at the Hockey Hall of Fame in Toronto showcasing women's hockey.

PROUD OF THE PROGRESS IN WOMEN'S HOCKEY

By Andrew Podnieks

My first hockey memory is probably riding on the toboggan to the rink to watch my dad play. He played terrible oldtimer's hockey. I remember getting my first pair of skates and he built us an outdoor rink in the backyard and that's how I learned to skate. In Shaunavon, Saskatchewan.

The skates were hand-me-downs from older kids around the neighborhood and I think I started on bob skates, the double-edge skates, and then moved to the molded Microns. But I remember skating on the outdoor rink in the winter and then public at the local Jubilee Arena.

We had a lot of kids around, so they all shared the rink and the arena. I think I was one of the only kids who really was a diehard and was out there hours and hours on end. But there were always other kids around. My younger brother, Ross, and my younger sister, Jane, were also there.

It was pretty natural right from the start to see girls playing hockey. In Shaunavon, there was myself and my best friend, Danielle, who played for a number of years. You know in those small towns, you were just another number to fill a team so there was no issue with girls playing hockey.

I think I knew I loved the game right from the start. Probably when I was seven or eight years old I started to realize, you know, that maybe I skated as well or better than a lot of the kids where I was growing up. I went to a hockey school in Regina when I was nine years old and it was my first experience being in a boys hockey school. Right away they accepted me. I slept in an ushers' room under a coat rack and my brother was there with me. I remember I was very nervous because I was the only girl. But it was a great experience to be around other players of my calibre. Lorne Davis, who was a scout with the Edmonton Oilers, gave me my first shot of going to that hockey school. I sort of knew then that against all these kids in Saskatchewan, I was one of the better players.

Sleeping in that coatroom was a little out of sorts, but the boys always treated me with respect and so did Lorne. I really credit him for giving me that opportunity, and I think he recognized I had some talent early on. That's really where I started my career.

I didn't even know women played hockey until I was 12 years old and I started with the Canada Games program in P.E.I. with Team Alberta. My heroes were Gretzky and Messier and the Oilers of the '80s. My dad was a big Messier fan and we watched all the games on *Hockey Night in Canada*. During intermission we'd go out and play hockey on the outdoor rink and come back in for the next period, and it was often the Oilers or Montreal or Calgary so that's who I grew up watching.

I had no real female models to look up to, but now it feels natural for me to have young girls have a chance to look up to female role models and have an Olympics to aspire to, which is essentially our Stanley Cup. That's the best that it gets. So I'm proud of that and I think that not only myself but a lot of women who have paved the way before me and I feel lucky in terms of timing that I kind of was at the right place and the right time with the game. So it's a natural evolution to see over 60,000 girls and women playing hockey in Canada right now. It makes me feel proud of what we've accomplished.

When I was 12, our family moved from Shaunavon to Calgary. I was in the process of trying out for Team Saskatchewan and switched to play for Team Alberta, and this was my first experience in the Canada Games program playing girls that were 16-17 years old. I was 12. We ended up winning the gold medal, and I actually scored the winning goal in the final game against Team B.C., so it was a wild experience.

That was my first introduction into women's hockey and the National Team program. That's where I got scouted, and this was around 1990, the same time they held the first World Women's Championship. I watched those games and I didn't know what I was going to do. I often thought about going to university and then finishing hockey and that would be it, but then about this time I was at a hockey school in B.C. and my mom came running in and said, "You'll never believe what happened — women's hockey is a full medal sport in 1998!" So I knew with the World Championships and the Olympics that I had a future in the game and it just motivated me. ∎

Team Canada stands at attention to sing the national anthem after winning gold at the 2006 Olympics in Turin. Hayley Wickenheiser (second from right, holding son, Noah) was named MVP for the second straight Olympics while captain Cassie Campbell (far right) was playing in her last event before retiring.

The Swedes couldn't replicate their heroics in the gold medal game, losing 4-1 to Canada. Hayley Wickenheiser's two assists gave her 17 tournament points, and she was named Olympic MVP just as she had been four years earlier.

"Tonight was our 52nd game of the year," coach Melody Davidson observed. "We played 46 games leading up to the Olympics. This allowed us to have some sort of real hockey season, and I think that was very important for our team."

Canada's cohesion and ability to integrate young players such as Meghan Agosta and Katie Weatherston with veteran stars kept it on top at the 2007 World Women's Championship in Winnipeg. Although the Americans looked every bit as tough

early in the tournament, Canada proved its resilience in a come-from-behind 5-4 shootout win when the two archrivals first clashed in the second round. In the gold-medal game, the host nation handled the USA with relative ease, posting a 5-1 victory. Wickenheiser was the tournament scoring leader and MVP again, and new attendance records of 15,003 (single-game) and 122,152 (overall) were set. Predictably, Sweden and Finland met in the bronze-medal game, Damkronor eking out a 1-0 win.

The future of international women's hockey is at once both promising and uncertain. While Canada and the USA boast some 66,000 and 53,000 registered players, respectively, the top European and Asian nations have much catching up to do. If anything, the North Americans have widened the gap

between themselves and the rest of the world in the last decade. While Sweden's remarkable Olympic silver medal in 2006 was a breath of fresh air, there is no immediate indication this was more than a miraculous result rather than signs of things to come. The other second-tier nation, Finland, enjoys a healthy rivalry with Sweden, but there is no overlap between the top rivalry and the second. Meanwhile, nations such as Germany, Russia, Switzerland, China, Kazakhstan, and Japan lag far behind and pose little threat to the Finns and Swedes, creating a three-tiered hierarchy that might take many years to break down.

Stars such as Hayley Wickenheiser and Angela Ruggiero have become recognizable names in the hockey world, but there is still a long way to go be-fore a full-fledged women's professional league becomes a viable option. Ultimately, that option will make it economically feasible for more women to devote their lives to the sport, and this in turn will provide more universal means for the game's development. Canada's NWHL has offered a small-scale glimpse of what could be, and NCAA athletic scholarships have empowered young women from both North America and Europe to aspire to a higher level of play. What must be remembered is that the men's game experienced growing pains of its own. To wit, between 1920 and 1994, only five nations won gold at the World Championships. Women's hockey deserves the time and opportunity to grow, and in the meantime if fans have the chance to enjoy the skills of Wickenheiser, Ruggiero, and Rooth, then the hockey world is a better place.

IIHF
Chapter 10
1998-2002

Nagano, the Czechs, the Slovaks

A DYNASTY AND A SEVENTH SUPERPOWER

By Pavel Barta

In the dying seconds of the gold-medal game at the 1998 Olympics in Nagano, Czech goaltender Dominik Hasek was waiting in front of his net, moving anxiously in metronomic rhythm in anticipation of the final horn. As the game ended, he threw his stick away in a sweeping motion, clipping teammate Richard Smehlik under the eye. Jiri Slegr joined the celebrations, and the rest of the team mobbed the goalie soon after.

The Czechs beat the Russians 1-0 in the finals at Big Hat Arena in Nagano on February 22, 1998, winning their first-ever Olympic gold at the first-ever Winter Games with full-scale NHL participation. It was, quite simply, the biggest win in the history of Czechoslovak and Czech hockey.

"When I saw the Czech flag and heard the national anthem, my whole hockey life projected in my mind at one moment," Hasek described later. It was he who almost single-handedly brought his country the victory, allowing only six goals on 135 shots in the tournament and winning the do-or-die shootout in the semi-finals against Canada by stopping all five shooters.

"While growing up, there was always the Olympics as the most outstanding competition," he added. "We didn't know much about the NHL. My heroes were playing in my country and when they went to the Olympics it was a big thing. Now I know the Stanley Cup is great. But when I went to North America for another season last summer, nobody talked about the NHL or playoffs with me. They all were talking about the Olympics," Hasek said.

By the time the 1998 Olympics were played, Hasek had already been in the NHL for eight

Peter Bondra holds the trophy high after Slovakia beat Russia 4-3 in 2002 to win its first world championship.

Jaromir Jagr kisses the World Championship trophy in 2005 after the Czechs defeated Canada 3-0 in the gold-medal game.

years, starring with the Buffalo Sabres for much of that time. He still had to wait another four cam-

Robert Reichel beats Patrick Roy for the only goal of the shootout in the semi-finals of the 1998 Olympics, giving the Czech a 2-1 win.

paigns to win his first Stanley Cup, with the Detroit Red Wings in 2002.

In the news conference after the final, Hasek and assistant captain Robert Reichel answered questions with wide, celebratory smiles. One reporter asked about money. Reichel replied into his microphone: "We don't care about money. We care about this." As he said it, he held up the gold medal hanging on his neck and smiled.

In winning, the Czechs exceeded all pre-tournament predictions. To many observers, they seemed

to be too small and too soft. Their defence was considered weak. They also had only eleven NHL players on their roster. "They can't play the left wing lock," was one observation offered by a hockey writer in the main media centre on the eve of the opening game of the Olympics.

In fact, the left wing lock had been used by the Czechs since the 1960s. Coaches Vladimir Kostka and Jaroslav Pitner developed the system of stifling mid-ice defence with the national team, but it took another 30 years for the rest of the world to catch on, a debt owed to Scotty Bowman who introduced the method in the NHL when he was coaching the Red Wings.

"We hated to repeat it at practice, but it worked in games," said Jiri Holik, one of the Czechs' greatest left wingers and a three-time World Champion.

The 1998 Olympics were the first to have complete NHL participation. For the first time, the league shut down to allow its players to represent

their countries. As a result, Canada and Russia were the pre-tournament favourites because of the wealth of talent those countries developed year after year.

Czechoslovakia had won the World Championship six times prior to Nagano, most famously in 1972 when Jaroslav Holik scored the winner in an historic 3-2-win in Prague that stopped the Soviets' nine-year gold medal streak.

After 1992, when the Czech Republic and Slovakia were formed, the Czechs started to dominate the world scene, winning the World Championship gold in 1996 and then three in a row, 1999-2001, on the heels of this historic Olympic gold. They won again in 2005. In addition, the junior team won back-to-back championships at the U20 in 2000 and 2001, leaving no doubt that the last great team of the 20th century and the first powerhouse of the new century was the Czech Republic.

Mild and unpredictable winters in middle Europe have ensured that Czech kids usually can't skate on frozen rivers, lakes, or backyard rinks every winter as is the case in Canada, Sweden, Russia, or

Dominik Hasek celebrates the first gold ever for the Czech Republic at the Olympics after beating Russia 1-0 in the finals.

Finland. There are fewer than eleven million people in the country and only about 80,000 registered players. The number of rinks is far below what the competing nations have. So why is the Czech Republic such a dominant hockey power? How is it that year after year the Czechs have more players in the NHL than any other European nation?

It's all in the history. Bohemia, the predecessor to

Czechoslovakia, joined the IIHF in its founding year, 1908, but clubs such as Slavia Prague and CLTK Prague played organized bandy even earlier. The Czechs held official national team games in hockey during the 1908-1909 season. They were European champions in 1911 and 1914. Hockey

Jaromir Jagr (far left) and his Czech teammates celebrate in the dressing room following their gold medal win in Nagano.

in Bohemia was played by athletes and not by dukes and counts, a sociological fact that allowed the game to flourish. After World War I, Czechoslovakia added another three European titles to its achievements and hockey continued to thrive after World War II despite two tragic events.

The Czechs won the World Championship (with Canada absent) in 1947 with a perfect record, and the next year they finished second to Canada at the Olympics. But five national team members died in a plane crash on November 5, 1948.

Still, Czechoslovakia was able to beat Canada at the 1949 World Championship to win the gold medal for the second time. Just two years after the communists had assumed power in the country, the entire team was not allowed to leave Czechoslovakia prior to the 1950 tournament in London amid accusations they planned to defect. The players were put on trial and 12 teammates were imprisoned for alleged treason and spying, their sentences ranging from eight months to 15 years. The first golden generation of Czech ice hockey was extinguished by the darkness of communism.

Czechoslovakia had to wait two decades for its next World Championship gold. Another great wave of star players came with the maturity of Vladimir Martinec, Milan Novy, and Ivan Hlinka in the 1970s. They reached the world throne three times in that decade, while finishing second on four

occasions, and won silver at the 1976 Olympics. They also made it to the finals of the Canada Cup that year, the first ever open tournament.

In the days of the three-decade long domination of international hockey by the Soviets, it was only the Czechoslovaks who occasionally could halt the "Big Red Machine." Between 1963 and 1986, when the Soviets won 18 World Championship titles, they lost the gold medal only four times — 1972, 1976, 1977, and 1985 — each at the hands of Czechoslovakia.

The winning ghost of another golden generation was evoked in 1996 under head coach Ludek Bukac, who also led the Czechoslovak squad to gold in 1985. The Czechs didn't lose a game in that championship in Vienna, and they won for the first time in eleven years. They failed miserably a couple of months later in the 1996 World Cup of Hockey, where, after being humiliated by Germany 7-1, they didn't even make the quarter-finals. In hindsight, that was probably the best thing that could have happened. Leading up to Nagano 1998, the Czech coaching staff learned a lesson. To be successful they needed a team, not an ensemble of all-stars.

"Something many people in North America may not realize is that after you get past the first seven or eight Czechs in the NHL, many of the Czechs playing in Europe are as good as the others in the NHL," co-coach Lener once said. "We learned from the World Cup disaster. And this was the reason the Czech team in Nagano had the fewest number of NHL players."

The philosophy embraced by the Czechs was one that all of the top teams preached but didn't necessarily practice: the best team, not the team with the biggest names, usually wins. Hlinka and Lener realized as much and put together a roster of top Czech players from available players in the NHL as well as Czechs playing in a variety of European leagues, including the 35-year-old Ruzicka whom they named captain.

Although there were some 40 Czechs playing in the NHL in 1997-98, only 12 were named to the Olympic team, the fewest of the "top six" nations. That number was reduced even further after Milan Hejduk, a winger with Pardubice, became the squad's youngest member, replacing Vaclav Prospal (of the Ottawa Senators) who broke his leg before the Olympics.

The team suffered only one defeat during the entire tournament in Nagano (to Russia in the preliminary round), while beating the best from Canada and USA and avenging the earlier loss to Russia with the 1-0 win in the finals.

Dominik Hasek's incredible performance was not the only reason for victory. Offensive stars such as Jaromir Jagr sacrificed their skills for team work. "Next time, write 68 D next to my name," joked Jagr with his typical sense of humour, referring to his uncharacteristic commitment to defence at Nagano.

After the semi-final shootout victory over Canada, the streets of Prague overflowed with joyous fans, many holding banners declaring "Hasek for President." After the finals, the Czech celebrants wanted to add the name Peter Svoboda to their streamers as he scored the only goal of the gold-medal game against Russia. His slapshot from the left point zipped past goalie Mikhail Shtalenkov midway through the third period.

It was fitting, too, that Svoboda scored the gold-medal goal. His family name means "freedom" in Czech. He had defected from communist

INTERVIEW WITH DOMINIK HASEK

THE DOMINATOR DEFINES GOALTENDING FOR A GENERATION

By Pavel Barta

Q: Do you think that the semi-finals in Nagano was even bigger than the gold medal game?
A: Maybe in the sense that Canada was considered the big favourite because they were able to send their best players to the Olympics for the first time ever. The tournament was widely covered in Canada, and everyone there was thinking that Canada would win.

Q: How did you feel during the shootout?
A: I didn't look at my teammates very much. I didn't see even one of our shooters. I had no idea about the order of our shooters; I was focusing on my own performance. I know that the players on the bench were holding each other arm in arm.

Q: Would you agree that the Czechs weren't that confident in the beginning of the playoffs against the U.S.?
A: Before the quarter-finals, we told ourselves that if we could win this game we could win a medal. The Americans were also favourites and that was the way the game began. We were very cautious in the first period, but I made three or four good saves and this helped the other guys get into the game, I think. After that, we started to trsut ourselves and in the end I think we deserved to win. But the first period was the turning point. We were down 1-0. Our captain, Vladimir Ruzicka, made a little speech in our dressing room during the intermission. He told us we couldn't keep playing the way we had in the first period. He told us to skate more, pass more, get more confident. He told us we could play as well as they could. He really woke the team up, and this was also an important factor in our victory.

Q: What about the finals against Russians?
A: Suddenly, we felt we had achieved something even before the game. After beating Canada, we knew we had a medal for sure. We still thought that we couldn't return home as the silver medal team, even though this would have been cause for celebration. We just didn't feel we could settle for silver, so we had nothing to lose in trying for gold. The finals was a game of more European hockey, more cautious. I don't want to say that we were the luckier team. We had more chances. In the end, a shot from blueline won the game, but Jaromir Jagr also hit the post with one shot and Josef Beranek also had a great scoring chance. Yes, the only goal of the game was a bit lucky, but our win was well-deserved. The great thing about the tournament was that we defeated the three strongest teams, the three biggest favourites. It was an incredible feeling.

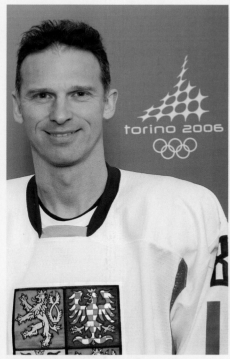

Goalie Dominik Hasek—without the mask.

Hasek stops Brendan Shanahan, the last of five Canadian shooters in the 1998 shootout, to earn the Czechs a place in the gold-medal game.

Q: You also played at the Olympics in 2002 and 2006. Was there a similar atmosphere to Nagano?

A: Nagano was really something different. The Olympics were open to all of the best players for the first time. Whether it was Gretzky, Forsberg, Sundin, Roenick, Modano, Bure. I don't think there is anything more attractive and beautiful in hockey than this. But when something happens for the first time, it's always a special.

Q: How do you look back at your career as a European goalie who won six Vezina Trophies and two Hart Trophies?

A: Back in the 1990s, the Russians were the best non-North American players. They were seen almost on a par with North Americans in the NHL. Occasionally someone from Sweden or the Czech Republic was in that group, someone like Jagr, Sundin, Forsberg. Those players proved that the NHL has changed, and I was the one among goaltenders.

Q: Do you feel that Chicago wasted your first two years in the NHL?

A: The situation in the NHL was completely different when I first started playing there. But goaltending is the most difficult position, and so much of success depends on chance and luck. When I was there, Eddie Belfour was there, so there was simply no place for me. When they traded me to Buffalo, they didn't really get anything for me. John Muckler, who was Sabres' GM at

the time, gave me a chance, but still it took him a while to fully trust me and trade Grant Fuhr. That took another two or three years, but that's the way it goes in goaltending. A forward can become a star right away if he scores 30 or 40 goals a year. A goaltender needs more of a chance because there's room for only one in the net.

Q: How did you develop your unique goaltending style?

A: I didn't imitate anyone. From the time I was ten, I watched every league game in my hometown, Pardubice. I watched goaltenders and tried different things later. The first goalie I really watched was Jiri Crha, but I wouldn't say he was my idol. My style has also changed over the years, even recently. It's never too late to change, even when you get older.

Q: Was there a shooter you really feared?

A: Mario Lemieux was the most difficult player. Anytime he came on the ice, I always shouted to my teammates, "Get Mario, get Mario!" so much that they laughed at me. I didn't care if there was someone else unchecked so long as Mario was still in the corner or behind the net. I always wanted the guy closest to him to check him right away. Jaromir Jagr scored more goals on me than any other player, I think. A defenceman named Ivan Cerny scored six goals in one season against me back in the Czechoslovak league. That was difficult to accept, especially since he was a defenceman. ∎

Wayne Gretzky is mobbed by reporters as Team Canada arrives for the 1998 Olympics in Nagano.

Former teammates Gretzky and Finland's Jari Kurri fight for the puck during the bronze-medal game.

David Moravec is mobbed by teammates after scoring the gold-medal winning goal in overtime at the 2001 World Championship, the third successive championship for the Czechs. Goalie Pasi Nurminen lies dejected in his crease.

Czechoslovakia as an 18-year-old in 1984 to play in the NHL. Amazingly, his appearance in Nagano at age 32 represented his senior national team debut for his homeland.

When the Czechs and Slovaks split in 1993, the Czechs, as IIHF members, remained in A pool to compete at the highest level. The Slovaks, however, had to start at the bottom and work their way to the top, which they did. They vaulted quickly from C pool to B and finally A pool in 1996 to assume a place among the top hockey nations. A country with just 10,000 registered players and a population of just five million, Slovakia nonetheless produced an extraordinary number of world-class hockey players.

In all, there were eleven Slovakian players, including national heroes Vladimir Dzurilla, Peter Stastny, and coach Jan Starsi, on the various teams that won gold at the World Championships during the communist regime of Czechoslovakia. Two other gold medalists — forward Vaclav Nedomansky and goaltender Jiri Holecek — played for league teams in Slovakia at that time.

The Slovaks placed sixth at the 1994 Olympics in Lillehammer, Norway, the first big tournament

Captain Robert Reichel of the Czech Republic holds the championship trophy in 2001.

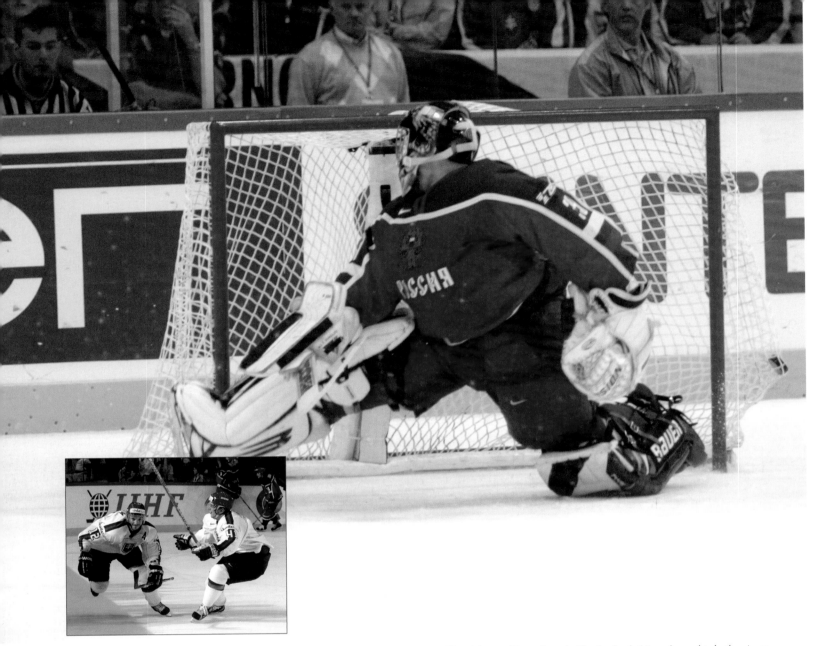

Maxim Sokolov watches Peter Bondra's shot get by him with just 100 seconds left in the 2002 gold-medal game. The goal put the Slovaks ahead, 4-3, and proved to be the winner, giving them their first ever World Championship title. (inset) Bondra (left) celebrates his goal with Richard Lintner.

they participated in as an independent nation. No one who witnessed that tournament will ever forget the scene when the teary-eyed 38-year-old Peter Stastny carried the Slovak flag during the opening ceremony. Six years after reaching the elite division, Slovakia was in a World Championship gold medal game — against the Czech Republic in St. Petersburg in 2000. The Czechs claimed their second consecutive title with a 5-3 win to become the first country to win back-to-back championships since Sweden in 1991 and 1992. It wasn't the dream ending the Slovaks had hoped for, but the silver medal was nevertheless the first by a non-top six hockey team since 1953 when the Swiss won a bronze (and there were only three teams competing that year).

The city and host organizers of the 2002 World Championship promised the winning team a parade in downtown Gothenburg, assuming Tre Kronor would win. Sweden didn't win, but organizers honoured their commitment and the winning Slovaks were welcomed by Slovakian and Swedish fans all the same.

On the night of May 11, 2002, however, the Slovak nation celebrated as one. The team downed Russia 4-3 in the gold medal game of the World Championship in Gothenburg, Sweden. And Slovakia, for the first time in its young, nine-year history, had become world champion. The hero was Peter Bondra who broke a 3-3 tie with a goal with 100 seconds left in the third period to send his millions of compatriots into frenzy while the team's general manager, Peter Stastny, celebrated from the stands.

"This means more than a Stanley Cup to me. The Cup is celebrated by one city, but this belongs to an entire nation," said Bondra, the Washington Capitals' sniper. The Swedish organizers, hoping

Miroslav Satan and goalie Jan Lasak lead their teammates in a celebratory "dance" after winning gold at the 2002 World Championship.

that the hometown Swedes would win, had arranged for the world champions to be paraded in an open bus cortege through the streets of Gothenburg and treated to a celebration in the main square. Despite a non-Swedish team winning, they still bestowed upon the Slovaks the same honour. Bondra, Miroslav Satan, Jan Lasak, Richard Lintner and the other players on the open bus couldn't believe when the people in the streets of Gothenburg, many of them dressed in Tre

Kronor's yellow and blue, celebrated the Slovak victory as if it were their own.

The win in Sweden came only three months after Slovakia, just like in Nagano 1998, missed the second round of the Olympic tournament at Salt Lake City. Their final placing in the 2002 Olympics was a dismal 13th. After the decisive 6-6-tie against Latvia in Salt Lake City — the game that cemented Slovakia's Olympic misery — head

coach Jan Filc was very sad, but composed, and said with astounding honesty: "I am sure that upon returning home I will be released of my duties as head coach of the Slovak national team," he said. "A failure like this will not be tolerated back home."

But the Slovak hockey authorities believed in Filc. Just 89 days after the Salt Lake City debacle,

Richard Lintner and Robert Petrovicky kiss the Scandinavium ice following the victory.

Slovakia was world champion. It was not only the defining moment in Slovak hockey history, but it also put an end to the concept of the "top six" ruling the hockey world. As of May 11, 2002, there were seven.

WHEN BONDRA STRUCK WITH 100 SECONDS LEFT

The year 2002 was both horrible and glorious for Slovakia. At the Olympics, the team was unable to put a decent roster on the ice and ended up in 13th place, not the finish GM Peter Stastny had had in mind when he played and fought to get his newly-independent nation into the top rung of countries during the mid-1990s as the nation was in its first years as an independent country.

Just a few weeks later, though, every available Slovak was determined to prove to the world how misleading that result in Salt Lake had been. The Slovaks beat Poland and Ukraine to start the 2002 World Championship in Gothenburg, and lost 3-1 to Finland. The first sign of better things to come occurred in their next game, against Sweden. The Swedes scored early and led 1-0 after two periods, but the Slovaks scored twice in the third to win. They then beat Austria and Russia to set up a quarter-finals date with Canada, Olympic gold medalists.

Canada built a 2-1 lead midway through the game and was playing solidly, but then the Slovaks scored at 19:59 of the second to tie the game and got the only goal of the third period to win, 3-2. In the semi-finals, against Tre Kronor again, they prevailed 2-1 in a shootout to face the Russians for gold. Slovakia held a 3-1 lead heading to the final period, but Russia scored twice to tie the game. Overtime seemed inevitable until Peter Bondra snapped a quick shot past goalie Maxim Sokolov with just 1:40 remaining in regulation time to give the Slovaks an historic gold medal.

They avenged their showing at the Olympics — where matters were beyond their control — and established once and for all that the new world of hockey consisted not of six great nations but seven.
— Andrew Podnieks

Captain Mario Lemieux poses with his best friend, his gold medal from the 2002 Olympics in Salt Lake City.

The Second Coming of Canada

GRETZKY PASSES THE TORCH

By Andrew Podnieks

To understand Canada's resurgence in the hockey world, one cannot start with the gold medal win at the 2002 Olympic Winter Games. One must go back four years earlier, to a stinging loss at the 1998 Olympics in Nagano. For Canadians, that experience is defined by the image of Wayne Gretzky on the bench, alone, head down, after five Canadians failed to beat Czech goalie Dominik Hasek even once during the semi-final shootout loss. Gretzky, the all-time leading goal scorer in NHL history, was not even selected to take one of the shots. His international career was now at an end (save a bronze-medal game against Finland a couple of days later which even Gretzky himself said was better for hockey that the Finns won), and a little more than a year later his NHL career would also be over.

The loss to the Czechs was a bitter pill for Canadians to swallow. The country had long believed that if the NHL were to shut down for the Olympics and allowed all of the best players in the world to play, Canada would surely win the gold. It was much the same as the confidence exuded leading up to the 1972 Summit Series when Canadians complained for a decade that the Soviets held an unfair advantage in who could and could not compete at the World Championships.

Leading up to 1998, Canada was clearly the favourite, even though it was coming off one of its most stunning losses, at the 1996 World Cup of Hockey, when USA defeated Canada 5-2 in the final game of a best-of-three finals, in Montreal. The only other best-on-best loss Canada had ever experienced was fully 15 years previous when the Soviets won the 1981 Canada Cup, precursor to the World Cup, by a humiliating 8-1 count in the final game.

In his last international game, a disconsolate Wayne Gretzky reflects after Finland won the bronze medal at the 1998 Olympics as team captain Eric Lindros skates away.

What few people at the time realized about the 1998 team was that even as general manager Bobby Clarke was selecting a team to defeat the Americans in Nagano, he was also selecting a team that could not compete on the bigger ice surface (Canada played all of its game in the World Cup on the smaller, North American ice) against European teams which were so well coached that players could come and go, stay within the "system," and still win consistently.

So, Clarke chose players such as Keith Primeau and Trevor Linden, power forwards and superstars in the NHL, to be sure, but slow and not as skilful on the bigger ice. Clarke also chose Rob Zamuner to the team, at the time one of the best defensive forwards in the game. Wisdom had it that a team needed such a player to check the other team's top stars, and perhaps if the Canadians had scored on Czech goalie Dominik Hasek and went on to win gold, it might have been a wisdom that proved genius. But they didn't, and it didn't. Perhaps most damning of Clarke, though, was his decision to name Eric Lindros as captain, an attempt to hand the torch from Gretzky to Lindros despite the Great One having earned the honour and Lindros not having made clear his ability to take over for Gretzky as the game's pre-eminent star.

This double loss in 1996 and 1998 represented a time of anguish for hockey in Canada and for its governing body, Hockey Canada. To sum up the last part of the 20th century: Mario Lemieux retired in the spring of 1996 and vowed never to play again; Canada lost the World Cup in September 1996 and then the Olympics in February 1998; Gretzky retired in April 1999. Meanwhile, the Czechs were winning the gold at the World Championships with regularity and were 1998 Olympic champions by playing a style of hockey defined by defence and opportunistic scoring. To make matters worse, the first round of the 1999 NHL Entry Draft featured only nine Canadians. Even the Canadian women failed to win gold at Nagano, another decisive blow to the country's self esteem. And at the junior level, Team Canada, which had reeled off an incredible five wins in a row (1993-97), was now unable to win another gold, coming up short to, usually, the Russians. As Hockey Canada saw it, something had to be done.

The media started to compare the Canadian system of player development to the European model. Journalists questioned the practice-to-games ratio which was so strong in Europe but so lop-sided toward games in Canada. Statistics were flouted about how nations such as the Czech Republic or Sweden, with smaller populations and fewer participating players, could produce so many world-class players per capita compared to Canada. Public opinion polls showed many Canadians believed the nation had lost its grip as the world power of the puck game. The result was the Open Ice Summit in August 1999 in Toronto. That was the first of a series of events which helped Canada reassert itself as the 20th century gave way to the 21st.

Gretzky was the honourary chair of this important three-day event, and the meetings included stars of today and yesterday, as well as parents, coaches, and kids at the grassroots level. The greatest debate focused on practice time versus playing time. In Canada, the emphasis was always on the latter, and the reasoning was simple and intelligent. Players must learn the game by playing games. In Europe, the message was the opposite, but equally intelligent. Players must develop and work on their skills if they are to play well during games.

The message Gretzky focused on was also equally simple. Let kids play with the puck. Skate, stick-handle, have fun. Forget about games and coaching

systems and hollering parents in the stands. Kids need to love the game, most of all, if they are to develop into great players. Let them "grab the puck and try to get it in the net," Gretzky summarized.

Although the Summit enabled some changes, it was more important that the most powerful people in the game came together and focused on the sport itself. Almost immediately after the event, Gretzky more or less disappeared from the hockey world for a year. He wanted to take a break from

Team Canada's on-ice portrait after its 5-2 win over USA for gold in Salt Lake 2002, the first win for Canada in half a century.

the game after retiring, but he promised he would be back and wanted to remain involved in hockey with the same passion in suit and tie as he had shown with skates and stick.

The next step in Canada's revival came on November 8, 2000, at a press conference in Calgary, when Hockey Canada hired Gretzky as executive director of hockey operations for the 2002 Olympics. The fancy title meant one thing — Gretzky would be in charge of everything related to hockey in Canada through to February 2002. His hiring immediately gave the sport even greater prominence — if that's possible — in Canada. His first words were a vow to forget about other countries, forget about tactics and systems and size and intimidation and defensive play. He made it clear Canadian players were more skilled than any other in the world, and he promised to build teams around speed, skill, creativity, scoring ability. He also promised to make the players accountable, and to connect this accountability from the juniors to the World Championships to the Olympics.

The first test during the Gretzky Era came right away, at the 2001 World Junior Championships. Coach Stan Butler selected a team built around speed, not size, scoring ability, not defensive play.

It doesn't look like it here, but Jarome Iginla (bottom left) beats Mike Richter with a deflection. It came late in the first period to give Canada a 2-1 lead in the 2002 gold-medal game against USA, won by the Canadians, 5-2.

The result was an exciting team that won its third medal since the Open Ice Summit, a bronze, to be sure. Nonetheless, it was a creative team, and it made clear the players were selected for the right reasons.

The bigger pre-Salt Lake City test for Gretzky came at the 2001 World Championship in Germany. Although Canada finished a distant fifth, its roster was perhaps the most impressive the country had ever sent to the tournament, which comes after a grueling NHL season and, for those who play, a disappointing early end to the season after being eliminated from the Stanley Cup playoffs. But the roster in 2001 was outstanding. Three players went on to play at Salt Lake — Eric Brewer, Michael Peca, Ryan Smyth — while seven younger members of that team later played at the 2006 Olympics — goalie Roberto Luongo, defenceman Wade Redden, forwards Vincent

Equipment flies through the air as Team Canada players empty the bench to celebrate their dramatic, tension-filled gold medal in the 2003 World Championship. Swedish goalie Mikael Tellqvist sits dejectedly in his crease after learning the decisive goal was allowed by video review.

A GOAL WORTH WAITING FOR

The 2003 World Championship gold medal game was decided in an historic manner. It was the first time an OT was played four skaters a side. And, more significant, it was the first time a gold-medal goal was decided by video review—and what a review it was!

Canada and Sweden were tied 2-2 after three periods of regulation. Midway through the 20-minute, sudden-death overtime, Canada's Anson Carter, wheeling around the Swedish goal guarded by young Mikael Tellqvist, wrapped the puck into the goal, and immediately started to jump for joy. His teammates poured off the ice to celebrate, but Tellqvist appealed to the referee who signaled he was going to 'go upstairs' for confirmation.

Then, the pause, the longest pause in IIHF history, as officials talked to the video goal judge to confirm Carter had, indeed, scored the gold-medal goal. The review took almost ten minutes, but after checking every angle and working with the TV production company to enlarge specific images, referee Vladimir Sindler confirmed Carter's immediate reaction, and Team Canada poured off the bench a second time to celebrate a 3-2 victory.

That was May 11, 2003, at the Hartwall Areena in Helsinki, Finland. The ending may have been surreal, but the referee and video judge, by taking their time and following proper protocol, made the right call. Indeed, one image in particular captured the puck nestled just inside the net over the goal line. Ten years ago, that play might have been ruled a goal—or might not have.
—Andrew Podnieks

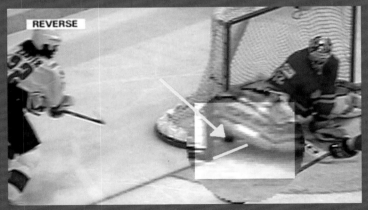

REVERSE

Finnish television YLE finally provided the IIHF with this angle which clearly shows that Anson Carter's shot squeezed between the post and Mikael Tellqvist's pad.

Lecavalier, Brad Richards, Joe Thornton, Kris Draper, and Smyth.

The 2002 Olympics were the culmination of four years' intense work. The Open Ice Summit exposed some weaknesses in the Canadian system which were corrected, at least in part; Gretzky was on board, symbolically and practically to select the team; the coaching staff was a capable one, as always; Mario Lemieux had come out of retirement and was named captain. Now, all that was left was execution. The players were capable of winning gold — now they had to go and do it. The NHL shut down again for 2002, and Team Canada was again the favourite.

Everything that went wrong in Nagano went right in Salt Lake, starting with leadership from Gretzky off ice and Lemieux on it, and continuing on with a team built for speed and skill and scoring. Gretzky and his management group didn't select the players with a particular opponent in mind, only with an intention to maximize ability. Whereas Clarke had selected Zamuner four years ago, Gretzky selected a top player, Michael Peca, knowing that coach Pat Quinn could make him a checker for two weeks, a checker with great offensive skills as well. The phi-

losophy was simple but brilliant: pick the best players and give them each a job.

Canada's victory in 2002 erased a half-century drought of Olympic gold, but it served as the cornerstone to a resurgence of the mother country as the top hockey nation. Both inspired by and inspiring to the women's team, Canada's women also won gold by beating the American women in a tense final. At the 2002 World Championship just ten weeks later, Canada's men finished sixth after a heart-breaking loss to the gold medalists from Slovakia in the quarter-finals. But starting in 2003, the Canadians went on a terrific run that saw the country play in four of the next five gold medal games at the World Championship, winning the first two and the last (2007) in impressive fashion and losing the third at the end of a lockout season in which most of Canada's players hadn't even played serious hockey all year.

In 2003, Canada had four players from the 2002 or 2006 Olympic team in the lineup — Brewer, Smyth, Luongo, Draper — plus an exceptional lineup of newcomers, notably the tandem of Dany Heatley and Daniel Brière, as well as Shane Doan, Mike Comrie, and Anson Carter. Thanks to

Czech photographer Jiri Kolis caught Anson Carter's goal from his position in the stands as Per-Johan Axelsson watches the play unfold.

Gretzky's initiatives, and the success in Salt Lake, Team Canada started to have more success recruiting players for a tournament that had traditionally been shunned by the top stars.

In 2003, it was a dramatic overtime goal by Carter that gave Canada a 3-2 win over Sweden for gold, and a year later it was Heatley who performed so well for Canada. The 2004 team also was loaded with talent, from defencemen Scott Niedermayer

"Captain Canada," Ryan Smyth, bites his gold medal playfully after victory in 2003. In the background hangs the famous photo of Paul Henderson's winning goal in 1972.

again. It was Olympic and world champions for men, Olympic and world champions for women, and it was champions of the World Junior tournament as well. Furthermore, Canada also had won the 2004 World Cup, again with Gretzky and Quinn heading the managerial and coaching teams, respectively. The IIHF had started a world ranking system in 2003, and for almost four years Canada was number one.

At the 2005 World Championship, Canada was bolstered by a lineup of players from Europe or the NHL who had been idle most of the year during the lockout. Goalie Martin Brodeur was in charge of the blue ice, and the team was led by the dominant duo of tournament MVP Joe Thornton and his linemate Rick Nash, a scoring machine, both of whom had led Davos to a Swiss-league championship during the year. The Czechs prevailed 3-0 in the final game with a lineup that had all been playing all season, but Canada's run during this three-year stretch was impressive, indeed.

and Jay Bouwmeester to forwards Glen Murray, Jeff Friesen, and Brendan Morrison. The gold-medal game against Sweden was again impressive as Canada stormed back in the third period to win, 5-3.

By early 2005, Canada had achieved a level of international success that might never be matched

Interestingly, this enormous and continued success helped Canada as a nation cope with its worst Olympic showing ever, at the 2006 event in Turin. Again Gretzky was in charge and again he named

FOCUS ON **RYAN SMYTH**

By Andrew Podnieks

He's called "Captain Canada" for a reason. Between 1999 and 2006, Ryan Smyth appeared in every international senior game for his country, a run of seven World Championships, two Olympics, and one World Cup. He had also appeared at the World Junior Championships in 1995 as an 18-year-old.

Smyth played his junior hockey in the WHL with Moose Jaw for four years, and it was in the last of these that he represented Canada for the first time at the U20 tournament in Red Deer, Alberta. Smyth had seven points in as many games, and Canada won the gold medal. He also played his first three NHL games with the Oilers that season, 1994-95, and the year after he made the team full-time. Smyth has never looked back.

Smyth had just two goals in 48 games in his rookie season, but the year after he played all 82 games, scored a staggering 39 goals, and developed into the best young player on the team. The Oilers won their first-round playoff series against Dallas in seven games but were eliminated in the conference semi-finals by Colorado in just five games.

The next two years saw a dramatic decline in production for Smyth as injuries slowed him down. His style of play, though, was endearing him to fans. Not big, he played with a giant heart, blocking shots, taking on bigger opponents in puck battles, and playing with unmatched intensity. He played at the senior World Championships for the first time in 1999, joining the players in Norway after a quick exit in the first round of the NHL playoffs. The team went to the bronze medal game before losing to Sweden, 3-2.

In 2000, the story was much the same. The Oilers lost to Dallas in five games, Smyth flew to Russia, and the team finished fourth again, losing to Finland this time, 2-1, in the bronze medal game. Smyth collected nine points in as many games that year.

The next year, the Oilers again had an early end to the season and Smyth again accepted the invitation to play for Canada. The team was loaded with talent but finished a disappointing fifth. Roberto Luongo was in goal, and forwards included Vincent Lecavalier, Brad Richards, Michael Peca, and Patrick Marleau.

In 2002, the Oilers didn't even make the playoffs, and Smyth was one of the first group of players named to the team. He was one of only two players to represent Canada that year at both the Olympics in Salt Lake City and the World Championship in Sweden (Eric Brewer was the other). Canada failed to win double gold, though. After an historic win at the Olympics, the country finished sixth after being eliminated by Slovakia in the quarter-finals.

Smyth's dedication paid off in 2003 when he captained Canada to the gold medal after a 3-2 overtime win against Sweden. He replicated his success in

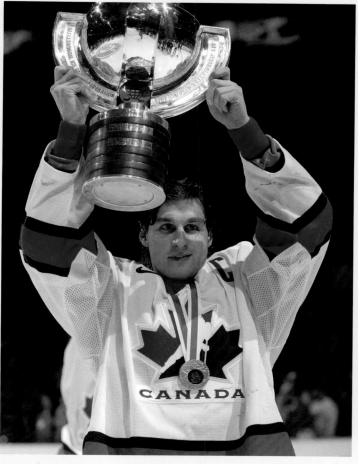

After several failed attempts, Smyth led Canada to consecutive World Championship titles in 2003 and 2004.

2004, again after a finals victory over Tre Kronor. Canada tried for a third successive title in 2005, the end of the lockout year, but Smyth and his teammates lost the gold-medal game to the Czech Republic. He also helped Canada win the 2004 World Cup of Hockey, scoring three goals in six games.

Smyth was unable to play the double international tournaments in 2006. He was named to the Olympic team, which followed its victory in 2002 with its worst showing ever—seventh place—but Smyth took his Edmonton Oilers to game seven of the Stanley Cup finals and was not available for Team Canada that year. He came within one game of becoming a member of the IIHF's exclusive Triple Gold Club (gold at the Olympics and World Championships, and Stanley Cup champion).

In all, Smyth played an incredible 78 straight games for his country, a record for a Canadian that might never be broken. ∎

Dany Heatley accepts the MVP trophy from IIHF president René Fasel after a brilliant performance in the 2004 World Championship.

the same managerial and coaching staff, but everything about the '06 Olympics was different. The team arrived in a cloud of controversy as Gretzky's wife, Janet, had been implicated in a gambling ring back in the U.S., and Gretzky himself came under scrutiny for naming Todd Bertuzzi to the team despite Bertuzzi's horrific, career-ending assault of Steve Moore in 2003 and Bertuzzi's very mediocre start to the 2005-06 season. Also, Lemieux had retired and the captaincy was given to the more

reserved, less spectacular Joe Sakic, and Gretzky received ample criticism for not selecting Sidney Crosby and Dion Phaneuf to the team, rookie teenagers in the NHL who were performing with extraordinary skill and maturity.

As a result, the team never focused, never performed, and never looked to be a serious contender. It lost 2-0 to Switzerland for the first time ever (a rivalry dating back to 1924 when

Rick Nash poses with the MVP trophy after his remarkable showing at the 2007 World Championship in Moscow.

Swiss forward Paul DiPietro is congratulated after scoring against Canada in the 2006 Olympics. A native Canadian, he scored both goals in a 2-0 win, the first ever by the Swiss over Canada at the Olympics.

At game's end, DiPietro shakes hands with his nemesis, Canadian goalie Martin Brodeur.

The Niedermayer brothers—Rob, left, and Scott, right—pose with the World Championship trophy after winning it together in 2004.

Canada beat the Swiss 33-0), and the decisive goal in the 2-0 loss to Russia in the quarter-finals was scored by Alexander Ovechkin early in the third period with, symbolically, Bertuzzi in the penalty box. Yet, despite the seventh-place finish in Turin, there was no call for overhauling the system, no criticism of practice-to-games ratio, no panic. Only disappointment and embarrassment.

Hockey Canada followed this poor performance in 2006 with another incredible year in 2007, virtually matching its dominance of early 2005. The juniors won gold at the 2007 WJC, and the women followed with a dominating 5-1 win over the Americans at the World Women's Championship in Winnipeg. Then, at the men's World Championship in Russia, coach Andy Murray led Team Canada to another gold, winning

Champagne showers the dressing room after Team Canada's gold medal victory in 2004 courtesy of Colby Armstrong.

all nine of its games, including a thrilling 4-2 victory over Finland in the deciding contest. The win was the result of tremendous performances from Rick Nash (tournament MVP) and the Staal brothers, Eric and Jordan, and marked a quick response to the poor Olympics showing.

Today, as Canada gets set to host the 2008 World Championship, its reputation has been restored, its place in hockey once again assuredly reaffirmed at the top. The women's national team has distanced itself even from the U.S. and is indisputably the best in the world, and the World Juniors have now won three straight gold medals and have appeared in six successive gold-medal finals. The men have erased the Turin result with gold in Moscow at the World Championship. The NHL is still represented by some 55% of Canadians, and the influx of Americans and Europeans has steadied.

Teen phenom Sidney Crosby celebrates Canada's gold medal at the World Junior Championship in January 2005 after defeating, Russia, 6-1.

The days of misery that were the post-Nagano period in Canada are long gone, and Canada remains a formidable opponent on hockey's world stage. The days of having to beg top players to play at the World Championships is a thing of the past, and as the gap between Canada and the rest of the world has gotten closer, Canada has still managed to win more than its share of glory. If the 2008 World Championship is successful — and who could say it won't be? — Canada could become part of the regular rotation to host the tournament, and this can only be a further boon to the nation and to the world of international hockey.

Team Canada coach Andy Murray has now led his country to gold three times after winning the title in 2007 in Russia, an unprecedented success for a Canadian coach. He won previously in 1997 and 2003.

Sweden's Double Gold Makes History

CENTENNIAL CIRCLE COMPLETED IN CANADA 2008

By Szymon Szemberg

Traditionally, the Olympics have rarely brought out the best of Swedish hockey. To put it simply, the Swedes never found a way to beat Canada during the pre-Soviet era and once the Soviets started to dominate after 1956, the Tre Kronor were never good enough to defeat the "Big Red Machine."

It took the Swedes 64 years to defeat Canada in an Olympic game (2-0 in Sarajevo in 1984) and they never managed an Olympic win over the Soviet Union as long as the country existed. The breakthrough came only after the Soviet empire crumbled and the less formidable Russia rose from the rubble. Only then did Sweden win, 4-3, in a semi-final game Lillehammer in 1994.

This was also the tournament which ended Sweden's 74-year wait for an Olympic hockey gold medal. Peter Forsberg's shootout goal on Canada's Corey Hirsch in the gold-medal game and Tommy Salo's save on Paul Kariya's last effort belong to Swedish sports lore.

But it was back to the bad old days when the Olympics opened for NHL players four years later. The collection of Swedish NHL stars failed miserably both in Nagano 1998 and in Salt Lake City 2002. The entire Olympic four-year cycle following the 4-3 quarter-final loss to Belarus in Salt Lake was a nightmare for Swedish hockey fans, almost to a degree of national trauma. The team that swept through the preliminary round, and defeated eventual gold medalist Canada 5-2 in the process, lost on Vladimir Kopat's shot from centre ice when the puck bounced off goaltender Tommy Salo's facemask and into the net. That moment is considered one of the lowest points in the country's sports history.

Members of the Swedish national team pour off the bench after the team's 3-2 win over Finland in the gold-medal game of the 2006 Olympics. Captain Mats Sundin, in what may have been his final game for Tre Kronor, leads the charge.

The Swedes pose for the traditional on-ice portrait after Olympic victory in 2006.

The same nation, with many different players, celebrates World Championship gold several weeks later.

Hockey (a bad 6-1 quarter-finals loss to the Czechs in Stockholm) only added to the misery.

The overall hockey morale in the country was so low leading up to Turin 2006 that many Swedish sports fans honestly believed Sweden, by no means a soccer power, had a better chance to win the World Cup in Germany that summer than win the Olympic hockey gold.

That Sweden in 2006 was second in the IIHF World Ranking was something no Swedish hockey fan cared to acknowledge. That the Tre Kronor was, by far, the most consistent of all national teams in the last 15-year period — three IIHF World Championships, six silver medals, four bronze, fourteen "final-four" appearances and one Olympic gold medal — was a nice statistic for the Swedish Ice Hockey Association, but it was not enough for the fans. They demanded a win. Because the core players such as Nicklas Lidstrom, 35, Mats Sundin 34, Daniel Alfredsson, 33, and Peter Forsberg, 32, weren't getting any younger, fans also knew that win would have to come either soon or not for a long time.

Sweden's beloved Tre Kronor didn't even make the final in the 2002 World Championship on home ice, a tournament labeled as "The Revenge of the Nation" following the Belarus debacle just weeks earlier. They lost consecutive gold-medal games to Canada in 2003 and in 2004 and they lost in the semi-finals to the Czechs in Austria in 2005. The monumental fiasco in the 2004 World Cup of

Everyone who had followed the fortunes of the

Swedish national team for the last four decades knew that Sweden's chances to strike gold in Turin increased dramatically after the 5-0 thrashing at the hands of the Russians in the preliminary round. It sounds funny, but all Swedish national teams, regardless of sport, perform better when there is no pressure. There is a saying in Swedish: "Att slå ur underläge," which, loosely translated, means "To strike from below." To strike from below has almost become a part of the Swedish national sports character.

After being outplayed by the Russians and then losing 3-0 to the Slovaks in a listless affair in the last preliminary round game, the Swedes positioned themselves exactly where they wanted to be. The pressure was off, and all attention was on Canada, Russia, and the streaking Finns and Slovaks. No one realized this better than national team coach Bengt-Ake Gustafsson. He knew that this was the perfect time to "strike from below."

After Sweden drew Switzerland as its opponent in the quarter-final — the preferred opponent for coach Gustafsson — the avenue to the gold was all but decorated in blue and yellow. As improved as the Swiss were, they were still inferior to a top

Belarus celebrates its greatest win ever, a 4-3 victory over Tre Kronor in the 2002 Olympics, sending shockwaves through Sweden at a time when the country could realistically have anticipated gold.

Sweden's coach, Bengt-Ake Gustafsson displays his Riga 2006 honours. He is one of only six men to win World Championship gold as both a player (1987) and coach.

Jorgen Jonsson displays the wares of his incomparable 2006 season—Olympic gold, World Championship gold, and his medal from the Swedish championship title with Farjestad.

Swedish selection as the 6-2 score proved. In the semi-finals, it was Sweden's turn to win an important game against the Czechs, 7-3, the first time since 1997 that Sweden won an "all-or-nothing" game against the Czechs. And, if there were a team that Sweden preferred to the play in a finals, it was Finland. With the exception of the 1995 World Championship final, Sweden has always held an important psychological advantage over their eastern neighbours.

In a moment appropriate to the occasion, the Olympic gold-winning goal, scored only ten seconds into the third period, was produced by the three most coveted Swedish players in modern history. Peter Forsberg skated in over the blueline and left the puck for Mats Sundin who dropped the puck to a trailing Nicklas Lidstrom. His tremendous one-timer flew past goaltender Antero Niittymaki who was named MVP of these Olympics. Since the World Cup of Hockey in

1996, Swedish hockey fans had been constantly asking, "How can our best players be rated so highly in the NHL and win all kinds of trophies, but when they play with the national team they aren't nearly as impressive?"

Finally the top players did perform at their highest level, and on February 26, 2006, the ghosts of Salt Lake City, Belarus, and Vladimir Kopat were banished. At last, Sweden's "Golden Generation" won gold. "Success breeds success" and seldom was the old proverb more fitting than when Tre Kronor followed this Olympic gold with a World Championship gold in Latvia, just 85 days later, becoming the first country to win the two titles in the same year.

Sweden's historic double gold, completed with a 3-0 win against the Czech Republic on May 21, 2006, was a feat that not even the superior Soviet teams of the 1970s managed to achieve. Prior to 2006, there were six times when the Olympics and the World Championships were played in the same year and on each occasion the challenge to win both proved too great. Historic wins often produce great trivia questions. Sweden's double victory from Turin and Riga in 2006 added this one to the history books: Which players were on both gold medal-winning teams? Answer: Henrik Zetterberg, Jörgen Jönsson, Kenny Jönsson, Niklas Kronwall, Mika Hannula, Mikael Samuelsson, Ronnie Sundin, and backup goalie Stefan Liv. Veteran Jörgen Jönsson went even one step further by winning the Swedish national championship with Färjestad on April 18, 2006, for a truly unique treble.

As the Swedes were dancing in streets celebrating the double gold, their archrivals Finland were again left wondering about what might have been. A silver medal from Turin and a bronze from Riga was still more than powerhouse nations like Canada and Russia took home, but there was an element of disappointment within the Finnish hockey community. Their national heroes were the best team in Turin for 23 out of 24 periods. They went through the preliminary round undefeated; and, they disposed of the Americans in the quarter-finals and thoroughly outplayed an excellent Russian team in the semis, 4-0, arguably one of the best games a Finnish team has ever played.

Just like Slovakia, Finland is a country of just over five million people that produces a disproportionate

Nicklas Lidstrom and teammates celebrate his goal just ten seconds into the third period of the gold-medal game at the 2006 Olympics. The goal held up, and Sweden won, 3-2. (inset) Lidstrom displays his medal in the dressing room after the game.

The Swedes spray their dressing room with champagne after winning Olympic gold in 2006.

Niklas Kronwall (aka "Lidstrom Light") gets his Olympic sweater signed by his mentor, Nicklas Lidstrom.

number of excellent hockey players, but the nation has always been one mental barrier away from being a legitimate top-three hockey power. The psychology factor has played a role in several decisive moments since the beginning of the 1990s when the Finnish teams have succumbed to pressure. During that period they have lost six World Championship gold medal games, the World Cup finals against Canada in 2004, and the Olympic final in Turin.

Some of the defeats were painful. They lost the 1994 World Championship final to Canada in a shootout, the 1998 final to Sweden despite allowing only one goal in two games in the best-of-two format, and the 1999 and 2001 finals both to the Czechs in overtime. Nobody knows what the outcome of the 2004 World Cup finals in

Toronto would have been had goaltender Miikka Kiprusoff not allowed two uncharacteristically soft goals against Canada. And what if Saku Koivu's stick hadn't broken on the opening faceoff in the third period of the Olympic final in Turin, an incident that left the Finns shorthanded for a moment that was enough for the Swedes to score the winning goal?

No Finnish fan will ever forget the quarter-finals against Sweden of the 2003 World Championship in Helsinki when the hosts where on their way to humiliating their fiercest rivals, only to see Tre Kronor stage the most remarkable come-from-behind victory in modern World Championship history, turning a 5-1 second period deficit into a 6-5-win.

At the 2007 World Championship in Moscow, the Finns had the chance to delete the "loser" label from their resume but, instead, they were defeated in yet another major final, to Canada, again, this time, 4-2. Until Finland manages to find a way to win these big games, the 1995 World Championship victory against Sweden in Stockholm will remain the defining moment in Finnish hockey history.

As the IIHF celebrates its centennial, there are many countries that are surging towards respectability, a process similar to what Finland experienced in the 1970s and '80s. When the Finns defeated Sweden in the 1970 World Championship for the first time in their history, the top pool of the IIHF's flagship event consisted of six teams, and the IIHF consisted of just 21 nations worldwide. Today, the elite division of the World Championship includes 16 nations, and the IIHF's entire men's world championship program now boasts 46 nations.

Approaching the centennial year, the IIHF has 65 member national associations and there are some twenty more working towards establishing active hockey programs with the aim of joining the IIHF

World Championship series. There are active national team programs in Macao, Hong Kong, Thailand, United Arab Emirates, Kuwait, Malaysia, and Liechtenstein that are just waiting for the opportunity to join teams from New Zealand, South Africa, Armenia, Ireland, Luxembourg and Mongolia, countries that have already taken part in official IIHF World Championship competition.

Thanks to the IIHF's annual world championship program for men, women, under-20 and under-18, the hockey world is getting both bigger and better. Everyone involved in hockey, from the lowest amateur ranks to the NHL, is a beneficiary. For example, at the inaugural Canada Cup in 1976, Team USA didn't have enough NHL players to fill the 25-man roster in the historic tournament — eight players had to be recruited from other leagues. More than 95 percent of all NHLers were Canadian at the time.

Today, hockey players are developed on all five continents and in recent years the NHL has signed players from 19 nations outside North America. Apart from the top European hockey nations, NHL clubs have recruited players who were developed in Germany, Switzerland, Belarus, Austria, Poland,

Finnish captain Saku Koivu suffers the pain of an Olympic finals loss in 2006.

Olli Jokinen remains inconsolable at the team bench.

Finnish Formula-1 star Kimi Raikkonen hugs Swedish friend Peter Forsberg after "Foppa" helped Tre Kronor to Olympic gold at Finland's expense.

Kazakhstan, Latvia, France, Norway, Ukraine, and Lithuania. During the 2006-2007 season, players from Slovenia, Denmark, and Japan added to the league's international flavour. Since the turn of the 21st century, some 30 percent of the league's players have come from outside North America.

The internationalization and increased quality of play has provided hockey with parity like never before. Between 1963 and 1986, only two nations won gold at the World Championships. In the ten years between 1993 and 2003, six nations claimed the title.

Almost every international event today is fiercely contested with none of the 30-0 results that marked international games in the 1920s and '30s. Belarus defeats Sweden; Switzerland shuts out the most talented Canadian team in many years, and that a couple of days after the Swiss edged the Czech Republic. Latvia defeats Russia; Denmark upsets USA. In international hockey of the 21st century, fans have come to expect the unexpected.

As Canada gave this beautiful game to the world at the beginning of the 20th century, it is only fitting that the world comes back to the motherland of

hockey in 2008 to show how the international community has managed to broaden the heritage. What started as a national leisure activity on the frozen ponds and lakes of Nova Scotia, Quebec, and Ontario, has become an international passion for millions of fans and players alike and the most watched sport of the Olympic Winter Games.

In 2008, the World Championship comes to Canada for the first time and marks a perfect completion of the centennial circle. The IIHF salutes the people who have paved the way for this century of unequalled passion of hockey, and it anticipates another century of the world's fastest sport. Indeed, the tradition continues.

GOLD AND GOLD—IN ONE YEAR!

There are eight players in the world who can boast winning Olympic and World Championship gold medals in the same year. When Sweden scored the unprecedented double in 2006 (Turin Olympics and Riga World Championships) these eight players were on both rosters: forwards Henrik Zetterberg, Jorgen Jonsson, Mikael Samuelsson, and Mika Hannula; defencemen Kenny Jonsson, Niklas Kronwall, and Ronnie Sundin; and, goaltender Stefan Liv. Zetterberg was instrumental in both wins, scoring six points in Turin and five in Riga. Kenny Jonsson proved that he was still one of the best defenceman in the world despite leaving the NHL and playing the 2005-2006 in Sweden's second division. He captained the Riga team while adding six points in scoring. Kenny's brother, Jorgen, was able to display his outstanding all-round abilities in both Turin and Riga, while Niklas Kronwall, who only played two games in the Olympics due to injury, won tournament MVP honours in Riga. Mika Hannula, who was just happy to be in Turin, scored four goals in Latvia. Vastly underrated Mikael Samuelsson had four Olympic points and added nine more in Riga. Ronnie Sundin had limited ice time in Turin but assumed bigger responsibility two months later, while Stefan Liv was a backup goalie in both events, playing only one game in each tournament. But, he won both of them.
—Szymon Szemberg

Stefan Liv

Ronnie Sundin

Niklas Kronwall

Kenny Jönsson

Jörgen Jönsson

Henrik Zetterberg

Mikael Samuelsson

Mika Hannula

INTERVIEW WITH **MURRAY COSTELLO**

IIHF Council member Murray Costello presents Mishigsuren Namjil with player of the game honours for the Mongolians after the team's game against New Zealand at the 2007 World Championship, Division III.

RINKS ARE THE KEY TO DEVELOPMENT

By Szymon Szemberg

Murray Costello had what he calls "the best seat in the house" during the 1956 Stanley Cup finals. Between the few shifts Costello enjoyed on ice, he watched "Rocket" Richard and his Montreal Canadiens from the Detroit Red Wings' bench.

Knowing that he would never be a star, Costello quit professional hockey at the age of 23 after having played 162 regular season NHL games for three teams in four seasons. He probably made the right choice. Costello was inducted into the Hockey Hall of Fame in 2005 for his contributions in developing youth and women's hockey as president of Hockey Canada, formerly the Canadian Amateur Hockey Association.

Costello joined the IIHF Council in 1998 and has since then been committed to the development of the game in countries that many hockey fans in traditional countries hardly know participate internationally in IIHF events.

"The key to all hockey development is building hockey rinks," said Costello, who is also chairman of the IIHF's Technical & Arena Committee. "If a country ever wants to develop a sustainable program, it needs facilities. No matter how much knowledge the IIHF assists with — if you don't have rinks, you won't get anywhere."

Few people can better judge the quality and development of the lower ranks of the IIHF's championship than Costello. As all IIHF Council members are obliged to do, Costello travels to Division II and III events every year to perform the duties of tournament chairman in countries such as Ireland, Iceland, New Zealand, and China.

In 2007, he was chairman of the IIHF World Championship Division III (men's lowest level) for the third time in four years, this time in Dundalk, Ireland, the country of his origins. The participating teams included Ireland, Luxembourg, Mongolia, New Zealand, and South Africa. Armenia was unable to play because of visa problems.

The championship was staged in the new Dundalk Ice Dome where a packed house — 1,522 fans — saw their home team earn promotion to Division II after a dramatic shootout win over Luxembourg in the final game.

In all, five teams from four continents displayed hockey's global appeal — and unmatched enthusiasm. If ever there were a truly amateur rank — playing for the love of the game — then Division III hockey is it. These players are at a comparable level as the IIHF pioneers who played in the inaugural European Championship in 1910 in Les Avants, Switzerland, the first international ice hockey event.

The players practise perhaps twice a week, and in most cases they do so at their own expense. Sometimes they have to take unpaid vacations to play in the World Championship; sometimes they have to collectively pay for the renting of the ice.

The question is: Can these nations develop high-quality programs and aim for world supremacy just as countries such as Bohemia, Sweden, Switzerland, Germany, and Finland once had to do many years ago? Or, does that even matter?

"This is the key question", says Costello. "Everything is really up to the people who run the game in that particular country. Some are content with remaining on an entirely amateur level while others are determined to build a program."

Costello mentions Iceland, New Zealand, and Ireland as countries with encouraging progress and China and South Korea as the countries with biggest growth potential in the game.

"The most important factor after having built some facilities is to organize a national league and create local rivalries," says Costello. "This immediately spurns public and media interest. Once you have reached so far, and simultaneously started youth development programs, you definitely have something going."

And just as it was with the pioneers in Les Avants in 1910, some countries that played in Dundalk in 2007 will strive for the next level and reach it, while others will continue approaching the game merely as a pastime. Either way, the IIHF will be there to organize and support tournaments for all countries for the next hundred years. ■

Team South Africa poses for a portrait during the 2007 World Championship, Division III. South Africa joined the IIHF in 1937.

New Zealand's Stacy Rout leads his team in a traditional Maori dance called the Haka prior to a game at the World Championship, Division III, in Dundalk, Ireland.

Members of the Irish national team pour off the bench after the team's dramatic 4-3 shootout win over Luxembourg in the 2007 World Championship, Division III in Dundalk, Ireland. Mark Morrison (centre, helmet off) scored the winning goal, and with the win the Irish moved up to Division II for 2008.

All Countries are Given the Chance for Olympic Gold

General belief is that only a few nations are ever given the chance to win Olympic gold, but the reality is that each and every country that is a member of the IIHF is given the opportunity to win every four years. But, to understand how this chance is available, one must understand the structure of the IIHF.

The first step for a nation to go to the Olympics is to be a member of the IIHF. This is done by applying, proving the seriousness of your desire to compete in international hockey, and backing it up with some facts. For instance, an applicant would help its cause by having an indoor arena with artificial ice and at least a core of players interested in representing that country.

Once the IIHF Congress has accepted the application, the next step could be to take part in the World Championship. As a new nation, you would be placed in Division III, the lowest tier. The top level features 16 teams competing for the

World Championship, and Divisions I, II, and III have two groups of, usually, six teams. Each year the top team from each group is promoted to the next highest level, and the bottom two demoted to the next lowest level.

So, if your country starts in Division III, it can advance to Division II the following year by winning its group. A win in Division II would move it to Division I, and another first-place finish would send your country to the top level. Usually, the top eight or nine teams in the IIHF World Ranking after the World Championship two years prior to the Olympics automatically qualify for the "five-ringed circus." For instance, teams that will receive automatic invitations to Vancouver 2010 will be determined following the 2008 IIHF World Championship.

However, even if your nation is not good enough to rise so remarkably through the divisions to qualify automatically, you still have an opportunity to go to

Very often the most thrilling games occur during the Olympic qualifications. Latvian players and fans go into a frenzy after their 5-4 win over Belarus on January 12, 2005 in Riga. The home team was behind 4-2 with six minutes left when Latvia pulled goaltender Edgars Masalskis. In the following 140 seconds, Latvia scored three goals to ensure participation at the 2006 Olympics in Turin. (inset) Alexander Semjonovs celebrates the game winner at 17:31 of the third period.

the Olympics because 12 teams in total make it to the Olympic games. The other three or four are determined through a series of qualifying tournaments.

Any country that participates in the World Championship program has the right to apply to compete in these qualifying tournaments. However, usually only about 20-25 teams apply. Division III teams don't usually have the funds to

either host or travel to a tournament, but they also realize they'd have to beat a top level team to advance, a highly unlikely scenario. Nonetheless, if your nation is ranked 65th of 65 in IIHF competition, it can play in qualifying tournaments, and if it keeps winning it can capture one of the four coveted places to the Olympics. Is it likely the 65th nation will ever make an appearance? No. But it's possible, and the opportunity is given.

History of Nations

LEVELS OF PLAY

In 2001, the IIHF changed levels of play from a "pool" system to a "division" system. A Pool became "World Senior" (World Women's for women's play), B Pool became Division I, C Pool became Division II, and D Pool became Division III.

Men

A Pool (World Senior)—1920 to present

B Pool (Division I)—1951-present

C Pool (Division II)—1961-present

D Pool (Division III)—1987-present

Women

A Pool (World Women's)—1990-present

B Pool (Division I)—1999-present

Division II—2001-present

Division III—2003-present

LEVELS OF MEMBERSHIP

There are three kinds of members in the IIHF. Full members participate annually in IIHF championships and have independent national associations specifically for hockey. Associate members are those that either do not have fully independent national associations or who do have independent associations but participate to only a limited extent in IIHF championships. Only full members have voting rights at the IIHF Congresses. And, Affiliate Members participate only in IIHF InLine events.

Hungary — an IIHF member since 1927 — has one of the most improved programs in recent years and also enjoys a loyal fan following.

HISTORY OF IIHF MEMBER ASSOCIATIONS

By Igor Kuperman, Szymon Szemberg, and Andrew Podnieks

ANDORRA 1995 (Associate Member)

Ice hockey did not begin in Andorra until the 1990s. Lack of ice (one indoor rink) and equipment slowed the development of the game, and there are only about 90 players in the country. A major step towards popularizing the sport was made when Andorra joined the IIHF on May 4, 1995, and hosted the D Pool World Championships in 1997, in the city of Canillo. Teams from Andorra currently play exhibition games only.

ARGENTINA 1998 (Affiliate Member)

In the 1970s, hockey was played around the Pampas mountains, mainly by European emigrants. The first indoor rink opened in 1981, in the capital of Buenos Aires. Recreational hockey was played there, but not much happened on the hockey front for nearly two decades. On May 31, 1998, Argentina became an IIHF member, but the country's IIHF membership is anchored mainly by its inline activities.

ARMENIA 1999 (Associate Member)

In 1962, in the town of Sverdlovsk (now named Yekaterinenburg) in Russia, the former Soviet Union hosted a tournament that featured all of the Soviet States. The Armenians participated and lost, 1-0, to Lithuania. Now its own nation, Armenia has returned to the hockey world. It became a member of the IIHF on September 22, 1999. Armenia made its international debut in 2004 when it took part in Division III of the World Championships. The first Armenian hockey championship took place in 2001 and was won by ASC Erevan.

AUSTRALIA 1938

The first recorded ice hockey game in Australia took place in 1907 when a group of young Melbourne skaters issued a challenge to the crew of the American battleship Baltimore. Although the home team was defeated, the groundwork for the future development of the sport was initiated. In 1908, games were played in the country's two indoor artificial rinks in Sydney and Melbourne. By 1909, there were four hockey clubs in the province of Victoria and two more in New South Wales. The first inter-provincial games in Australia were played that year, as Melbourne (Victoria) defeated Sydney (New South Wales) two games to one. This early chapter in Australian hockey history came to a close with the outbreak of World War I in 1914.

Melbourne player John Goodhall established the Cup bearing his name in 1921. This went on to become Australia's pre-eminent interstate championship trophy. New South Wales and Victoria dominated the trophy for decades until Queensland's victory in 1977.

Australia joined the IIHF on February 11, 1938, though the Australian Ice Hockey Federation was not founded until 1954. The world caught its first glimpse of the Australian national team when it competed at the 1960 Squaw Valley Olympics. The Aussies lost all six of their preliminary and consolation round matches by an aggregate score of 88-10. Two years later, at the B Pool tournament, they defeated Denmark but lost badly to Japan, Austria, and France. The national side did not compete again for another ten years. Australia continued to experience difficulties at the C Pool World Championships in 1974 and 1979. A source of pride for the Australian hockey program occurred in 1989 when Sydney hosted the C Pool tournament. Today, Australia competes mainly in Division II of the IIHF World Championship.

AUSTRIA 1912

The first mention of hockey in Austria occurred on January 12, 1896, when the Vienna newspaper *Allgemeine Sport-Zeitung* printed an article about bandy. Bandy debuted in Austria in 1899 when a game was played in Vienna. During this same period, three Austrian clubs organized an ice hockey committee. Though the new sport could not yet match the popularity of bandy, it made huge strides and superseded its rival sport by 1911. Ice hockey received a huge boost when the first artificial ice rink opened, in Vienna, on November 10, 1909.

The Austrian Hockey Union was created on January 15, 1912, and was admitted to the IIHF two months later, on March 18. Austria played its first international hockey game on February 2, 1912, losing 5-0 to Bohemia at the European Championship. In the aftermath of World War I, Austria was removed from the IIHF and was not reinstated until in 1925.

In 1922, the country held its first national ice hockey championship. That year, Wiener EV captured its first of nine consecutive titles. Austria attained its first major international success by winning the 1927 European Championships, a feat it duplicated in 1931. This brought an increase in ice rink construction and a wider domestic audience.

Following World War II, Austria won the bronze medal at the 1947 World Championship but soon lost contact with the elite hockey powers. A string of mediocre performances saw the Austrians placed in the inaugural B Pool tournament in 1951.

Austria spent most of the 1960s competing in the B Pool World Championships but found itself in C Pool a decade later. Improved results occurred in the 1980s under the guidance of coaches Rudi Killias and Dr. Ludek Bukac. The Austrians qualified for the Olympics in 1984, 1988, and 1998. Today, Austria frequently ranks among the top 16 hockey nations.

AZERBAIJAN 1992

The Ice Hockey Federation of the Republic of Azerbaijan was founded in 1991 as a part of the Soviet Ice Hockey Federation. After the breakup of the Soviet Union, Azerbaijan achieved independence in 1992. The federation joined the IIHF on May 6, 1992. There is no organized national hockey league in Azerbaijan, and the country has not yet played in IIHF tournaments.

BELARUS 1992

Hockey in the Soviet Republic of Belorussia (now the independent Belarus) became very popular right after World War II when ice hockey made its first inroads in the Soviet Union. In 1946, Torpedo Minsk (later Dynamo Minsk) was formed and began to play in the top Soviet division.

Federatsiya Hokkeya Belarusi (Ice Hockey Federation of the Republic Belarus) became independent in 1992, after the breakup of the Soviet Union. Belarus became a member of the IIHF on May 6, 1992, and staged its first independent national championship in 1992-93. Dynamo Minsk won this title and finished 10th in the KHL of the Commonwealth of Independent States.

Belarus showcased its national team for the first time in November 1992 when it hosted the Group 2 Qualification Tournament for the 1993 C Pool World Championship. Belarus enjoyed a strong debut at the 1994 C Pool World Championship in Slovakia by defeating the Ukraine, Kazakhstan, Slovenia, Hungary, and Bulgaria to claim the silver medal.

The following year, Belarus won the tournament to qualify for B Pool. The Belorussians completed their quick rise to A Pool by winning the 1997 B Pool tournament in Poland. The 1998 Nagano Olympics saw Belarus win its preliminary round group and lose a respectable 4-1 decision to eventual silver medalist Russia in the quarter-finals. The country's biggest success came at the 2002 Olympics in Salt Lake City when Belarus upset Sweden 4-3 in the quarter-finals. It finished fourth after losing the bronze-medal game to Russia.

BELGIUM 1908

Bandy was first played in Belgium in Brussels and Antwerp in 1899. Soon, bandy players began learning to play ice hockey and in 1908 the Koninklijke Belgische Ijshockey Federatie (Royal Belgian Ice Hockey Federation — Federation Royale Belge der Hockey sur Glace) was founded. The Belgians were very active during the early days of ice hockey in Europe. On December 8, 1908, Belgium joined France, Bohemia, Great Britain and Switzerland as the fifth member of the Ligue Internationale de Hockey sur Glace (LIHG).

Hockey quickly became a popular sport in Belgium and the first national championship was held in 1912. At the first official European Championship in 1910, Belgium tied gold medal-winning Great Britain 1-1 and earned the bronze medal. The country repeated this achievement in 1911 and 1914. Belgium won the European Championship in Munich in 1913 and earned a silver medal in 1927.

Paul Loicq, who was president of the IIHF for 25 years (1922 to 1947), is the most famous Belgian in the history of international hockey. He was a member of the 1913 European championship squad. The country's most legendary hockey player was Jef Lekens of Antwerp. He played in nine World and European championships between 1929 and 1955 and was also an international referee during the 1950s.

By the 1990s, the Belgian Ice Hockey Federation boasted nearly 1,000 players, and today the national team usually plays in Division II.

BOSNIA AND HERZEGOVINA 2001

Bosnia and Herzegovina became the 61st member of the IIHF on May 10, 2001, during the Annual Congress held in Hanover, Germany. The country made its debut at the World Championship in 2003, when its U18 team played in Division III, the only level the country has played to date. There is no organized national hockey championship in Bosnia and Herzegovina.

BRAZIL 1984 (Affiliate Member)

A former hockey player from Munich, Erwin Dietenhofer emigrated to Brazil in the 1950s. His successful business ventures enabled him to finance the building of the first hockey rink in the country at Petropolis. The first official games in Brazil were played in 1967 in the ice hall of the Hotel Quitandinha in this city, 40 miles from Rio de Janeiro. Games took place there for eight years until the hotel was closed. During that time, the CCEG Rio de Janeiro team was the best in Brazil.

Hockey resumed in Brazil in 1978 with teams playing on a rink used for the Holiday on Ice show. Once again it was Dietenhofer whose efforts made possible the creation of the Confederacao Brasileira de Desportos Terrestres (Brazil Ice Sport Union) and the organization Brazil Hockey as part of the sports union. He served as the first president of both Brazil Hockey and the Brazil Ice Sport Union. Brazil joined the IIHF on June 26, 1984. Today, Brazil's IIHF membership is based on its inline participation.

BULGARIA 1960

Hockey in Bulgaria began in 1929 when the Bulgarian Skating Club was created. A handful of players took part in a few intramural games and later played on two other teams, AS-23 and FC-13. The Bulgarian national team played its first international game, against Yugoslavia, on January 17, 1942, winning 4-2.

The Bulgarian Skating and Ice Hockey Federation was founded in 1946. Sofia's Yunak sports arena was converted into a hockey rink in 1949 in preparation for the country's first tournament. Four teams participated — Spartak, Slavia, Levski, and Sredec.

Hockey became increasingly popular in Bulgaria, and in 1950 five new sports clubs were founded, each with its own hockey team. In 1952, the country's first national championship took place on the ice of a frozen lake near the Musala mountains.

Bulgaria's first artificial ice rink opened in Sofia in 1960. After joining the IIHF on July 25, 1960, Bulgaria began to play regularly at the World Championships. It debuted at the 1960 C Pool Championships and remained chiefly at that level until 1991 after which it played mostly in C and D Pools.

CANADA 1920

Hockey was born in Canada. Conflicting claims surround the origins of the game, but it is generally accepted that the rules of the game were first codified and the sport itself first flourished in Montreal. The first organized game was played at Montreal's Victoria Skating Rink on March 3, 1875. The game rapidly took root in Montreal, Ottawa, and Toronto, but the sport's popularity quickly spread from coast to coast.

In 1893, Canada's Governor-General, Lord Stanley of Preston, donated a silver bowl to be awarded to the top senior amateur team in the country. This Dominion Hockey Challenge Cup soon came to be known by the name of its patron.

By the turn of the century hockey was played in every part of Canada. Even before 1910, openly professional players were competing for the Stanley Cup. Accounts of the exploits of storied teams such as the Ottawa Silver Seven, Montreal Wanderers, and Renfrew Millionaires filled newspapers of the day. The National Hockey League was established in 1917 and by the end of its first decade stood alone as the game's finest professional circuit.

As hockey in Canada become increasingly professional, the Allan Cup was donated by Sir Montagu Allan in 1908 to honour Canada's senior amateur champions. In 1914, the Canadian Amateur Hockey Association was created and in 1920 the CAHA was accepted by the IIHF as Canada's governing body in international hockey. Canada competed at the 1920 Olympics in Antwerp, Belgium and was represented by the Allan Cup champion Winnipeg Falcons which easily won the gold medal at the event which was later considered to be the first World Championships. Canada offically joined the LIHG on April 26, 1920.

By using top amateur club teams, Canada was able to remain the dominant nation in international hockey until 1954. That year, the Senior B East York Lyndhursts were defeated by the Soviet national team when the USSR made its debut at the World Championships. Senior clubs continued to carry Canada's colors into the early 1960s with teams like the Penticton Vees and Whitby Dunlops still able to defeat the Soviets. However, the Trail Smoke Eaters would be the last Canadian senior amateur club for 33 years to win the World Championship when they captured the title in 1961.

In the early 1960s, the CAHA accepted a proposal by Father David Bauer, coach of the 1961 Memorial Cup-winning St. Michael's junior team in Toronto, to develop a Canadian national hockey team. The Nats were a good program, but the Soviet hockey system was in full flower during the 1960s. The best finish by Father Bauer's squad was a bronze medal at the 1968 Olympics.

Canada withdrew from international competition in 1970 due to a fundamental disagreement with the IIHF over the amateur rule. Hockey Canada was created that year to improve Canada's performance in international play. Beginning with the 1972 Summit Series against the Soviet Union, professional players began to participate in some international events. Canada returned to the IIHF World Championship in 1977 and in 2002 the motherland of hockey ended a 50-year drought by winning gold at the Salt Lake City Olympics. Canada has dominated women's hockey, winning nine World Championships and two Olympic golds.

CHILE 2000 (Affiliate Member)

Little is known about ice hockey in Chile, but it is believed that the sport was played in the harbour city of Valparaiso during the 1970s.

CHINA 1963

The roots of Chinese ice hockey date back to 1915 when a few games took place in Sen Jan province. The next appearance of hockey was not until January 26, 1935, when the country's first tournament took place as part of the First Winter Spartakiade Games.

The Ice Hockey Association of the People's Republic of China was founded in 1951. Two years later, the first national championship was held. In 1956, the National Winter Sports Federation was founded and in March of that year the Chinese national team made its international debut at the Universiade in Wroclaw, Poland.

China joined the IIHF on July 25, 1963. It played its first game in the C Pool World Championship in Miercurea Ciuc, Romania on March 3, 1972. The country's first victory came at the expense of Bulgaria by a 4-3 score. Since that time the national team has played at either the B or C Pool competitions (more recently, Division I or II). Domestic hockey has been centred in the northern provinces bordering the USSR, and Harbin has been the chief base. With women's hockey enjoying rapid growth in the 1990s, China has seen more people involved in the game. The Chinese women made their debut in 1994. Their finest placing was fourth at the 1998 Olympics in Nagano.

CHINESE TAIPEI 1983

The Chinese Taipei Skating Association was founded in 1980. Two years later, in 1982, the first national championship took place. In 1983, Chinese Taipei became a member of the IIHF.

The debut of the Chinese Taipei national team took place in 1987, in Perth, Australia, when the team played at the D Pool World Championship. The results with Chinese Taipei didn't count in the final standing. The national team tied 2-2 with Hong Kong in its first official game on March 13, 1987.

CROATIA 1992

The roots of ice hockey in Croatia go back to 1906 when the first hockey team in Yugoslavia (HASK — the Croatian Academic Sports Club) was formed in the city of Zagreb. Dr. Franjo Bucar was a key figure in the introduction of the sport. The first official hockey games also took place in Zagreb, in 1916-17, when HASK played a two-game series against I.HSK (I. Croatian Sports Club). In 1930, the Yugoslav Ice Hockey Federation was founded in Zagreb.

In 1991, Hrvatski Savez Hokeja na Ledu (Croatian Ice Hockey Association) was founded and the first Croatian national championship was won by MK Zagreb in 1991-92. The newly-independent nation joined the IIHF on May 6, 1992, and the Croatian national team made its debut in the 1994 C Pool World Championships in Barcelona, Spain. Today, Croatia plays mostly in Division I or II.

CZECH REPUBLIC 1908 (AS BOHEMIA)

Josef Rossler-Orovsky introduced bandy as Bohemia in 1890 when the country was still known as Bohemia. He brought sticks and a ball home from Paris and translated rules that were imported from England. Ice hockey was demonstrated for the first time at Prague in 1905 by Canada's Ruck Anderson. The country's bandy background provided players with a solid basis for the new game.

Another key figure at this time was Karlov University professor Josef Gruss who translated Canadian rules into Czech. In the summer of 1908, Gruss began establishing the first hockey clubs in Prague — I. CLTK, Slavia, AC Sparta, ASK and others — which led to the formation of the Czech Hockey Union (Cesky Svaz Hokejovi) on November 6, 1908. Bohemia joined France as the second member of the LIHG on November 15, 1908.

The Bohemian national team won the European Championship in 1911 and again in 1914. When Bohemia became Czechoslovakia after World War I, it was re-admitted to the IIHF under its new name on April 26, 1920. Czechoslovakia won European titles again in 1922, 1925, 1929, and 1933.

The first artificial ice rink opened in Prague on January 17, 1931, where the University of Manitoba played LTC Prague in the inaugural game while en route to representing Canada at the World Championship in Poland. Also in 1931, Slovakia's Hockey Union merged with the Czech Hockey Union to form the Czechoslovakian Hockey Union.

The Soviet Union emerged as a world power in 1954, but Czechoslovakia continued to rank among the best teams in Europe. It often rivaled or bettered the USSR, particularly in the 1970s. Czechoslovakia triumphed at the World Championships in 1972, 1976, and 1977.

After the fall of Communism, the Czech Republic and Slovakia split, and the Czech Republic replaced Czechoslovakia in the IIHF program. The Czech Republic's first major triumph took place at the 1996 World Championship when the team won gold on a last-minute goal versus Canada. The high point in Czech hockey circles was the stunning gold medal victory at the 1998 Nagano Olympics. They also won gold at the World Championships in 1999, 2000, 2001, and 2005.

DENMARK 1946

The first mention of hockey (bandy) in Denmark dates back to the beginning of the 20th century when the members of KSF Copenhagen (Copenhagen Skating Club, founded in 1869) tried the new game. Informal games were played in Copenhagen as early as the 1920s. In 1929, a select team representing the city played the Sodertalje club from Sweden. The popularization of the game was enhanced by the creation of the Dansk Ishockey Union on November 27, 1949. Prior to that date, Denmark had become a member of the IIHF on April 27, 1946.

The first appearance of Danish hockey players on the world stage resulted in what still remains the worst defeat in the history of international hockey at its highest level. On February 12, 1949, Denmark was defeated 47-0 by Canada at the World Championship in Stockholm, Sweden. After its difficulties in 1949, the national team did not return to the World Championships until the 1962 B Pool tournament. Between 1963 and 1991 the Danes competed for the most part in C Pool. They hosted and won the 1991 C Pool competition and finished a respectable fourth at the 1992 B Pool event. The Danes were among the most improved hockey countries at the turn of the 21st century, and have played in the top division of the World Championship every year since 2002.

DPR KOREA 1963

Ice hockey in the People's Democratic Republic of Korea (North Korea) became popular during the 1950s when Soviet and Chinese workers taught the game and its rules in the capital city of Pyongyang. North Korea became a member of the IIHF on August 8, 1963.

The North Korean national team did not make its debut until 1974 when it competed in the C Pool World Championships. The team lost its first official game to Italy 11-2 on March 8, 1974, but rebounded by defeating China and Australia. North Korea did not re-appear at the C Pool competition until the 1980s.

North Korea's first national championship was held in 1956 and was won by Amnokang Pyongyang. Approximately 30 clubs existed in the country by the mid-1980s, the top eight competing for the national title. Pyongyang had the only regulation ice surface as well as all the teams.

The North Korean women's team made its international debut in 2000. Since 2001, the team has played in Division I. The men's team plays at the Division II level while North Korea's junior teams appear sporadically at IIHF events.

ESTONIA 1935/1992

As in so many European nations, hockey in Estonia developed out of bandy which was being played in the capital of Tallinn prior to World War I. By the 1930s, there were many hockey clubs in Estonia, and most of the teams concentrated in Reval (now Tallinn) and the university town of Dorpat (now Tartu). The first national championship took place in 1935 and was won by Kalev Tallinn. Later, Kalev, the Tartu academic sport club, and Sport Tallinn dominated competition in Estonia.

The Eesti Jaahoki Federatsiooni (Estonian Ice Hockey Federation) was founded in 1921 when Estonia was an independent country and was re-founded in 1991 as a part of the Soviet Ice Hockey Federation. Estonia originally joined the IIHF on February 17, 1935, but was removed following World War II on April 27, 1946. During this time, Estonia never sent its national team to the World and European Championships and restricted its play to exhibition games against other Baltic countries and Finland.

The Estonian national team played its first game on February 20, 1937, losing 2-1 to Finland in Helsinki. The country's last international game before World War II was a 3-0 victory over Lithuania in February 1941. After becoming part of the Soviet Union, the best Estonian club (Dynamo Tallinn) played in the top division of the Soviet league from 1946 to 1953. After 1955, Dynamo Tallinn played only for the Estonian Republic Championship.

The newly-independent nation of Estonia again became a member of the IIHF on May 6, 1992 and played in D Pool World Championship in 1994. It won the bronze medal as hosts of the 1997 C Pool tournament. Today, Estonia plays most often at the Division I level, and the nation has yet to compete in women's events.

FINLAND 1928

The first attempt to introduce hockey in Finland was made by professor Leonard Borgstrom at the end of the 19th century. Training sessions were held in the North Harbour area (Pohjoisranta) of Helsinki.

Interest in the new sport waned, however, and the second coming of hockey to Finland did not occur until 1927 under the direction of the Finnish Skating Union. Skaters had long been unhappy with bandy because the large playing surfaces that the game required was taking ice away from the speed skaters. After seeing 'Canadian' hockey in Sweden and at the Olympic Games in Antwerp in 1920, the Finnish speed skating organization concluded that this game could be played without interfering with their skating competitions. As a result, hockey was added to the program of the Finnish Skating Union. This organization published the first set of rules for hockey in Finland based on the standards of the IIHF. The first club game was played in Tampere on January 15, 1928. Finland was admitted to the IIHF on February 10, 1928.

While the best players in Europe had long been practicing on artificial ice rinks, Finnish players were still totally dependent on natural rinks and the weather. The first artificial rink in Finland did not open until November 22, 1955, in Tampere. Two defining results for the Finns were a 5-2 win over Canada in the 1968 Olympics, and a 3-1 win over Sweden at the 1970 World Championship, their first win over arch-rivals Sweden.

Finland's national team became a force at the international level in the 1960s. By the 1980s players such as Jari Kurri, Esa Tikkanen, and Reijo Ruotsalainen were NHL stars. The 1988 Calgary Olympics saw the Finns upset the USSR 2-1 to earn the silver medal, and four years later they finished second to Sweden at the World Championship. Teemu Selanne arrived in the NHL in 1992-93 and made the greatest individual impact in the league by a Finnish player, shattering Mike Bossy's rookie goal-scoring record by an amazing 26 goals, finishing the year with 76 goals. Selanne also notched 132 points, breaking Peter Stastny's rookie point record of 109.

Finland won the bronze medal at the 1994 Lillehammer Olympics and reached an all-time high at the 1995 World Championship by defeating host Sweden 4-1 in the gold medal game. Finland also stunned Canada 3-2 in the bronze medal game at the 1998 Nagano Olympics. Since that time, Finland has been among the top four most dominant teams, winning one Olympic silver medal (Turin 2006), four World Championship silver medals, two World Championship bronze medals, and finishing runner-up to Canada at the 2004 World Cup of Hockey. Finland's women's team competes most frequently with Sweden for the bronze medal at the top level.

FRANCE 1908

France was one of the few European countries to begin playing hockey towards the end of the 19th century. The game was introduced to France by Canadian George Meagher, who brought a rule book and coaching instructions to Paris in 1894. Meagher began running practices to teach the fundamentals of hockey to the French, but the first official game did not take place until 1903 when a team from Paris beat a Lyon squad, 2-1.

France held its first national hockey championship in 1904, making it the second country in Europe — behind Great Britain — to stage a national championship. Patineurs de Paris were France's first title holders. The French national team played its first game against Belgium in 1906. In 1907, an ice hockey association was founded as part of the Federation Francaise des Sports de Glace (French Federation of Ice Sports). One year later, France, Great Britain, Belgium, and Switzerland founded the Ligue Internationale de Hockey sur Glace, forerunner of the IIHF. On October 20, 1908, France became the first member of the new organization, and Frenchman Louis Magnus became its first president.

France's best showing at the World Championships occurred when it finished fifth at the 1924 and 1928 Olympics. The French remained near the bottom of the top grouping until the 1950s when they were relegated to B Pool. They alternated between B and C Pools in the 1960s before settling into the latter between 1970 and 1985. France won the 1985 C Pool competition to earn promotion to B Pool where it played for five years. The late Jean Ferrand worked tirelessly to improve the national team during this period. They competed in A Pool throughout the 1990s, their best finish an eighth in 1995. Their best-known players were Philippe Bozon and Antoine Richer. Bozon played 144 NHL games for the St. Louis Blues from 1991 to 1995. Today, France ranks as a Division I team that occasionally makes appearances at the top level.

GERMANY 1909/1990

The beginning of ice sports in Germany goes back to 1888 when the country's National Skating Union was founded in Berlin. Among its duties, the union was in charge of bandy in Germany. The first game of hockey in the country took place on Lake Halensee in Berlin on February 4, 1897. By 1901, the first hockey team had been created with players practicing at a rink on the grounds of the Berlin Zoo. Germany's first indoor arena opened in Berlin in 1909, and by 1910 hockey had become so popular that the capital held its first city championship.

On September 19, 1909, Germany became the sixth nation to join the League Internationale de Hockey sur Glace (forerunner of the International Ice Hockey Federation). In 1910, the Germans won the silver medal at the first official European Championship. Its players quickly became among the best in Europe and never failed to win a medal at the European Championships through 1914. So popular was hockey in Germany at this time that the European tournament was held in Berlin in both 1911 and 1914 and in Munich in 1913. Germany was expelled from the IIHF from 1920 until January 11, 1926. However, even during this period, German teams continued

to play internationally at the Spengler Cup. Berliner SC won that tournament in 1924 and again in 1926 and 1928.

The success of Berliner SC on the international scene was no surprise. The team, with players such as Canadian Lawrence Roche and Swedes Nils Molander, Gustaf Johansson, and Birger Holmqvist, were the main factor for the international success. Stocked mainly by players from Berliner SC, the German national team earned a bronze medal in its return to the European Championship in 1927. Prior to World War II, Germany won two European Championship gold medals, three silver medals, and seven bronze medals. Germany also won a silver medal at the 1930 World Championship and bronze medals at the 1932 Olympics and 1934 World Championship.

Germany was again excluded from the IIHF after World War II but was reinstated as the Federal Republic of Germany (West Germany) on March 10, 1951. West Germany's finest success came at the 1976 Olympics in Innsbruck when it won the bronze medal. Following the re-unification of the country, it nearly pulled off an upset at the 1992 Olympics in Albertville when it extended Canada to a shootout in the quarter-finals.

GREAT BRITAIN 1908

In 1876, the world's first artificial ice rinks were opened in London. The first hockey game played outside of Canada is believed to have been Cambridge University against Oxford University at St. Moritz, Switzerland in 1885. Oxford won 6-0 in a match that was fairly primitive.

The "Founding Father" of the sport in the United Kingdom is considered to be Major B.M. "Peter" Patton. It was he who approached Admiral Maxe, founder of the Prince's Skating Club in London, and asked for permission to form a hockey team at the rink. The first game took place in February 1897. Patton, 21 at the time, did not retire from the game until 1931 when he was 55 years old. Over the years, the teams he formed often represented Great Britain abroad. The Prince's won an international bandy tournament in Davos, Switzerland, in 1904 and also beat France in Lyon that same year. In November 1908, the Prince's gave Great Britain victory in the first indoor international ice hockey tournament when if defeated Germany and France in Berlin. The first official European Championship was held in Switzerland in 1910 and Peter Patton was on hand to captain Great Britain to victory. In 1913, he founded the British Ice Hockey Association (BIHA). He revived it in 1923 after it had been disbanded during World War I.

On November 19, 1908, Great Britain joined France, Belgium, and Switzerland in founding the Ligue Internationale de Hockey sur Glace, forerunner of the IIHF. That same year, the first hockey games were played in Scotland at the old Crossmyloof rink in Glasgow. The Scottish Ice Hockey Association was formed in 1929. Some of the best domestic clubs over the years were Scotland's Falkirk Lions and Fife Flyers and England's Harringay Racers and Streatham Redskins.

Britain remained a hockey power in Europe until World War II. The culmination of its success took place at the 1936 Garmisch-Partenkirchen Olympics when the team stunned Canada 2-1 en route to the gold medal. The British national team's performances dropped significantly after the war. It finished fifth at the 1948 Olympics, the last time the British competed at the quadrennial event. The same decline was mirrored at the World Championships after Britain slipped to B Pool in 1952. Between 1954 and 1960 it did not participate at the tournament. Since the early 1960s, Britain has either passed on the competition or played chiefly in C or D Pool. The modern national team peaked in 1993 when it earned promotion to the top pool for the following year it Italy, but its stay was short-lived. Today, Britain remains a distinctly Division I level team.

GREECE 1987 (Associate Member)

Ice hockey in Greece was introduced in Thessaloniki by Czechoslovak emigrants in the early 1980s. Romanians and Canadians built ice rinks in Greece, but most of these arenas were not of standard size. A regulation-sized facility did exist at the sports stadium at Neo Faliro but the space was used more often for basketball. Ice was only available for about two or three weeks in November.

Despite the difficulties, Greece joined the IIHF on April 29, 1987. The first Greek national hockey championship took place in 1988-89 and was won by Aris Thessaloniki. In 1989, Greece's ice hockey association became a section of the Greek Ice Sports Federation (Elliniki Omospondia Pagodromion–Hellenic Ice Sports Federation). Three years later, the Greek national team made its first international appearance at the C Pool World Championship in South Africa. Greece enjoyed a successful debut when it defeated Turkey 15-3 on March 21, 1992, in Johannesburg. There has been no hockey activity in Greece since 2001 after the country's lone arena closed. In March 2007, however, plans to build a new rink in Athens were announced, ushering in a more hopeful future for hockey in the country.

HONG KONG (CHINA) 1983

The Hong Kong Ice Hockey Association, was founded on August 8, 1980. Hong Kong joined the IIHF on April 30, 1983, and made its debut on the world stage at the D Pool World Championship in Perth, Australia, in 1987. Hong Kong tied Taiwan 2-2 in its first international game on March 13, 1987.

Although there was plenty of hockey activity in Hong Kong, local teams (usually stocked with Canadian and American players) did not compete for a national championship until 1995-96. The first title was won by a team sponsored by Planet Hollywood. In 2002, Hong Kong had six ice hockey teams. The national team has not yet participated in the IIHF World Championship program, but Hong Kong has competed at the Asian Winter Games, most recently in 2007 when it finished 10th of eleven teams.

HUNGARY 1927

Hockey was introduced to Hungary by Englishman John Dunlop in 1925. The first real hockey game in the country was staged on December 26 of that year between BKE and a team from Vienna with the latter winning, 1-0.

The Hungarian Winter Sports Federation was founded in 1908 and ice hockey was given a division within the federation. Hockey in Hungary is represented today by the Magyar Jegkorong Szovetseg — Hungarian

Ice Hockey Federation. Hungary joined the IIHF on January 24, 1927, and that same day the Hungarian national team played its first game, losing 6-0 to Austria.

Hungary's first artificial ice rink was built outdoors at Budapest in 1926. At the European Championship in Vienna in 1927, the national team finished last. Two years later, Hungary hosted the tournament during the bitterly cold winter of 1929, and by the 1930s the Hungarians became one of the top teams in Europe. In 1934, a touring Canadian team could manage only a scoreless tie against the Hungarian national squad in an exhibition game at Budapest. The Hungarians posted a 1-1 tie against the eventual gold medal-winning Canadian team at the 1938 World Championship in Prague. The big hero of the Hungarian team was goaltender Istvan Hircsak, who was considered one of the best in Europe at the time.

World War II stopped the development of hockey in Hungary for nearly ten years, but interest in the game rose again by the late 1940s. In subsequent years, training methods were significantly improved by Czechoslovakian coach Vladimir Kominek, who led the Hungarian national team between 1959 and 1964. The Hungarians were promoted to B Pool in 1964 but slipped back to C Pool five years later. They have made slow but steady progress over the last decade, establishing themselves as a consistent and contending Division I team.

ICELAND 1992

Hockey in Iceland dates back to 1937. The main hockey-playing centre was the North Sea port of Akureyri followed by the capital, Reykjavik. The former was the home of Gudmundur Petursson, the "father of hockey" in Iceland. During the late 1930s, the official rules of the game were translated into Icelandic for the first time. Local pickup games were the only sign of hockey in the country for the next three decades.

The Icelandic Skating Association, as a part of the Ithrottasambaud Islands (Sports Union of Iceland), was created in 1987 and included an Ice Hockey Division. Iceland joined the IIHF on May 6, 1992, and made its debut on the world stage in 1997 when its national junior team played at the D Pool European Junior Championship. The country recorded its first win at an IIHF tournament by defeating Turkey, 4-2, to finish fifth out of six teams. In 1998, Iceland sent a team to the D Pool U20 Championship and in 1999 it debuted in the men's World Championship where it placed ninth in the D Pool. Today, the country is of Division II calibre and improving steadily.

The first artificial ice rink didn't open until 1988 in Reykjavik, and a couple of years later a second rink in Akureyri opened. Iceland got its first indoor rink, in Reykjavik, in 1998. At present there are four indoor rinks in Iceland.

INDIA 1989

The Winter Games Federation of India was founded in 1979 and became a member of IIHF on April 27, 1989. The first two clubs to play ice hockey in India were Bombay IHC and Madras IHC, although the majority of hockey in the country has been played by two other clubs, the Shimla Ice Skating Club in the Himalayan mountains and the Ladakh Ice Skating Club in Leh near the Tibet border. The distance

between these two cities is about 1,000 miles. There are about 100 ice hockey players in India. Currently, there are no national championships.

The Shimla Ice Skating Club has existed since 1920 when an open air rink was created. The Ladakh Winter Sports Club, however, is considered the first functional hockey club in India. It was established in 1995 by a group of local hockey fans. The club can't afford any equipment, but in 2002, the NHL Players' Association equipped the team with 50 sets of hockey equipment.

The Ladakh Winter Sports Club organizes the National Ice Hockey Championship. It has taken place three times since 2001. The tournament takes place at Leh Karzoo ice hockey rink, an open-air ice rink (India doesn't have any indoor rinks) situated some 3,474m (11,500 feet) above sea level. The games last 40 minutes (two 20-minute periods), a very demanding test at this altitude.

IRELAND 1996

The first ice hockey game on Irish soil was played in December 1939 at the Kings's Hall, Balmoral, in Belfast, between two Wembley junior teams, the Terriers and Colts. The first game involving an Irish team was played April 21, 1982, between Irish team Dublin Stags IHC and British team Liverpool Leopards. In 1999, Ireland made its IIHF debut playing in Division II of the European U18 Championship. It had joined the IIHF on September 26, 1996.

Domestic competition flourished and cross-border leagues between, Dublin, Belfast, and Coleraine provided a platform to compete at a high level. By the year 2000, however, the two ice rinks in Dublin had closed down. In 2001, the Dublin City Council recruited the IIHA to help out in running an outdoor rink in the centre of Dublin over the festive season. The rink flourishes every year and provides a training ground for all the IIHA members and stars of the future.

The IIHA submitted its first senior men's national squad to IIHF competition in Reykjavik, Iceland, in March 2004 (Division III). Ireland hosted the Division III World Championship in 2007 in a newly-built rink in Dundalk.

ISRAEL 1991

Israel's first ice skating rink was opened in January 1986 in the Haifa suburb of Kiryat Motzkin in northern Israel. Hockey practices began in April of that year with former Canadian players as instructors. Shortly after formal coaching began, hockey started and attracted many players who formerly lived in Canada, United States, Soviet Union, and other traditional hockey countries.

In May 1988, a new and larger skating rink opened in the city of Bat Yam near Tel Aviv. That same year, the Israel Ice Hockey and Figure Skating Association was founded, and Isreal joined the IIHF on May 1, 1991.

Israel's national team played its first game in 1989-90 when a team of Israeli Selects met a team made up of Canadian UN Forces posted in the Golan Heights. Although the Israeli team featured several immigrant Jewish players

from North America and the USSR, it was native Gal Assa who scored the country's first goal during the 20-2 loss.

The Israel Ice Hockey and Figure Skating Association (now the Ice Hockey Federation of Israel) joined the IIHF on May 2, 1991. Paul Shindman and David Popko were key figures behind this historic membership. The national team made its debut at the C Pool World Championship in 1992. It lost its first game 23-4 against Spain in Johannesburg on March 22, 1992. A few days later, Israel recorded its first win at an IIHF championship when it defeated Turkey, 8-2. Israeli hockey has received a major boost in recent years with the opening of an Olympic-sized skating rink at the Canada Centre in Metulla in 1995. In 2005, the team was led by former Stanley Cup-winning coach Jean Perron, winning Division II and earning a promotion to Division I, playing alongside Germany and France for one year.

ITALY 1924 (Associate Member)

The first hockey teams started to appear in Italy during the early 1920s and the country's first indoor ice rink opened in Milan on December 28, 1923. The Hockey Club Milano (which had previously played roller hockey) was soon playing ice hockey in the new arena. Italy's first hockey association was created in 1924 and was later admitted into the IIHF On January 24, 1924. In 1925, the Federazione Italiana Sport del Ghiaccio (Italian Federation of Winter Sports) was founded. The hockey association became a part of FISG in 1926. Hockey is played mainly in the South Tyrol region and in Milan.

The Italian national team competed for the most part in the B Pool World Championships. It finished seventh in A pool in 1933 and 1956 but slipped to C pool six times between 1966 and 1979. Through most of the 1990s the squad maintained a place in A Pool including a sixth place finish as hosts in 1994. Italy's best finish at the Olympics was seventh place as hosts at Cortina d'Ampezzo in 1956. Today, Italy struggles between the top pool and Division I, often not quite good enough for the former but superior for the latter.

JAPAN 1930

Ice hockey was brought to Japan by the English at the beginning of the 20th century. Games were held as early as 1912 and the new sport gained popularity, particularly in the northern regions of the country. Teams from Tokyo, Waseda, and Tomakomai founded the Japan Ice Hockey Federation in 1929.

Japan became a member of the IIHF on January 26, 1930. That same year, the IIHF made a decision to hold the World Championship in conjunction with the European Championship if a team was present from Canada, the United States, or Japan. The Japanese national team played its first international game at the World Championship in Davos, Switzerland in 1930, losing to Great Britain, 3-0. Japan continued to participate in major tournaments including the 1936 Garmisch-Partenkirchen Olympics where goaltender Teiji Honma surprised everyone by wearing a mask.

In the aftermath of World War II, Japan was barred from the IIHF from April 27, 1946 until March 10, 1951. The Japanese competed in six consecutive Olympics between 1960 and 1980. Japan hosted the 1972 Sapporo Olympics and finished ninth after defeating West Germany and Yugoslavia. Between 1999 and 2004, Japan enjoyed special status as the top Asian team, competing in the top level of the World Championship. When this privilege ended, however, the team was relegated to Division I.

In 2003-04, the Asian Hockey League was founded, allowing Japan's top teams to play against teams from Korea and China. Japanese goalie Yutaka Fukufuji made history in early 2007 when he played in a game for the Los Angeles Kings, the first Japanese player to appear in the NHL.

KAZAKHSTAN 1992

Hockey in Kazakhstan dates back to the 1950s when the first teams were created in what was then a Soviet Republic. Torpedo Ust-Kamenogorsk became Kazakhstan's best team, and in 1987-88 it made its debut in the top Soviet league after playing in lower divisions for many years.

Federatsiya Hokkeya Kazakhstana (the Kazakhstan Ice Hockey Federation) was created as part of the Soviet Ice Hockey Federation in 1991. It became a separate organization when Kazakhstan gained its independence in 1992, uniting the region's four teams — Torpedo Ust-Kamenogorsk, ShVSM Ust-Kamenogorsk, Bulat Temirtau, and Automobilist Karaganda (later Bulat Karaganda). The Kazakhstan national team made its debut at the St. Petersburg Grand Prix tournament on April 14, 1992, by beating Ukraine, 5-1.

On May 6, 1992, Kazakhstan became a member of the IIHF and in 1993 the national team made its World Championship debut by winning the bronze medal at the C Pool World Championships in Slovenia. In 2000, at the B Pool Championship, Kazakhstan continued its ascent with a second place finish to claim the silver medal. Kazakhstan's first major upset on the international stage took place when it stunned Canada in the fifth-place game at the 1998 World U20 Championship. A few weeks later, at the Olympics, the team earned respect by winning its preliminary round group ahead of Slovakia and losing 4-1 to Canada in the quarter-finals. The Kazakhs also qualified for the 2006 Olympics and have played in the top pool of the World Championships since 2004.

KOREA 1960

The earliest known hockey game in Korea took place in 1928 when the Yonsan Railway Club of Seoul faced the Tokyo University team. The members of this railway club organized informal games and soon had a rival in the Kyungsung University team. A key administrator at this time was Chun Yoo-Ryang. The Korean Ice Hockey Association was founded in 1928. Two years later, the Chosun Hockey League began play and Yonsei University was crowned the inaugural champion.

The modern Korea Ice Hockey Association was founded in 1947. The country joined the IIHF on July 25, 1960. The following year, the Dongdaemun Rink was opened as the country's first artificial ice facility. In 1965, the first IIHF- sanc-

tioned match took place when a university team from Japan played the Koreans.

The national team debuted with a seventh-place finish at the 1979 C Pool World Championship. Korea remained at this level until 1996 when it was relegated to D Pool, though it would be a short stay as the Koreans returned to C Pool in 1998. In 1984, to mark the opening of the new Taenung ice rink in Seoul, the South Korean national team hosted an invitational tournament featuring the French club Viry-Chatillon, a team from Tokyo, and the University of Alaska-Anchorage. The next season, Seoul hosted the Asia-Oceania Junior Championship. Today, Korea usually plays in Division II of the World Championship.

LATVIA 1931/1992

The Latvijas Hokeja Federacija (Latvian Ice Hockey Federation) was founded on January 5, 1923 and became a member of the IIHF on February 22, 1931. Prior to World War II, Latvia took part in five World Championships, including the 1936 Olympic Games in Garmisch-Partenkirchen, Germany. The most successful Latvian player of this time period was Leonid Vedejs.

Following its incorporation into the Soviet Union after World War II, the best Latvian teams began to play for the USSR championship. The most successful Latvian team was Dynamo Riga which was coached from 1971 to 1977 by the legendary national team coach Viktor Tikhonov. The first well-known Latvian player was Helmut Balderis, who starred for the Soviet national team from 1976 to 1983. Latvians Arturs Irbe and Sandis Ozolinsh were top NHL players in the 1990s.

After re-gaining its IIHF membership on May 6, 1992, following the breakup of the Soviet Union, Latvia rose quickly through the World Championship pool system. Latvia won the C Pool tournament in 1993 and the B Pool competition three years later. It finished seventh at its first A Pool World Championship in 1997.

While not a medal contender, the Latvian team has produced some upsets over the top teams in World Championships, defeating the USA twice (in 1998 and 2001) and archrival Russia twice (in 2000 and 2003). Latvia has also competed in the 2002 and 2006 Olympics. In May 2006, Latvia hosted the World Championship for the first time with the spectacular new Arena Riga as the main venue.

LIECHTENSTEIN 2001 (Associate Member)

The Principality was admitted to the IIHF on October 4, 2001, at the Semi-Annual Congress in Malmö, Sweden. Not having any indoor ice rink in the tiny nation of 33,000 inhabitants nestled between Switzerland and Austria, the top club team EHC Vaduz-Schellenberg has been playing in the Swiss fourth division. Four years after the Liechtenstein Ice Hockey Association joined the IIHF, the country listed over 100 active players, and on March 11, 2007, Liechtenstein played its second national team game against Luxembourg, losing 4-2 at the Mittelrheintal arena in the Swiss village of Widnau, some 20km from Liechtenstein (the first game took place in April 2003). The close score against Luxembourg, ranked 43rd by the IIHF, was an indication that Liechtenstein might soon be ready to join the IIHF World Championship program.

LITHUANIA 1938/1992

The first ice hockey activity in Lithuania took place in the 1920s. Teams were formed in the cities of Kaunas and Memel (now Klaipeda) and the first national championship was held in 1926. LFLS Kaunas won Lithuania's first title. After the country became a part of the Soviet Union, Spartak Kaunus (later Zalgiris Kaunas) played in either the first or second division of the Soviet league. After 1955, the team played only in the Lithuanian Republican Championship.

The Lietuvos Ledo Ritulio Federacija (Lithuanian Ice Hockey Federation) was founded on October 14, 1932, and Lithuania joined the IIHF on February 19, 1938. It was expelled on April 26, 1946, after becoming a part of the Soviet Union. The newly-independent Lithuania had its hockey federation reinstated in 1991 and rejoined the IIHF on May 6, 1992.

The Lithuanian national team played its first international game on February 27, 1932, a 3-0 loss to Latvia. Lithuania debuted at the World Championships in Prague in 1938 and beat Romania 1-0 for its only victory. The country played its last international game before the war in Kaunus in 1941 and suffered a 3-0 loss to Estonia. The Lithuanians returned to the world stage in 1995 at the C Pool World Championship where they finished 11th and were relegated to D Pool. The nation's greatest success to date was a second-place finish at the 2006 World Championship, Division I, in Tallinn, Estonia.

LUXEMBOURG 1912

The Federation Luxembourgeoise de Hockey sur Glace (Luxembourg Ice Hockey Federation) is one of the oldest in Europe, having been formed in 1912. Although Luxembourg joined the IIHF on March 23, 1912, the popularity of hockey in the country grew slowly. Luxembourg did not hold its first national championship until 1978.

Ice hockey in Luxembourg has been played since the late 1960s and the first team was HC Beaufort. There are three rinks in the country. One is Kockelsheuer (just south of the capital), one in Remich, and one in Beaufort. The only indoor rink is Kockelsheuer with a capacity of 1,000. Luxembourg's most prominent visit came when Detroit Red Wings' English farm team, the London Lions, played two exhibition games in Luxembourg during the 1973-74 season.

Luxembourg's national team appeared first on the international scene at the C Pool World Championship in 1992. The team lost its first game to South Africa 23-0 on March 21 in Johannesburg. In 1998, Luxembourg iced a national U20 team at the D Pool European U20 Championship. The senior national team is on Division III level.

MACAU 2005 (Associate Member)

The former Portuguese colony on the coast of mainland China was admitted as member on May 12, 2005, at the IIHF Annual Congress in Vienna, Austria. The national team's first official participation was at the 2007 Asian Winter Games when Macau finished last in the eleven-nation tournament.

FYR MACEDONIA 2001 (Associate Member)

The former Yugoslav republic was admitted to the IIHF at the 2001 Semi-Annual Congress in Malmö, Sweden. The country has not recorded any national team games, nor has it staged any official national club competition.

MALAYSIA 2006 (Associate Member)

The Sunway Pyramid Ice Rink is the only hockey arena in Malaysia, and the Adun Subang Jaya ice hockey league represents the only formal hockey in the country. There have been four editions of a national championship in the country (2001, 2002, 2005 and 2006). Malaysia became an IIHF member at the 2006 Congress in Athens, Greece, on September 28, 2006.

MEXICO 1985

The Federacion Mexicana de Deportes Invernales A.C. (Mexican Federation of Winter Sports) was founded in 1984, although hockey had been played there as early as 1964. Mexico joined the IIHF the following year on April 30, 1985. At the time, Mexico boasted two indoor rinks — one in Mexico City and one in Guadalajara — and six hockey teams. The first national championship was held in 1988-89 and was won by the Association del Estado de Mexico. Currently, there is no Mexican national championship. Mexico competed internationally for the first time in 1997 when the national junior team competed in the D Pool World U20 Championship. It returned to the same tournament the following year with somewhat improved results. Under the guidance of Canadian Daniel Gendron, the national junior team gained valuable experience in November 1997 when it toured Canada.

MONGOLIA 1999

The history of Mongolian hockey started in the mid-1960s when guest workers from ally Soviet Union introduced the game, mostly in the region around the capital Ulaanbaatar. The first national competition (with eight teams) was the Ulaanbaatar championship in 1970. The Mongolian Ice Hockey Association was established on November 30, 1991, and the first official Mongolian championship was played in February the following year. The Mongolian Hockey League was introduced in 1998. The country became an IIHF member in 1999 and in the same year the national team participated in the Asian Winter Games. The first-ever Mongolian participation in an official IIHF-event was at the 2000 IIHF Asia Oceanic U18 Championship, Division II, in Bangkok. Mongolia also participated in the 2007 IIHF World Championship, Division III, in Dundalk, Ireland.

NAMIBIA 1998 (Affiliate Member)

Namibia joined the IIHF on May 31, 1998. To date, it does not have any hockey activity beyond InLine participation.

THE NETHERLANDS 1935

Hockey was introduced in the Netherlands in the early 1930s. The country's first artificial ice rink was build in the Hague in 1937, although the first indoor arena was not built until 1961, in Amsterdam.

The Nederlandse Ijshockey Bond (Dutch Ice Hockey Union) was founded on September 6, 1934, and the Netherlands joined the IIHF on January 20, 1935. The best teams in the country began competing for a national championship in 1937, but no such championship was held from 1950 to 1963 because of a lack of teams.

The Dutch national team made its debut on the international scene with a 4-0 loss to Belgium in Amsterdam on January 5, 1935. Two weeks later, the Netherlands made its first appearance at the World and European Championships in Davos, Switzerland. The Netherlands lost its first game 6-0 to Hungary on January 19. The Dutch made their initial Olympic appearance when they tied for ninth place out of twelve teams at the 1980 Lake Placid Games. Included on their roster was Dick Decloe who had won a Memorial Cup with the Toronto Marlboros in 1973. The 1981 World Championship was the only other time the Dutch played in the top pool, but it was relegated in its first year. Today, the Dutch play comfortably in Division I.

NEW ZEALAND 1977

Ice hockey has been played in New Zealand for over 60 years. Many of the early games were played on the frozen ponds in the South Canterbury mountains and teams were made up of local farm workers who had regular access to the ice. The first organized hockey tournament in New Zealand was held at Opawa near Albury in 1937.

New Zealand became a member of the IIHF on May 2, 1977. The inaugural club competition for the Norm Hawker Shield was held at the Big Apple rink in Christchurch. The tournament featured ten teams and took place from June 19-21, 1987. The Manuwai Warriors of Auckland won the title. Also in 1987, the New Zealand national team made its debut in the D Pool World Championship. The first official game took place in Perth, Australia, on March 13, 1987, and resulted in a 35-2 loss to Korea. The national team gained valuable experience but did not reappear until the 1995 D Pool World Championship. Today, New Zealand is a Division III nation.

NORWAY 1935

The first Norwegian national championship was played in 1934-35 and was won by the Trygg SFK, Oslo. The 1934-35 season also saw the formation of the Norges Ishockeyforbund (Norwegian Ice Hockey Union) on September 18, 1934, and the inclusion of Norway in the IIHF on January 20, 1935.

The Norwegian national team began its official history on February 13, 1937, in London, when it was defeated 13-2 by Switzerland in the first game of the World and European Championship. However, Norway later made its mark on the international scene by winning a bronze medal at the European

Championship in 1951 and 1962. The Norwegians turned in a particularly strong performance at the 1951 World Championship in Paris when they finished fourth.

Norway played mainly in B Pool between 1961 and 1991 but returned to and remained in A Pool for most of the 1990s. The team managed an eighth place finish at the 1972 Sapporo Olympics. Recently, the most prominent national team player has been forward Espen Knutsen who has played in the NHL with the Mighty Ducks of Anaheim and the Columbus Blue Jackets. In addition, several Norwegians have had an impact in Swedish league play, and Norway was promoted to the top pool of World Championship play in 2005.

POLAND 1926

Four clubs in Warsaw established the Polski Zwiazek Hokeja na Lodzie (the Polish Ice Hockey Union) in January 1925. Poland joined the IIHF on January 11, 1926. In 1931, an outdoor hockey arena was built in Katowice.

Poland first participated in international competition in 1926 and has been entering official IIHF tournaments ever since. Polish hockey flourished during the late 1920s and early 1930s, and the national team was bolstered by the use of Polish-Canadians who had returned to their native country. Among these players was Polish national team captain Tadeusz Adamowski.

Polish hockey was slow to recover after World War II, but the construction of the country's first indoor artificial ice rinks in the early 1950s helped rekindle interest in the game. The national team played at the World Championships A Pool level in the 1950s but slipped to B Pool in 1961. Since that time Poland has alternated between these two levels. It did manage a fourth-place finish in the 1932 Olympics and four sixth-place finishes between 1948 (St. Moritz) and 1976 (Innsbruck), but it has not been in the top pool since 2002. Poland's most recent Olympic appearance came in 1992. It performed one of the greatest upsets in the history of the game at the 1976 World Championship, defeating the mighty Soviets 6-4 in Katowice, Poland.

PORTUGAL 1999 (Associate Member)

Portugal's ice hockey history is short. In the summer of 1996 a large Portuguese company named Visabeira finished the construction of a huge complex in Viseu that included a shopping mall, ice rink, swimming pools, and other sports facilities. Soon the first ice hockey team emerged — "Lobos do Palacio do Gelo" — which consisted of roller-hockey players.

The first hockey games ever played in Portugal occurred during the opening festivities of the Palacio, on November 29-30 and December 1, 1996. The "Lobos" played against an in-line all-star team, and the games were attended by some 900 fans.

The Associacao Nacional de Deporteos no Gelo e InLine Hockey was founded on March 25, 1998, and Portugal joined the IIHF on May 13, 1999.

ROMANIA 1924

Ice hockey began in Romania in 1921 when the first games took place in Miercurea Ciuc. The popularity of the game grew quickly, and in 1924 the Romanian Ice Hockey Association was founded. On January 24, 1924, Romania joined the IIHF. Today, the Federatia Romana de Hochei pe Gheata (Romanian Ice Hockey Federation) is the national governing body.

Romania's first national hockey championship was held in 1925 and won by the provincial club Brasovia Brasov. The popularity of the sport increased after the country's first artificial ice rink was built in 1931, though many games continued to be played on natural ice surfaces in the country's mountain areas. Throughout most of the 1930s the capital of Bucharest was home to all of the top domestic clubs — HC Roman, Roman Tennis Club, Club Venus, Club Telefon, and HC Bragadiru.

Major steps towards developing the game took place in the 1940s and '50s, including the construction of new ice rinks in Bucharest, Galati, and Miercurea Ciuc in 1958. Romania made its international debut at the World and European Championships in Poland in 1931, losing its first game to the United States, 15-0.

In the aftermath of this poor showing, the national team withdrew from international hockey for more than a decade. Romania has played mainly in B and C pool since the 1960s. They qualified for A Pool in 1977 and the 1980 Lake Placid Olympics. Today, Romania's prime objective is to remain competitive in Division I.

RUSSIA 1952 (AS SOVIET UNION)/1992

The first demonstration of 'Canadian' hockey in the former Soviet Union took place at Moscow in March 1932, shortly after the Lake Placid Olympics. A German workers' union team called "Ficheti" played a series of exhibition games against the Central Red Army Sports Club and the Moscow Selects. The Soviet Union joined the IIHF on April 1, 1952, although they didn't play internationally for two more years.

The first official Soviet championship began on December 22, 1946, but a major turning point in Soviet hockey occurred in February 1948 with the historic visit of the LTC Prague team of Czechoslovakia. Almost every player on the Prague team had been a member of the Czechoslovak squad which had received a silver medal at the recently concluded St. Moritz Olympics. The results of the three-game series surprised many as the Moscow Selects won 6-3, lost 5-3, and tied, 2-2. Even more startling was the success of the Soviet national team when it entered the World Championships for the first time in 1954. The USSR defeated Canada 7-2 in the gold-medal game in a contest that permanently altered the complexion of international hockey. Soviet coach Anatoli Tarasov was crucial to the rapid progress made by the national team. Some of the early Soviet stars were forward Vsevolod Bobrov, defenceman Nikolai Sologubov, and goalie Nikolai Puchkov.

Backed by strong support from the country's sports authorities, the Soviet

national team became the strongest power that international hockey has ever seen. Between 1954 and 1990, the Soviets won 22 gold medals at the World Championship and eight Olympic gold medals. Some of the most prestigious wins came in games against rivals Canada, notably a 7-3 win over the home side in game one of the historic Summit Series in 1972 and an 8-1 drubbing in the finals of the 1981 Canada Cup, both in Montreal. The Soviet domination came to an end with the collapse of the Soviet Union in 1991 as sports no longer enjoyed strong political backing.

The famous CCCP was replaced by Russia in 1992 and the country won its first World Championship a year later. That win, however, marked the end of an era, not the beginning. Between 1994 and 2007, Russia won a silver and a bronze medal at the Olympics but no men's World Championships.

SERBIA 1939 (AS YUGOSLAVIA)/2004

The roots of ice hockey in Yugoslavia go back to 1906 when the first hockey team in Yugoslavia (HASK — the Croatian Academic Sports Club) was formed in the city of Zagreb. Dr. Franjo Bucar was a key figure in the introduction of the sport in the country. The first official hockey games took place in Zagreb in 1916-17 when HASK played a two-game series against I.HSK (I. Croatian Sports Club). In 1930, the Yugoslav Ice Hockey Federation was founded in Zagreb and the country's first IIHF World Championship participation was in 1939 where Yugoslavia finished 13th. It had its strongest period in the late 1960s and early 1970s when the national team finished 9th at the 1968 Olympics in Grenoble and placed 8th (2nd in B pool) in the 1974 IIHF World Championship.

In 1992 most of the former Yugoslav republics became independent sport bodies. Yugoslavia competed under this name until 2004 when it changed to Serbia and Montenegro. In 2006, Montenegro gained independence and the country continued its IIHF membership as Serbia, where the game is centered around the capital Belgrade and Novi Sad.

SINGAPORE 1996 (Associate Member)

The first ice hockey games in Singapore were played in the 1970s. Singapore joined the IIHF on May 2, 1996, but has not yet played at IIHF tournaments.

It was not until 1988 that an ice skating rink, the Fuji Ice Palace, was built in Singapore. In the mid-1990s, the Fuji Ice Palace found a new location at Jurong East Entertainment Center (near the Jurong East MRT Station) where it has operated until the present. As of 2006, this is the only operational ice skating rink in Singapore. In 1997, a local league began at Fuji, organized by the Ice Hockey Association, Singapore (IHAS), with six teams. Due to the high costs for players, the league shut down after one year. Between that time and the formation of the AIHA and NIHL in late 2000, "pick-up" sessions of informal games were organized by various local and expatriate players. The Canadian Association of Singapore has also run various hockey activities over the years, most recently a comprehensive youth hockey program since 2001.

SLOVAKIA 1993

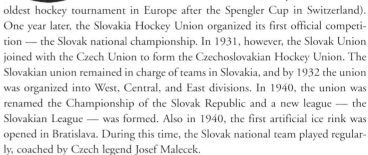

The first organized game of hockey took place January 1921 in the Bratislava suburb of Petrzalka. Hockey became more popular after the 1925 European Championships were held in Stary Smokovec and won by Czechoslovakia. In 1929, the Tatra Cup was held in Czechoslovakia for the first time. (Today, it is the second oldest hockey tournament in Europe after the Spengler Cup in Switzerland). One year later, the Slovakia Hockey Union organized its first official competition — the Slovak national championship. In 1931, however, the Slovak Union joined with the Czech Union to form the Czechoslovakian Hockey Union. The Slovakian union remained in charge of teams in Slovakia, and by 1932 the union was organized into West, Central, and East divisions. In 1940, the union was renamed the Championship of the Slovak Republic and a new league — the Slovakian League — was formed. Also in 1940, the first artificial ice rink was opened in Bratislava. During this time, the Slovak national team played regularly, coached by Czech legend Josef Malecek.

After World War II, the Slovak clubs began playing in the Czechoslovakian League. Three of these teams became national champions: Slovan Bratislava (1979), VSZ Kosice (1986 and 1988) and Dukla Trencin (1992). These clubs produced international stars such as Vladimir Dzurilla, Jozef Golonka, Vaclav Nedomansky, the Stastny brothers (Peter, Marian, Anton), Vincent Lukac, Darius Rusnak, Igor Liba, Dusan Pasek, Robert Svehla, Peter Bondra, and Zigmund Palffy.

Shortly after the separation of Czechoslovakia into two independent countries in 1993, Slovakia qualified for its first Olympics by winning a qualification tournament held in Great Britain. Peter Stastny, who played for Czechoslovakia at the Lake Placid Olympics in 1980, carried Slovakia's flag at the opening ceremonies of the 1994 Lillehammer Games. The Slovaks finished a respectable sixth at the tournament. Later that year, Slovakia made its debut at the World Championships in the C Pool competition. Within two years it earned promotion to the A Pool level.

The Slovaks also competed at the inaugural World Cup in 1996 where they nearly prevented Canada from reaching the playoffs for the first time in the history of the Canada Cup/World Cup. The team disappointed at the 1998 Nagano Olympics by finishing second to Kazakhstan in the preliminary round. This result prevented Slovakia from participating in the medal round. The young country's greatest sports triumph came when it won the World Championship in Sweden in 2002. Slovakia also took silver in 2000 and bronze in 2003.

SLOVENIA 1992

The history of hockey in Slovenia officially began on February 7, 1929, when the new hockey section of the Ilirija Sports Club in Ljubljana played against a team from the nearby town of Kamnik. Ilirija won the game 15-1 as the Kamnik team had only been thrown together for this one match.

Credit for introducing hockey to Slovenia is given to Stanko Bloudek, who brought the first hockey equipment to Ljubljana from Vienna in 1928 and

founded the Ilirija hockey club with Viktor Vodisek. After the demise of Kamnik, the Ilirija team sought opponents in Austria where they played games against KAC Klagenfurt and VSV Villach.

Hokejska Zveza Slovenije (the Ice Hockey Federation of Slovenia) was founded in 1991 and the newly independent nation of Slovenia joined the IIHF on May 6, 1992. Slovenia held its first national championship (won by Acroni Jesenice) that year and the Slovenian national team played its first international game on March 20, 1992, losing to Austria 1-0 in Klagenfurt. The country's debut in the C Pool of the World Championship took place on home ice in Ljubljana and Bled in 1993. After winning the silver medal at the 1997 C Pool competition, Slovenia did the same as hosts of the B Pool tournament in 1998.

The nation earned special glory in 2004 when it won the World Championship, Division I, gaining promotion to the top pool where it competed in 2005 and 2006 (it had also played in the top division in 2002). It was at these tournament that saw the emergence of the first world-class superstar from Slovenia, Anze Kopitar. He was just 17 when he played for his country in 2005 in Austria, and a year and a half later he was the first Slovenian player to appear in the NHL, with the Los Angeles Kings. Kopitar led Slovenia to the Division I title to earn promotion to Canada 2008.

SOUTH AFRICA 1937

The South African Ice Hockey Association was founded on July 20, 1936 and became a member of the IIHF on February 25, 1937. During that first year of ice hockey, the new South African Ice Hockey Association organized a three-team league. The Mohawks won first South African Championship. In July 1938, top Austrian club Wiener EV visited Johannesburg and played eight exhibition games, winning seven.

South Africa played its first official game at the C Pool World Championship in Lausanne, Switzerland on March 3, 1961, when it lost 12-3 to Yugoslavia. It finished fifth at this tournament and did not reappear until a third-place finish in 1966. Political sanctions against South Africa's apartheid policies left the country out of international hockey until the 1990s. After experiencing difficulties in C Pool from 1992 to 1995, South Africa withdrew for two years. It re-emerged in 1998 as hosts of the D Pool World Championship.

In recent years, the construction of additional rinks in Johannesburg, Pretoria, Krugersdorp, and Cape Town, has seen an increase in the number of people becoming involved in hockey. Presently, there are five rinks in South Africa including three of international size. The centre of hockey in South Africa is the province of Gauteng (former Transvaal) from where some 80 percent of the approximately 1,000 players in South Africa come.

SPAIN 1923

In the early days of Spanish ice hockey, the game was played on natural rinks in the Pyrenees Mountains and the region of Cataluna. The game first made an impact in the country at the beginning of the 20th century with a series of exhibition games featuring Canadian and British players. Spain's first indoor rink with artificial ice was built in Madrid in 1924. The Federacion Espanola Deportes de Invierno (Spanish Winter Sports Federation) was founded in 1923. On March 10, 1923, Spain joined the IIHF. The country participated at the 1924 European Championship in Madrid but lost 12-0 to Switzerland in its first international game on March 12, 1924. Spain also played at the 1926 European Championship.

Over the next 25 years, ice hockey was rarely played in Spain though roller hockey was very popular. In 1971, Spain's first modern indoor arena opened in San Sebastian, and in 1972-73 that city's Real Sociedad team won Spain's first official national championship. A rink in Barcelona opened in 1972.

In 1986, the national team ceased operations. It returned to the D Pool championships in 1989 and 1990. The Spaniards won the bronze medal at the latter competition and played in C Pool from 1992 to 1995. Since then, Spain has played mostly in Division III with occasional forays to Division II.

A list of the top Spanish players is headed by forward Frank Gonzalez. After growing up in Canada, he starred with FC Barcelona, Casco Viejo, and Puigcerda. He also captained the national team, served as an IIHF referee, and became the Spanish delegate to the IIHF Council.

SWEDEN 1912

American Roul La Mat is credited with introducing the game of hockey to Sweden. La Mat was a movie distributor who arrived in Stockholm in 1919. Already familiar with "Canadian" hockey, La Mat became fascinated by the game of bandy, which had been played in Sweden since 1896. He was impressed with the talent of the local players and believed their excellent skating skills would make them successful in hockey as well. It was La Mat's idea to enter Sweden at the Olympic hockey tournament in 1920, although Sweden had joined the IIHF on March 23, 1912.

Hockey found many supporters in Sweden after the Olympic tournament. As a reward for its team's strong showing, the Swedes were named host of the European Championship in 1921. They won the event but, in all fairness, Czechoslovakia was the only other team to participate. Regardless, this success boosted the development of hockey in Sweden, and on November 17, 1922, seven teams from Stockholm founded the Swedish Ice Hockey Association.

National championships have been held in Sweden since 1922, with the first title being won by IK Gota, a team which included several players from the 1920 Olympic team. In 1927 interest in Swedish hockey brought the first visit of a Canadian team to the country with the arrival of the Victoria Hockey Club of Montreal. The first artificial ice rink in Sweden was built inside an airplane hangar in 1931 in Stockholm, and it remained the country's only indoor arena until 1938, hosting 1,032 games over that time.

The Swedish Ice Hockey Association was instrumental in making hockey one of the most popular sports in the country. It also maintained a unique list of the greatest players in the country's history. The "Stor Grabb" (Great Men) are determined according to a special system of points. Fittingly, the list is headed by Swedish hockey pioneer Nils Molander of the 1920 national team, who is accorded the title of "Stor Grabb" #1. Over the years, Sweden's national team has come

to be known as Tre Kronor (Three Crowns) for the emblem on its uniform. To date, Sweden has won the World Championship in 1953, 1957, 1962, 1987, 1991, 1992, 1998, and 2006, and won Olympic gold medals in 1994 and 2006. The year 2006 was an historic one for Tre Kronor as it became the first nation to win both Olympic gold and World Championship gold in the same year, while the women's team won an historic bronze medal in the 2006 Olympics. Swedish players were also at the forefront of European representation in the NHL. Defenceman Thommie Bergman became the first European-trained player to become a regular in the NHL, with Detroit in 1972-73, and the next year Borje Salming and Inge Hammarstrom signed with the Toronto Maple Leafs. Salming had a Hall of Fame career in Toronto and proved Europeans had the skill—and the toughness—to play at a high level year after year.

SWITZERLAND 1908

Switzerland played its first international matches against the French club Lyon on December 19, 1904. The teams split the series by identical 3-1 scores and the Swiss roster included future IIHF President Max Sillig. Through the initiative of Sillig and Louis Dufour, Switzerland became the fourth member of the League Internationale de Hockey sur Glace (forerunner of the IIHF) on November 23, 1908.

Switzerland took part in Europe's first international hockey tournament at Chamonix, France in 1909 along with Belgium, Bohemia, England and the host country. A 3-0 loss to tournament champion Great Britain represented the debut of the Swiss national team. A year later, Switzerland hosted the first official European Championship. Games were played in Les Avants, near Montreux. By the end of the first decade of the 20th century, hockey had gained a strong foothold in all parts of Switzerland.

In 1923, Davos resident Dr. Carl Spengler founded a tournament and trophy bearing his name, the Spengler Cup, Europe's oldest hockey tournament. Davos became the site of the first artificial ice rink in 1926 and the setting for Switzerland's first European Championship that same year. The Swiss also claimed European titles in 1935, 1939, and 1950 along with a silver medal the 1935 World Championship and bronze medals at the 1928 and 1948 Olympics. During the 1930s the "Ni-Sturm" and "Er-Sturm" forwards lines gained formidable reputations. The former consisted of Richard "Bibi" Torriani along with brothers Ferdinand and Hans Cattini. This troika represented Switzerland for the first time in 1934 and faced Canadian clubs frequently in exhibition games. The second trio consisted of Hans Lohrer and the Kessler brothers. These two combinations led the Swiss to a bronze medal at the 1937 World Championship and gold at the European Championship two years later.

The Swiss remained in the top level of World Championship competition until the 1950s. Between 1950 and 1991, they competed mainly in B Pool with the odd excursion into A and C Pools. During the early 1990s, they enjoyed a brief renaissance and finished as high as fourth during the 1992 A Pool World Championship, a feat they repeated in 1998.

Since hosting the 1998 World Championship, Switzerland has established itself among the top eight nations in the world. La Suisse defeated Canada for the first time ever at the 2006 Olympics, 2-0, just a couple of days after beating the Czechs, 3-2. Goaltenders David Aebischer and Martin Gerber and defenceman Mark Streit established themselves in the NHL in the early years of the 21st century.

THAILAND 1989

The Thai Ice Hockey Association was founded in 1976 and the affiliation to the IIHF came thirteen years later, on April, 27, 1989. Thailand had a national club competition going between 1999 and 2003 but since then no official champions have been crowned. The country's governing body of ice hockey lists 200 active players and three indoor rinks. The 2003 Asian Winter Games was Thailand's first international experience. The national team finished fifth in Aomori, Japan after defeating Mongolia 4-2 in the game for fifth place. Thailand also took part in the 2007 Asian Winter Games and placed ninth out of eleven participants.

TURKEY 1991

The first ice hockey rinks in Turkey were built in the late 1980s at Ankara and Istanbul. Turkiye Buz Sporlari Federasyonu (the Turkish Ice Sports Federation), formerly known as the Turkish Skating and Skiing Union, was created in 1991 and included a hockey component. On May 1, 1991, Turkey became a member of the IIHF. The national team made is debut at the 1992 C Pool World Championship where it suffered a series of resounding defeats. Omer Arasan became the first Turkish player to earn the reputation as a legitimate goal scoring threat. In 1995, the Turkey's national junior team debuted at the C Pool of the European Junior Championship. In 1997-98, the Turkish national team played in the D Pool World Championship and a junior team competed in the D Pool World U20 Championship. Today, Turkey is a Division II-level country.

UKRAINE 1992

Ukrainian hockey began in 1946 when the game began to catch on in the Soviet Union. Spartak Uzhgorod played games against Vodnik Arkhangelsk in the Dynamo soccer stadium in Kiev and the team was invited to participate in the first Soviet championship in 1946-47. Prior to World War II, Uzhgorod had been part of Czechoslovakia, a country with a long hockey heritage. Players from Uzhgorod had excellent equipment and could compete well against other Soviet clubs during the first championship.

Before the breakup of the Soviet Union, the Federatsiya Hokkey Ukrainy (Ukrainian Ice Hockey Federation) was part of the Soviet Ice Hockey Federation. It became an independent federation in 1992 and joined the IIHF on May 6, 1992. The Ukrainian national team had made its debut at the St. Petersburg Grand Prix on April 13, 1992, tying the Russian national B-team, 3-3. The Ukraine made its first appearance at the World Championship at the C Pool tournament in 1993. Between 1993 and 1996, the Ukrainians won either silver or bronze at this tournament. They captured the gold medal at the 1997 tournament in Estonia to earn promotion to B Pool. The following year, the Ukraine continued its dramatic rise by winning the B Pool tournament in Slovenia. This triumph qualified them for the A Pool for the first time in their history, and it is there they have maintained position for most of the time since.

The first Ukrainian player to reach the NHL was Alexander Godynyuk, who made his debut with the Toronto Maple Leafs in 1990-91. Dimitri Khristich, Alexei Zhitnik, and Oleg Tverdovsky are other Ukrainians who have played in the NHL.

UNITED ARAB EMIRATES 2001
(Associate Member)

The first hockey games were played in United Arab Emirates (UAE) in the 1970s. The first national league was played in 1979, but after a few years the development of hockey in the country slowed down and there were no national championships until the beginning of the 1990s. The UAE Ice Hockey Committee was founded in 1998 and UAE joined the IIHF on May 10, 2001.

The UAE has not yet participated at a World Championship, but the national team has played at other international tournaments. Having acquired their IIHF membership in 2001, United Arab Emirates is focused on increasing participation in the sport. There were four clubs in 1999, and the number grew to 14 by 2001 when a national championship was established. Desert Snake Abu Dhabi were champions during the 1999-2000 season, while Dubai Amro Green Wings took top honours the following year. During the 1999 Asian Hong Kong International Ice Hockey Cup, UAE claimed the title during their first ever international competition. The Emirates finished a respectable sixth out of eleven teams at the 2007 Asian Winter Games.

UNITED STATES OF AMERICA 1920

Hockey's origins in the United States are almost as old as they are in Canada, though it was not until Canadian teams began to tour the northeastern United States in the late 19th century that the game really caught on. Canadians were also paid to play in the U.S. as part of hockey's first professional league in the early 1900s. The United States did not meet teams from outside North America until 1920. That year, the Americans made their international debut at the Antwerp Olympics. Led by Hall of Fame member Moose Goheen, they took the silver medal, losing only to Canada.

Until the creation of the United States Amateur Hockey Association in 1920, amateur hockey had been controlled by the International Skating Union. In 1924, the Americans repeated as silver medallists at the Chamonix Olympics. In 1924-25, the Boston Bruins became the first U.S.-based team in the National Hockey League.

The first entirely all-American team to represent the country internationally was the Boston Olympics, a squad composed entirely of Massachusetts-born players. The team placed second behind Canada in the 1931 World Championship and won another silver medal at the 1932 Olympics in Lake Placid. The USA finally upset Canada in 1933 to win its first and so far only World Championship in a non-Olympic year.

The 1960 Winter Olympics, staged in Squaw Valley, California, were a spectacular success for American hockey. Led by goaltender Jack McCartan, the Americans defeated Canada and the Soviet Union en route to the gold medal.

The U.S. won a surprising silver medal at the 1972 Olympics with a team that included Mark Howe and Robbie Ftorek, but the late 1960s and 1970s were not a good time for American hockey. In 1969, the United States sent more men to the moon than it did to the National Hockey League. Internationally, using a team built around a nucleus of college players, the USA was relegated to the IIHF's B Pool twice, in 1969 and 1971, not returning until 1975.

The biggest upset in the history of international hockey changed all that. Team USA's Miracle on Ice victory over the Soviet Union at the 1980 Olympics in Lake Placid was not only a ground-breaking achievement, it also motivated a new generation of children in the U.S. to take up the sport. The USA teams that won the 1996 World Cup of Hockey title and later won a silver medal at the 2002 Olympics were comprised of players who credited the 1980 victory as their main inspiration for playing the game in the first place. By 2007, there were some 170 Americans in the NHL, and the USA national teams of both the men and women are often medal contenders at the most important international tournaments—Olympics, World Championships, U20, and U18.

Zach Parise, here celebrating the goal that gave USA its first-ever World U18 Championship gold in 2002, is one of many great young players that have come up through USA Hockey's development system. Parise is the son of J-P Parise.

Presidents and Congresses

IIHF PRESIDENTS

The IIHF President is elected by the General congress and chairs all congresses and council (board) meetings. The council is the IIHF's highest executive body. The president represents the interests of the IIHF in all external matters and is responsible for ensuring that all decisions are made in accordance with the federation's statutes, bylaws, and regulations. He has the right to sign on behalf of the IIHF in all matters that that have been approved by council.

Louis Magnus (FRA)	1908-1912
Henri van den Bulcke (BEL)	1912-1914
Louis Magnus (FRA)	1914
B.M. Patton (GBR)	1914
Henri van den Bulcke (BEL)	1914-1920
Max Sillig (GER)	1920-1922
Paul Loicq (BEL)	1922-1947
Fritz Kraatz (SUI)	1947-1948
George Hardy (CAN)	1948-1951
Fritz Kraatz (SUI)	1951-1954
Walter Brown (USA)	1954-1957
John Francis Ahearne (GBR)	1957-1960
Robert LeBel (CAN)	1960-1963
John Francis Ahearne (GBR)	1963-1966
Thayer Tutt (USA)	1966-1969
John Francis Ahearne (GBR)	1969-1975
Günther Sabetzki (GER)	1975-1994
René Fasel (SUI)	1994-present

IIHF GENERAL SECRETARIES

The IIHF General Secretary is the IIHF's highest ranked employee and has the role of the federation's chief executive officer.

Walter Wasservogel (AUT)	1977-1986
Jan-Ake Edvinsson (SWE)	1986-2006
Horst Lichtner (GER)	2006-present

IIHF Presidents — top row: (l to r) Louis Magnus, Henri van den Bulcke, B.M. Patton, second row: Max Sillig, third row: Paul Loicq, Fritz Kraatz, George Hardy, fourth row: Walter Brown, John Francis Ahearne, Robert LeBel, fifth row: Thayer Tutt, Günther Sabetzki, René Fasel

IIHF General Secretaries — (l to r) Walter Wasservogel, Jan-Ake Edvinsson, Horst Lichtner

IIHF GENERAL CONGRESSES

The General Congress is the IIHF's highest legislative body and makes decisions about the rules of the game, the statutes and bylaws. The General Congress, which is made up by representatives from all IIHF member associations, elects the president and the council. With some exceptions, the General Congress is held every fourth year. The General Congress was held for the first time in 1975. Prior to that, the federation elected the president and the council at the Annual Congress that usually was held in conjunction with the IIHF World Championship.

1975 Gstaad, Switzerland

1978 Sirmione, Italy

1982 Nice, France

1986 Colorado Springs, USA

1990 Saint Vincent, Italy

1994 Venice, Italy

1998 Lausanne, Switzerland

2003 Marbella, Spain

2008 Montreal, Canada

IIHF Hall of Fame Honour Roll

NAME	COUNTRY	INDUCTED	CATEGORY
Hans Dobida	AUT	2007	Builder
Josef Puschnig	AUT	1999	Player
Walter Wasservogel	AUT	1997	Builder
Paul Loicq	BEL	1997	Builder
Father David Bauer	CAN	1997	Builder
Roger Bourbonnais	CAN	1999	Player
Mike Buckna	CAN	2004	Builder
Wayne Gretzky	CAN	2000	Player
William Hewitt	CAN	1998	Builder
Derek Holmes	CAN	1999	Builder
Fran Huck	CAN	1999	Player
Marshall Johnston	CAN	1998	Player
Gordon Juckes	CAN	1997	Builder
Dave King	CAN	2001	Builder
Bob LeBel	CAN	1997	Builder
Vic Lindquist	CAN	1997	Player
Barry MacKenzie	CAN	1999	Player
Seth Martin	CAN	1997	Player
Jackie McLeod	CAN	1999	Player
Terry O'Malley	CAN	1998	Player
Gordon Renwick	CAN	2002	Builder
Harry Sinden	CAN	1997	Player
Harry Watson	CAN	1998	Player
Quido Adamec	CZE	2005	Referee
Vladimir Bouzek	CZE	2007	Player
Vlastimil Bubnik	CZE	1997	Player
Ludek Bukac	CZE	2007	Builder
Josef Cerny	CZE	2007	Player
Jaroslav Drobny	CZE	1997	Player
Karel Gut	CZE	1998	Player
Ivan Hlinka	CZE	2002	Player
Jiri Holecek	CZE	1998	Player
Jiri Holik	CZE	1999	Player
Vladimir Kostka	CZE	1997	Builder
Oldrich Machac	CZE	1999	Player
Josef Malecek	CZE	2003	Player
Vladimir Martinec	CZE	2001	Player
Vaclav Nedomansky	CZE	1997	Player
Frantisek Pospisil	CZE	1999	Player
Miroslav Subrt	CZE	2004	Builder
Frantisek Tikal	CZE	2004	Player
Vladimir Zabrodsky	CZE	1997	Player

NAME	COUNTRY	INDUCTED	CATEGORY
Jorgen Hviid	DEN	2005	Builder
Timo Jutila	FIN	2003	Player
Matti Keinonen	FIN	2002	Player
Jari Kurri	FIN	2000	Player
Harry Lindblad	FIN	1999	Builder
Pekka Marjamaki	FIN	1998	Player
Lasse Oksanen	FIN	1999	Player
Esa Peltonen	FIN	2007	Player
Goran Stubb	FIN	2000	Builder
Jorma Valtonen	FIN	1999	Player
Juhani Wahlsten	FIN	2006	Player
Unto Wiitala	FIN	2003	Referee
Urpo Ylonen	FIN	1997	Player
Jacques Lacarriere	FRA	1998	Player
Louis Magnus	FRA	1997	Builder
Rudi Ball	GER	2004	Player
Heinz Henschel	GER	2003	Builder
Gustav Jaenecke	GER	1998	Player
Udo Kiessling	GER	2000	Player
Josef Kompalla	GER	2003	Referee
Erich Kuhnhackl	GER	1997	Player
Hans Rampf	GER	2001	Player
Dr. Gunther Sabetzki	GER	1997	Builder
Alois Schloder	GER	2005	Player
Xaver Unsinn	GER	1998	Builder
Joachim Ziesche	GER	1999	Player
Bunny Ahearne	GBR	1997	Builder
Carl Erhardt	GBR	1998	Player
Peter Patton	GBR	2002	Builder
Gyorgy Pasztor	HUN	2001	Builder
Enrico Calcaterra	ITA	1999	Builder
Shoichi Tomita	JPN	2006	Builder
Kawabuchi Tsutomu	JPN	2004	Builder
Yoshiaki Tsutsumi	JPN	1999	Builder
Helmuts Balderis	LAT	1998	Player
Tore Johannessen	NOR	1999	Builder

NAME	COUNTRY	INDUCTED	CATEGORY
Henryk Gruth	POL	2006	Player
Eduard Pana	ROM	1998	Player
Veniamin Alexandrov	RUS	2007	Player
Vsevolod Bobrov	RUS	1997	Player
Arkady Chernyshev	RUS	1999	Builder
Vitaly Davydov	RUS	2004	Player
Igor Dimitriev	RUS	2007	Builder
Vyacheslav Fetisov	RUS	2005	Player
Anatoli Firsov	RUS	1998	Player
Yuri Karandin	RUS	2004	Referee
Valeri Kharlamov	RUS	1998	Player
Viktor Konovalenko	RUS	2007	Player
Viktor Kuzkin	RUS	2005	Player
Konstantin Loktev	RUS	2007	Player
Sergei Makarov	RUS	2001	Player
Alexander Maltsev	RUS	1999	Player
Boris Mayorov	RUS	1999	Player
Boris Mikhailov	RUS	2000	Player
Vladimir Petrov	RUS	2006	Player
Alexander Ragulin	RUS	1997	Player
Nikolai Sologubov	RUS	2004	Player
Andrei Starovoitov	RUS	1997	Builder
Vyacheslav Starshinov	RUS	2007	Player
Anatoli Tarasov	RUS	1997	Builder
Viktor Tikhonov	RUS	1998	Builder
Vladislav Tretiak	RUS	1997	Player
Valeri Vasiliev	RUS	1998	Player
Alexander Yakushev	RUS	2003	Player
Vladimir Yurzinov	RUS	2002	Builder
Vladimir Dzurilla	SVK	1998	Player
Josef Golonka	SVK	1998	Player
Ladislav Horsky	SVK	2004	Builder
Jan Starsi	SVK	1999	Builder
Peter Stastny	SVK	2000	Player
Ernest Aljancic Sr.	SLO	2002	Player
Sven Bergkvist	SWE	1999	Player
Curt Berglund	SWE	2003	Builder
Lars Bjorn	SWE	1998	Player
Ove Dahlberg	SWE	2004	Referee
Rudolf Eklow	SWE	1999	Builder
Arne Grunander	SWE	1997	Builder
Bengt-Ake Gustafsson	SWE	2003	Player
Anders Hedberg	SWE	1997	Player
Leif Holmqvist	SWE	1999	Player
Tomas Jonsson	SWE	2000	Player
Hakan Loob	SWE	1998	Player

NAME	COUNTRY	INDUCTED	CATEGORY
Mats Naslund	SWE	2005	Player
Kent Nilsson	SWE	2006	Player
Nisse Nilsson	SWE	2002	Player
Ronald Pettersson	SWE	2004	Player
Thomas Rundqvist	SWE	2007	Player
Borje Salming	SWE	1998	Player
Ulf Sterner	SWE	2001	Player
Roland Stoltz	SWE	1999	Player
Arne Stromberg	SWE	1998	Builder
Sven Tumba-Johansson	SWE	1997	Player
Ferdinand Cattini	SUI	1998	Player
Hans Cattini	SUI	1998	Player
Jakob Kölliker	SUI	2007	Player
Cesar Luthi	SUI	1998	Builder
Bibi Torriani	SUI	1997	Player
Anatoli Khorozov	UKR	2006	Builder
Herb Brooks	USA	1999	Builder
Walter Brown	USA	1997	Builder
Bill Christian	USA	1998	Player
Bill Cleary	USA	1997	Player
Gerry Cosby	USA	1997	Player
Jim Craig	USA	1999	Player
Mike Curran	USA	1999	Player
Mark Johnson	USA	1999	Player
John Mayasich	USA	1997	Player
Jack McCartan	USA	1998	Player
Lou Nanne	USA	2004	Player
Bob Ridder	USA	1998	Builder
Jack Riley	USA	1998	Builder
Hal Trumble	USA	1999	Builder
Thayer Tutt	USA	2002	Builder

PAUL LOICQ AWARD
For outstanding contributions to international ice hockey.

NAME	COUNTRY	INDUCTED
Wolf-Dieter Montag	GER	1998
Roman Neumayer	GER	1999
Vsevolod Kukushkin	RUS	2000
Isao Kataoka	JPN	2001
Pat Marsh	GBR	2002
George Nagobads	USA	2003
Aggie Kukulowicz	CAN	2004
Rita Hrbacek	AUT	2005
Bo Tovland	SWE	2006
Bob Nadin	CAN	2007

Triple Gold Club

19 MEMBERS AS OF 2007

These nineteen players form a unique group that has won an IIHF World Championship gold medal, an Olympic gold medal, and the Stanley Cup (listed chronologically).

1. TOMAS JONSSON
(SWE 12.04.60)
WS 91
OG 94
SC 82, 83 (NY Islanders)

2. HAKAN LOOB
(SWE 03.07.60)
WS 87, 91
OG 94
SC 89 (Calgary)

3. MATS NASLUND
(SWE 31.10.59)
WS 91
OG 94
SC 86 (Montreal)

4. VALERI KAMENSKY
(RUS 18.04.66)
WS 86, 89, 90
OG 88
SC 96 (Colorado)

5. ALEXEI GUSAROV
(RUS 08.07.64)
WS 86, 89, 90
OG 88
SC 96 (Colorado)

6. PETER FORSBERG
(SWE 20.07.73)
WS 92, 98
OG 94, 06
SC 96, 01 (Colorado)

7. VYACHESLAV FETISOV
(RUS 20.04.58)
WS 78, 81, 82, 83, 86, 89, 90
OG 84, 88
SC 97, 98 (Detroit)

8. IGOR LARIONOV
(RUS 03.12.60)
WS 82, 83, 86, 89
OG 84, 88
SC 97, 98, 02 (Detroit)

9. ALEXANDER MOGILNY
(RUS 18.02.69)
WS 89
OG 88
SC 00 (New Jersey)

10. VLADIMIR MALAKHOV
(RUS 30.08.68)
WS 90
OG 92
SC 00 (New Jersey)

11. JOE SAKIC
(CAN 07.07.69)
WS 94
OG 02
SC 96, 01 (Colorado)

12. BRENDAN SHANAHAN
(CAN 23.01.69)
WS 94
OG 02
SC 97, 98, 02 (Detroit)

13. ROB BLAKE
(CAN 10.12.69)
WS 94, 97
OG 02
SC 01 (Colorado)

14. SCOTT NIEDERMAYER
(CAN, 31.08.73)
WS 04
OG 02
SC 95, 00, 03 (New Jersey),
07 (Anaheim)

15. JAROMIR JAGR
(CZE, 15.02.72)
WS 05
OG 98
SC 91, 92 (Pittsburgh)

16. JIRI SLEGR
(CZE, 30.05.71)
WS 05
OG 98
SC 02 (Detroit)

17. NICKLAS LIDSTROM
(SWE, 28.04.70)
WS 91
OG 06
SC 97, 98, 02 (Detroit)

18. FREDRIK MODIN
(SWE, 08.10.74)
WS 98
OG 06
SC 04 (Tampa Bay)

19. CHRIS PRONGER
(CAN, 10.10.74)
WS 97
OG 02
SC 07 (Anaheim)

2007 IIHF World Ranking

The IIHF World Ranking is a tool to reflect the long-term quality of countries' national team program. The ranking is calculated by on awarding points for the final positions in the last four IIHF World Championships and in the last Olympic ice hockey tournament. The 2007 world ranking is thus based on the performance at the 2006, 2005, 2004, and the 2003 World Championships and at the 2006 Olympics.

Young hockey nation Belarus holds on to tenth position in the IIHF World Ranking thanks to emerging international stars like Mikhail Grabovsky who signed with the Montreal Canadiens in 2006.

MEN

RANKING	COUNTRY	POINTS
1	SWE	2640
2	CZE	2575
3	FIN	2480
4	CAN	2470
5	RUS	2415
6	SVK	2350
7	USA	2315
8	SUI	2250
9	LAT	2115
10	BLR	2105
11	KAZ	2020
12	GER	1965
13	NOR	1920
14	UKR	1920
15	DEN	1915
16	ITA	1915
17	AUT	1855
18	SLO	1840
19	FRA	1745
20	POL	1655
21	JPN	1605
22	HUN	1560
23	NED	1515
24	EST	1485
25	LTU	1485
26	ROU	1370
27	CRO	1290
28	CHN	1280
29	BUL	1120
30	SRB	1115
31	GBR	945
32	ISR	800
33	KOR	780
34	AUS	740
35	BEL	700
36	PRK	660
37	ESP	610
38	NZL	560
39	MEX	515
40	ISL	500
41	RSA	490
42	TUR	470
43	LUX	410

Men (continued)

RANKING	COUNTRY	POINTS
44	ARM	390
45	IRL	390
46	MON	0

WOMEN

RANKING	COUNTRY	POINTS
1	CAN	1780
2	USA	1730
3	SWE	1705
4	FIN	1655
5	GER	1585
6	RUS	1545
7	SUI	1495
8	CHN	1480
9	KAZ	1465
10	JPN	1405
11	ITA	1360
12	CZE	1335
13	FRA	1330
14	LAT	1330
15	NOR	1265
16	SLO	1145
17	DEN	645
18	PRK	600
19	SVK	595
20	NED	560
21	AUT	555
22	GBR	530
23	AUS	505
24	BEL	500
25	HUN	495
26	KOR	450
27	ROU	435
28	RSA	310
29	NZL	290
30	ISL	270
31	CRO	0
32	EST	0
33	TUR	0

International Hockey Timeline

1873 – James Creighton devises informal rules for a new winter game in Montreal, a game which later became known as ice hockey.

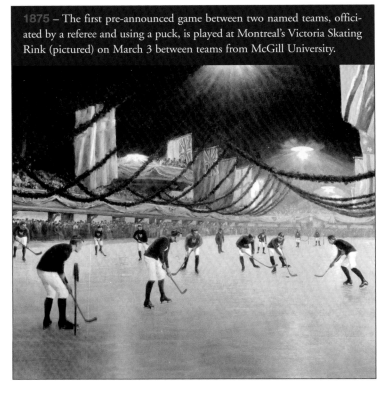

1875 – The first pre-announced game between two named teams, officiated by a referee and using a puck, is played at Montreal's Victoria Skating Rink (pictured) on March 3 between teams from McGill University.

1877 – McGill University in Montreal forms the first organized hockey team on January 31. On February 27, the *Montreal Gazette* publishes the first rules — seven in all — for hockey.

1881 – The McGill University team poses at Montreal's Crystal Palace Rink for what remains the world's first extant photograph of a hockey team.

1893 – The first Stanley Cup games are played with Montreal AAA Winged Wheelers being the first winners.

1897 – Canadian champion skater George Meagher travels to Paris, France and brings hockey equipment with him. He oversees a series of friendly games between Paris's Palais de Glace Club and bandy clubs from London and Glasgow.

1902 – The first real ice hockey games in Europe are played at the Prince's Skating Club in Knightsbridge, England.

1905 – Two international games between Belgium and France are played in Brussels on March 4. Ice hockey games, with no unified set of rules, are also played in Switzerland that year.

1908 – The Ligue Internationale de Hockey sur Glace (LIHG—later IIHF), is founded in Paris, France on May 15. France, Belgium, Switzerland, Great Britain, and Bohemia are the founding members. The first LIHG-organized games are played in Berlin, Germany, on November 3-5.

1910 – The first LIHG European Championships take place in the Swiss winter resort of Les Avants on January 10-12. Great Britain wins the tournament.

1911 – The LIHG adopts "Canadian rules" for all levels of play on March 14.

1917 – The National Hockey League is formed consisting of four teams— Montreal Canadiens, Toronto Arenas, Ottawa Senators, and Montreal Wanderers.

1920 – The Olympic Summer Games in Antwerp, Belgium, hosts the first international ice hockey tournament with North American participation. Canada (Winnipeg Falcons) wins gold. On April 26, the LIHG decides to eliminate the rover position making international hockey a six-man game.

1921 – The first LIHG European Championship after World War I is contested. Only Sweden and Czechoslovakia take part in the Stockholm event, won by the Swedes, 7-4.

1923 – The LIHG adopts a new set of rules. The game is now played with five skaters and a goalie and the games consist of three, 15-minute periods.

1930 – The first IIHF World Championship outside the Olympics takes place in Chamonix, Berlin, and Vienna.

1933 – USA becomes the first country other than Canada to win the IIHF World Championship.

1936 – The three zones of the hockey rink are introduced. Players must carry the puck to another zone, not pass it. Body-checking is allowed only in the defensive zone. Rink size is changed to 60m x 30m. Great Britain wins gold in Garmisch-Partenkirchen

1939-47 – There is no World Championship or Olympic play during World War II.

1946 – The red line at centre ice and the modern offside rule are introduced. Body-checking is allowed only in the defensive half of the ice. All games now consist of three, 20-minute periods.

1947 – Czechoslovakia becomes the first non-North American team to win the IIHF World Championship.

1948 – Canada wins its fifth Olympic gold, but only on goal difference with Czechoslovakia. The world is closing in.

1952 – Canada (Edmonton Mercurys) wins its sixth Olympic gold. It would be Canada's last Olympic hockey gold medal for 50 years.

1953 – Sweden wins the IIHF World Championship for the first time, but only three teams finish the event held in Zurich, Switzerland.

1954 – The Soviet Union enters the IIHF World Championship and strikes gold in Stockholm, Sweden, by defeating Canada in the last game.

1956 – The Soviet Union wins its first Olympic gold, in Cortina, Italy.

1957 – The largest hockey crowd ever for an international game, more than 50,000 spectators at Moscow's Lenin Stadium watch Sweden win World Championship gold after a 4-4-tie against the Soviet Union.

1960 – USA wins its first Olympic gold, at Squaw Valley, California.

1961 – The Trail Smoke Eaters' World Championship gold by Canada in Geneva, Switzerland, is the nation's last for 33 years.

1963 – The Soviet Union begins its streak of nine consecutive IIHF World Championship gold medals.

1964 – Father David Bauer's National Team starts representing Canada in international play.

1968 – The Soviet Union wins its third Olympic gold, in Grenoble, France. Canada's bronze was the country's last international medal for ten years.

1969 – Body-checking is allowed in all three zones in international hockey, a rule change that paves way for future confrontations between "amateurs" and "professionals."

1970 – Canada leaves international hockey after a disagreement with the IIHF over the amateur rule. Sweden hosts the World Championship, initially allocated to Canada (Montreal and Winnipeg). The World Championship in Stockholm is the first where helmets are mandatory for skaters.

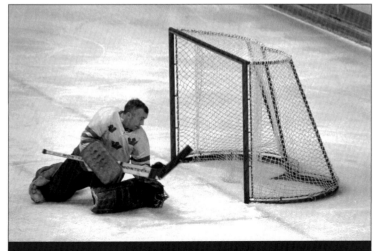

1971 – Czechoslovakia's Marcel Sakac, Sweden's Leif Holmqvist (above) and Christer Abrahamsson, and USA's Carl Wetzel are the last goaltenders to play without a face mask in the World Championships.

1972 – Czechoslovakia wins its first world championship gold in 23 years and ends the Soviet Union's streak of nine consecutive world titles. This is the first year where there is both an Olympics and World Championship tournament. Hockey history is written in September as the Soviet Union takes on a fully professional Team Canada in the eight-game "Summit Series." Canada's Paul Henderson wins the series for Canada with just 34 seconds remaining in Game 8 in Moscow. Team USA becomes the first national squad to wear namebars on their sweaters at the Olympics in Sapporo. Swedish defenceman Thommie Bergman becomes the first European-trained player to occupy a regular roster spot and play a full season in the NHL, for Detroit. Goaltenders' face masks become mandatory in Olympics and World Championships.

1973 – Swedish defenceman Borje Salming becomes the first European-trained player to achieve star status in the NHL, playing for Toronto.

1975 – CSKA Moscow and the Montreal Canadiens play to an historic 3-3 tie at the Montreal Forum on New Year's Eve, one of the finest hockey games ever played.

1976 – The inaugural "open" international hockey tournament — the Canada Cup — is staged for the first time. Darryl Sittler's overtime goal in game two of the best-of-three finals against Czechoslovakia in Montreal wins the cup for Canada. It is the first international tournament officiated by one referee and two linesmen as opposed to the two-referee system.

1977 – Canada re-enters the World Championship with a professional squad in Vienna, Austria, after a seven-year absence. Czechoslovakia becomes the first country other than Canada and the Soviet Union to win two consecutive World Championship gold medals. It is the first World Championship which is officiated by one referee and two linesmen. The IIHF introduces the World Junior (U20) Championship as a formal, annual event.

1979 – The Soviet Union shocks the NHL All-Star Team in the Challenge Cup by winning the third and decisive game 6-0 at New York's Madison Square Garden.

1980 – The biggest upset in international hockey history: A collegian Team USA defeats the Soviet Union 4-3 at Lake Placid en route to a gold medal. The Soviets' silver breaks what would have been a streak of eight consecutive Olympic gold medals by the Soviet Union/Russia.

1981 – The Soviet Union beats Sweden 13-1 in the most lopsided World Championship game to decide the gold medal and four months later defeats Team Canada 8-1 in the one-game Canada Cup final in Montreal, arguably the most crushing defeat in Canada's international hockey history.

1983 – Legendary Soviet goalie Vladislav Tretiak (above) is selected by Montreal in the NHL's Entry Draft, though he is never allowed to join the team. Tretiak retires following the next season at age 32 as the most successful player in the history of international hockey with ten World Championship gold medals, two silver and one bronze, including three Olympic golds and one silver.

1984 – The Soviet Union sweeps through the Sarajevo Olympics undefeated, claiming its sixth Olympic gold. Canada makes up for its 1981 defeat by winning this year's Canada Cup. Mike Bossy's dramatic overtime goal in the semi-final inflicts the Soviets their first loss since Lake Placid 1980.

1987 – Sweden wins its first World Championship gold in 25 years, in Vienna, Austria. Canada wins the fourth Canada Cup after a three-game series against the Soviet Union where all games end with the same score, 6-5. Canada's Mario Lemieux and Wayne Gretzky dominate the series.

1988 – The Soviet Union wins its seventh and last Olympic hockey gold, in Calgary, Canada.

1989 – Alexander Mogilny becomes the first Soviet hockey defector as he leaves the team immediately following the World Championship in Stockholm to play in the NHL.

1990 – The first IIHF-sanctioned World Women's Championship takes place in Ottawa, Canada.

1992 – Sweden wins consecutive World Championship gold medals for the first time. The Commonwealth of Independent States (CIS, above) — the former Soviet Union and the future Russia – wins Olympic gold in Albertville, France. The IIHF introduces a playoff/elimination system with quarter-finals, semi-finals, and final.

1993 – Russia wins its first World Championship gold, but it also marks the end of the Soviet Union/Russian dominance after 39 years.

1994 – Sweden wins its first Olympic gold, in Lillehammer, Norway, after Peter Forsberg's daring shootout goal against Canada, a goal so famous that it eventually became a postage stamp in Sweden.

1994 – Canada wins its first World Championship gold in 33 years, in Milan, Italy, becoming the first team to win in a shootout. Luc Robitaille is the shootout hero in the final against Finland.

1995 – Finland becomes the seventh nation to win the IIHF World Championship trophy (held here by Timo Jutila) as it defeats arch-rival Sweden in Stockholm.

1996 – USA wins the inaugural World Cup of Hockey (trophy hoisted by Chris Chelios), which replaced the Canada Cup. It's the USA's biggest international success since the 1980 Olympic "Miracle on Ice."

1997 – IIHF Congress decides to take away the red line for the purpose of allowing the two-line pass, the most important rule change in international hockey since 1969. The new rule is implemented for the first time at the 1999 World Championship in Norway. The IIHF Hall of Fame is established.

1998 – For the first time since its founding in 1917, the National Hockey League takes a break during the season to allow its players to participate in the Olympic Winter Games. The Czech Republic wins its first Olympic gold in Nagano, Japan. Women's hockey makes its debut on the Olympic program and USA wins the historic gold medal, defeating arch-rival Canada.

1999 – Jan Hlavac becomes the first player to decide a World Championship gold medal game in overtime as Czechs defeat Finland in Lillehammer, Norway.

2001 – The Czech Republic becomes the first nation other than Canada and the Soviet Union to win three consecutive World Championships.

2002 – Canada ends a 50-year drought by winning Olympic gold in Salt Lake City, USA. The country strikes a double as Canada's women also win. Slovakia becomes the eighth nation to win the World Championship, in Gothenburg, Sweden.

2004 – Canada wins consecutive World Championship titles for the first time since 1959. The Canadians defeat Sweden in both 2003 and 2004.

2006 – Sweden becomes the first country in international hockey history to win Olympic gold and the World Championship in the same year, capturing the titles in Turin and Riga, respectively. The Swedish women also make history by defeating USA in a shootout in the semi-finals, earning a silver medal and marking the first time a women's final featured a matchup other than Canada-USA.

2007 – The World Championship in Moscow is the first IIHF flagship event where a regulation-time win is awarded with three points. Canada wins its 24th men's world title, surpassing Soviet Union/Russia's 23 titles. The IIHF decides to introduce the four-man officiating system for the upcoming season.

2008 – Canada hosts its first World Championship to mark the centenary of the IIHF. Quebec City (celebrating its 400th anniversary) and Halifax host the 56 games played by 16 countries.

Most National Team Games in IIHF History

HELMINEN'S RECORD ONE FOR THE AGES

1. Raimo Helminen, FIN	330		16. Valeri Kharlamov, URS	287
2. Udo Kiessling, GER	320		17. Jörgen Jönsson, SWE	285
3. Jiri Holik, TCH	319		18. Boris Mikhailov, URS	282
4. Alexander Maltsev, URS	316		19. Lasse Oksanen, FIN	282
5. Sergei Makarov, URS	315		19. Valeri Vasiliev, URS	282
5. Dietmar Peters, GDR	315		21. Vasili Pervukhin, URS	280
7. Vyacheslav Fetisov, URS	314		22. Esa Peltonen, FIN	277
8. Alexei Kasatonov, URS	299		23. Vladimir Petrov, URS	276
9. Denis Perez, FRA	297		23. Vladimir Lutchenko, URS	276
10. Dieter Frenzel, GDR	296		25. Antoine Richer, FRA	274
11. Oldrich Machac, TCH	293		26. Roland Peters, GDR	273
12. Henryk Gruth, POL	292		27. Jonas Bergqvist, SWE	272
13. Dieter Hegen, GER	290		28. Frank Braun, GDR	270
14. Vladimir Martinec, TCH	289		29. Thomas Rundqvist, SWE	267
15. Vladislav Tretiak, URS	288		30. Frantisek Pospisil, TCH	262

Finland's Raimo Helminen set a world record for national team games with 321 on May 4, 2002, at the World Championship in Gothenburg, Sweden. On that occasion Helminen was presented with a commemorative plate by IIHF President René Fasel (right) and Vice President Kalervo Kummola (left). Before retiring from the Finnish national team, Helminen added nine games for the current record of 330. Just two months prior to this ceremony, Helminen took part in a record sixth Olympic ice hockey tournament in Salt Lake City 2002.

Sweden's Pelle Lindbergh was the first European goalie to win the Vezina Trophy as the NHL's best goaltender, in 1984-85, with the Philadelphia Flyers. He died in a car accident in Somerdale, New Jersey in November 1985. Here, Lindbergh tends Tre Kronor's goal at the 1980 Olympics in Lake Placid.

Roger Christian puts the winning goal past Nikolai Puchkov in the Soviet net with six minutes left to lead Team USA to a sensational 3-2 victory at the 1960 Olympics in Squaw Valley. It was a key win in USA's gold medal march during the original "Miracle on Ice."

GAMES OF THE VIIth OLYMPIAD & 1st WORLD CHAMPIONSHIP
April 23-September 12, 1920
(hockey played April 23-29, 1920)
Antwerp, Belgium

FINAL PLACING
1. Canada
2. United States
3. Czechoslovakia
4. Sweden

RESULTS
Gold Medal Round

April 23	Sweden 8	Belgium 0
April 24	Canada 15	Czechoslovakia 0
April 24	United States 29	Switzerland 0
April 25	Canada 2	United States 0
April 25	Sweden 4	France 0
April 26	Canada 12	Sweden 1

Silver Medal Round

| April 27 | United States 7 | Sweden 0 |
| April 28 | United States 16 | Czechoslovakia 0 |

Bronze Medal Round

| April 28 | Sweden 4 | Switzerland 0 |
| April 29 | Czechoslovakia 1 | Sweden 0 |

1st OLYMPIC WINTER GAMES & 2nd WORLD CHAMPIONSHIP
January 25-February 5, 1924
Chamonix, France

FINAL PLACING
1. Canada
2. United States
3. Great Britain
4. Sweden
5. Czechoslovakia
5. France
7. Belgium
7. Switzerland

FINAL STANDINGS
Preliminary Round
Group A

	GP	W	T	L	GF	GA	P
Canada	3	3	0	0	85	0	6
Sweden	3	2	0	1	18	25	4
Czechoslovakia	3	1	0	2	14	41	2
Switzerland	3	0	0	3	2	53	0

Group B

	GP	W	T	L	GF	GA	P
United States	3	3	0	0	52	0	6
Great Britain	3	2	0	1	34	16	4
France	3	1	0	2	9	42	2
Belgium	3	0	0	3	8	45	0

FINAL STANDINGS
Medal Round

	GP	W	T	L	GF	GA	P
Canada	3	3	0	0	47	3	6
United States	3	2	0	1	32	6	4
Great Britain	3	1	0	2	6	33	2
Sweden	3	0	0	3	3	46	0

2nd OLYMPIC WINTER GAMES & 3rd WORLD CHAMPIONSHIP
February 11-20, 1928
St. Moritz, Switzerland

FINAL PLACING
1. Canada
2. Sweden
3. Switzerland
4. Great Britain
5. France
6. Czechoslovakia
7. Belgium
7. Austria
9. Poland
10. Germany
11. Hungary

PRELIMINARY ROUND FINAL STANDINGS
Pool A

	GP	W	T	L	GF	GA	P
Great Britain	3	2	0	1	10	6	4
France	3	2	0	1	6	5	4
Belgium	3	2	0	1	9	10	4
Hungary	3	0	0	3	2	6	0

Pool B

	GP	W	T	L	GF	GA	P
Sweden	2	1	1	0	5	2	3
Czechoslovakia	2	1	0	1	3	5	2
Poland	2	0	1	1	4	5	1

Pool C

	GP	W	T	L	GF	GA	P
Austria	2	1	1	0	4	4	3
Switzerland	2	1	0	1	5	4	2
Germany	2	0	1	1	0	1	1

FINAL STANDINGS
Medal Round

	GP	W	T	L	GF	GA	P
Canada	3	3	0	0	38	0	6
Sweden	3	2	0	1	7	12	4
Switzerland	3	1	0	2	4	17	2
Great Britain	3	0	0	3	1	21	0

4th WORLD CHAMPIONSHIP
January 29-February 10, 1930
Chamonix, France/Berlin, Germany/Vienna, Austria

FINAL PLACING
1. Canada
2. Germany
3. Switzerland
4. Austria
5. Poland
6. Czechoslovakia
6. France
6. Hungary
6. Japan
10. Belgium
10. Great Britain
10. Italy

RESULTS
First Round

January 31	Hungary 2	Italy 0
January 31	Germany 4	Great Britain 2
January 31	France 4	Belgium 1

Second Round

February 1	Germany 4	Hungary 1
February 1	Poland 5	Japan 0
February 1	Austria 2	France 1
February 1	Switzerland 3	Czechoslovakia 1

Third Round

| February 2 | Germany 4 | Poland 1 |
| February 2 | Switzerland 2 | Austria 1 |

Fourth Round

| February 9 | Germany 2 | Switzerland 1 |

Fourth-place Game

| February 5 | Austria 2 | Poland 0 |

Gold Medal Game

| February 10 | Canada 6 | Germany 1 |

5th WORLD CHAMPIONSHIP
February 1-8, 1931
Krynica, Poland

FINAL PLACING
1. Canada
2. United States
3. Austria
4. Poland
5. Czechoslovakia
6. Sweden
7. Hungary
8. Great Britain
9. France
10. Romania

RESULTS & FINAL STANDING
First Qualification Round

| February 1 | Austria 1 | Great Britain 0 (OT) |
| February 1 | Czechoslovakia 4 | Hungary 1 |

Second Qualification Round

February 1	Canada 9	France 0
February 1	United States 15	Romania 0
February 2	Czechoslovakia 4	Poland 1
February 2	Sweden 3	Austria 1

Third Qualification Round

| February 3 | Austria 7 | Romania 0 |
| February 3 | Poland 2 | France 1 (OT) |

Medal Round

	GP	W	T	L	GF	GA	P
Canada	5	4	1	0	15	0	9
United States	5	4	0	1	7	3	8
Austria	5	2	0	3	5	13	4
Poland	5	1	1	3	3	6	3
Czechoslovakia	5	1	1	3	2	5	3
Sweden	5	1	1	3	1	6	3

3rd OLYMPIC WINTER GAMES & 6th WORLD CHAMPIONSHIP
February 4-13, 1932
Lake Placid, United States

FINAL PLACING
1. Canada
2. United States
3. Germany
4. Poland

FINAL STANDINGS

	GP	W	T	L	GF	GA	P
Canada	6	5	1	0	32	4	11
United States	6	4	1	1	27	5	9
Germany	6	2	0	4	7	26	4
Poland	6	0	0	6	3	34	0

7th WORLD CHAMPIONSHIP
February 18-26, 1933
Prague, Czechoslovakia

FINAL PLACING
1. United States
2. Canada
3. Czechoslovakia
4. Austria
5. Germany
5. Switzerland
7. Hungary
7. Poland
9. Romania
10. Latvia
11. Italy
12. Belgium

FINAL STANDINGS

Group A

	GP	W	T	L	GF	GA	P
Czechoslovakia	3	3	0	0	13	2	6
Austria	3	2	0	1	11	3	4
Italy	3	1	0	2	3	6	2
Romania	3	0	0	3	1	17	0

Group B

	GP	W	T	L	GF	GA	P
Germany	2	2	0	0	8	0	4
Poland	2	1	0	1	1	2	2
Belgium	2	0	0	2	0	7	0

Group C

	GP	W	T	L	GF	GA	P
Switzerland	2	2	0	0	6	1	4
Hungary	2	1	0	1	3	1	2
Latvia	2	0	0	2	1	8	0

Semi-final Group D

	GP	W	T	L	GF	GA	P
United States	3	3	0	0	17	0	6
Czechoslovakia	3	2	0	1	2	6	4
Switzerland	3	1	0	2	3	9	2
Poland	3	0	0	3	1	8	0

Semi-final Group E

	GP	W	T	L	GF	GA	P
Canada	3	3	0	0	12	1	6
Austria	3	2	0	1	3	4	4
Germany	3	1	0	2	4	7	2
Hungary	3	0	0	3	1	8	0

Semi-finals
February 24   Canada 4   Czechoslovakia 0
February 24   United States 4   Austria 0

Bronze Medal Game
February 26   Czechoslovakia 2   Austria 0

Gold Medal Game
February 26   United States 2   Canada 1 (OT)

8th WORLD CHAMPIONSHIP
February 3-11, 1934
Milan, Italy

FINAL PLACING

1. Canada
2. United States
3. Germany
4. Switzerland
5. Czechoslovakia
6. Hungary
7. Austria
8. Great Britain
9. Italy
10. Romania
11. France
12. Belgium

FINAL STANDINGS

Group A

	GP	W	T	L	GF	GA	P
Switzerland	3	3	0	0	30	3	6
France	3	1	0	2	4	6	2
Romania	3	1	0	2	6	13	2
Belgium	3	1	0	2	5	23	2

Group B

	GP	W	T	L	GF	GA	P
Hungary	2	1	0	1	2	1	2
Czechoslovakia	2	1	0	1	2	2	2
Great Britain	2	1	0	1	2	3	2

Group C

	GP	W	T	L	GF	GA	P
Austria	2	1	0	1	2	2	2
Italy	2	1	0	1	3	3	2
Germany	2	1	0	1	4	4	2

Semi-final Group A

	GP	W	T	L	GF	GA	P
United States	2	2	0	0	2	0	4
Czechoslovakia	2	1	0	1	4	1	2
Austria	2	0	0	2	0	5	0

Semi-final Group B

	GP	W	T	L	GF	GA	P
Switzerland	2	2	0	0	4	0	4
Hungary	2	0	1	1	0	1	1
Italy	2	0	1	1	0	3	1

Semi-final Group C

	GP	W	T	L	GF	GA	P
Canada	2	2	0	0	15	0	4
Germany	2	1	0	1	4	6	2
France	2	0	0	2	0	13	0

Semi-finals Qualifying Group

	GP	W	T	L	GF	GA	P
Germany	2	2	0	0	2	0	4
Czechoslovakia	2	1	0	1	1	1	2
Hungary*	2	0	0	2	0	2	0

*Hungary withdrew from the group & forfeited both games, 1-0

Relegation Round

	GP	W	T	L	GF	GA	P
Austria	3	2	1	0	7	4	5
Great Britain	3	2	0	1	7	4	4
Italy	3	1	1	1	6	6	3
Romania	3	0	0	3	2	8	0

Semi-finals
February 10   Canada 2   Switzerland 1 (OT)
February 10   United States 3   Germany 0

Bronze Medal Game
February 11   Germany 2   Switzerland 1 (2OT)

Gold Medal Game
February 11   Canada 2   United States 1

9th WORLD CHAMPIONSHIP
January 19-27, 1935
Davos, Switzerland

FINAL PLACING

1. Canada
2. Switzerland
3. Great Britain
4. Czechoslovakia
5. Sweden
6. Austria
7. France
8. Italy
9. Germany
10. Poland
11. Hungary
11. Romania
13. Latvia
14. Belgium
14. Netherlands

FINAL STANDING

Group A

	GP	W	T	L	GF	GA	P
Switzerland	3	2	1	0	11	2	5
Sweden	3	2	0	1	10	6	4
Hungary	3	1	1	1	7	4	3
Netherlands	3	0	0	3	0	16	0

Group B

	GP	W	T	L	GF	GA	P
France	3	2	1	0	6	4	5
Italy	3	1	2	0	4	2	4
Poland	3	1	1	1	6	5	3
Germany	3	0	0	3	2	7	0

Group C

	GP	W	T	L	GF	GA	P
Czechoslovakia	3	3	0	0	28	3	6
Austria	3	2	0	1	9	4	4
Romania	3	1	0	2	5	7	2
Belgium	3	0	0	3	2	30	0

Group D

	GP	W	T	L	GF	GA	P
Canada	2	2	0	0	18	2	4
Great Britain	2	1	0	1	7	5	2
Latvia	2	0	0	2	1	19	0

Semi-final Group A

	GP	W	T	L	GF	GA	P
Canada	3	3	0	0	16	3	6
Czechoslovakia	3	2	0	1	8	4	4
Sweden	3	0	1	2	4	8	1
Italy	3	0	1	2	2	15	1

Semi-final Group B

	GP	W	T	L	GF	GA	P
Switzerland	3	2	1	0	7	2	5
Great Britain	3	2	0	1	5	2	4
Austria	3	1	1	1	6	6	3
France	3	0	0	3	2	10	0

9-15 Placement Group A

	GP	W	T	L	GF	GA	P
Germany	3	3	0	0	11	1	6
Romania	3	2	0	1	9	5	4
Latvia	3	1	0	2	10	6	2
Netherlands	3	0	0	3	0	18	0

9-15 Placement Group B

	GP	W	T	L	GF	GA	P
Poland	2	1	1	0	13	3	3
Hungary	2	1	1	0	7	2	3
Belgium	2	0	0	2	3	18	0

Semi-finals
January 26   Canada 6   Great Britain 0
January 26   Switzerland 4   Czechoslovakia 0

Bronze Medal Game
January 27   Great Britain 2   Czechoslovakia 1

Gold Medal Game
January 27   Canada 4   Switzerland 2

4th OLYMPIC WINTER GAMES & 10th WORLD CHAMPIONSHIP
February 6-16, 1936
Garmisch-Partenkirchen, Germany

FINAL PLACING

1. Great Britain
2. Canada
3. United States
4. Czechoslovakia
5. Germany
5. Sweden
7. Austria
7. Hungary
9. Italy
9. France
9. Japan
9. Poland
13. Belgium
13. Latvia
13. Switzerland

FINAL STANDINGS

Round One

Group A

	GP	W	T	L	GF	GA	P
Canada	3	3	0	0	24	3	6
Austria	3	2	0	1	11	7	4
Poland	3	1	0	2	11	12	2
Latvia	3	0	0	3	3	27	0

Group B

	GP	W	T	L	GF	GA	P
Germany	3	2	0	1	5	1	4
United States	3	2	0	1	5	2	4
Italy	3	1	0	2	2	5	2
Switzerland	3	1	0	2	1	5	2

Group C

	GP	W	T	L	GF	GA	P
Czechoslovakia	3	3	0	0	10	0	6
Hungary	3	2	0	1	14	5	4
France	3	1	0	2	4	7	2
Belgium	3	0	0	3	4	20	0

Group D

	GP	W	T	L	GF	GA	P
Great Britain	2	2	0	0	4	0	4
Sweden	2	1	0	1	2	1	2
Japan	2	0	0	2	0	5	0

Round Two

Group A

	GP	W	T	L	GF	GA	P
Great Britain	3	2	1	0	8	3	5
Canada	3	2	0	1	22	4	4
Germany	3	1	1	1	5	8	3
Hungary	3	0	0	3	2	22	0

Group B

	GP	W	T	L	GF	GA	P
United States	3	3	0	0	5	1	6
Czechoslovakia	3	2	0	1	6	4	4
Sweden	3	1	0	2	3	6	2
Austria	3	0	0	3	1	4	0

Final Round

	GP	W	T	L	GF	GA	P
Great Britain	3	2	1	0	7	1	5
Canada	3	2	0	1	9	2	4
United States	3	1	1	1	2	1	3
Czechoslovakia	3	0	0	3	0	14	0

11ᵗʰ WORLD CHAMPIONSHIP
February 17-27, 1937
London, Great Britain

FINAL PLACING

1. Canada	7. France
2. Great Britain	8. Poland
3. Switzerland	9. Norway
4. Germany	9. Romania
5. Hungary	9. Sweden
6. Czechoslovakia	

FINAL STANDINGS

Group A

	GP	W	T	L	GF	GA	P
Great Britain	3	3	0	0	24	0	6
Germany	3	1	1	1	6	10	3
Hungary	3	1	1	1	6	10	3
Romania	3	0	0	3	3	19	0

Group B

	GP	W	T	L	GF	GA	P
Canada	3	3	0	0	29	2	6
Poland	3	2	0	1	12	9	4
France	3	1	0	2	3	20	2
Sweden	3	0	0	3	1	14	0

Group C

	GP	W	T	L	GF	GA	P
Switzerland	2	1	1	0	15	4	3
Czechoslovakia	2	1	1	0	9	2	3
Norway	2	0	0	2	2	20	0

Semi-final Group A

	GP	W	T	L	GF	GA	P
Canada	3	3	0	0	21	1	6
Germany	3	2	0	1	7	6	4
Czechoslovakia	3	1	0	2	9	6	2
France	3	0	0	3	2	26	0

Semi-final Group B

	GP	W	T	L	GF	GA	P
Great Britain	3	3	0	0	19	0	6
Switzerland	3	2	0	1	5	5	4
Poland	3	1	0	2	4	12	2
Hungary	3	0	0	3	2	13	0

5-8 Placement Group

	GP	W	T	L	GF	GA	P
Hungary	3	2	1	0	10	1	5
Czechoslovakia	3	2	1	0	4	1	5
France	3	1	0	2	7	8	2
Poland	3	0	0	3	0	11	0

Final Group

	GP	W	T	L	GF	GA	P
Canada	3	3	0	0	10	1	6
Great Britain	3	2	0	1	7	3	4
Switzerland	3	1	0	2	7	4	2
Germany	3	0	0	3	0	16	0

12ᵗʰ WORLD CHAMPIONSHIP
February 11-20, 1938
Prague, Czechoslovakia

FINAL PLACING

1. Canada	7. Poland
2. Great Britain	7. United States
3. Czechoslovakia	10. Austria
4. Germany	10. Latvia
5. Sweden	10. Lithuania
6. Switzerland	13. Norway
7. Hungary	13. Romania

FINAL STANDINGS

Group A

	GP	W	T	L	GF	GA	P
Switzerland	4	4	0	0	31	2	8
Poland	4	3	0	1	15	8	6
Hungary	4	2	0	2	13	6	4
Lithuania	4	1	0	3	3	33	2
Romania	4	0	0	4	2	15	0

Group B

	GP	W	T	L	GF	GA	P
Great Britain	4	3	1	0	15	2	7
United States	4	3	1	0	10	2	7
Germany	4	2	0	2	9	2	4
Latvia	4	1	0	3	4	8	2
Norway	4	0	0	4	2	26	0

Group C

	GP	W	T	L	GF	GA	P
Canada	3	3	0	0	9	2	6
Czechoslovakia	3	1	1	1	1	3	3
Sweden	3	0	2	1	3	4	2
Austria	3	0	1	2	1	5	1

Semi-final Group A

	GP	W	T	L	GF	GA	P
Great Britain	2	2	0	0	10	3	4
Sweden	2	1	0	1	3	3	2
Poland	2	0	0	2	1	8	0

Semi-final Group B

	GP	W	T	L	GF	GA	P
Czechoslovakia	2	2	0	0	5	2	4
Switzerland	2	1	0	1	3	3	2
United States	2	0	0	2	0	3	0

Semi-final Group C

	GP	W	T	L	GF	GA	P
Canada	2	1	1	0	4	3	3
Germany	2	1	0	1	3	3	2
Hungary	2	0	1	1	1	2	1

Semi-finals

February 19	Canada 1	Germany 0	
February 19	Great Britain 1	Czechoslovakia 0	

Bronze Medal Game

February 20	Czechoslovakia 3	Germany 0

Gold Medal Game

February 20	Canada 3	Great Britain 1

13ᵗʰ WORLD CHAMPIONSHIP
February 3-12, 1939
Basel/Zurich, Switzerland

FINAL PLACING

1. Canada	8. Great Britain
2. United States	9. Italy
3. Switzerland	10. Latvia
4. Czechoslovakia	11. Belgium
5. Germany	11. Netherlands
6. Poland	13. Finland
7. Hungary	13. Yugoslavia

FINAL STANDINGS

Group A

	GP	W	T	L	GF	GA	P
United States	3	3	0	0	13	0	6
Germany	3	1	1	1	12	5	3
Italy	3	1	1	1	5	7	3
Finland	3	0	0	3	3	21	0

Group B

	GP	W	T	L	GF	GA	P
Switzerland	3	3	0	0	36	0	6
Czechoslovakia	3	2	0	1	33	1	4
Latvia	3	1	0	2	6	21	2
Yugoslavia	3	0	0	3	0	53	0

Group C

	GP	W	T	L	GF	GA	P
Canada	2	2	0	0	12	0	4
Poland	2	1	0	1	9	4	2
Netherlands	2	0	0	2	0	17	0

Group D

	GP	W	T	L	GF	GA	P
Great Britain	2	2	0	0	4	1	4
Hungary	2	1	0	1	8	2	2
Belgium	2	0	0	2	2	11	0

Semi-final

	GP	W	T	L	GF	GA	P
Canada	3	3	0	0	15	1	6
Czechoslovakia	3	1	1	1	4	3	3
Germany	3	1	1	1	2	10	3
Great Britain	3	0	0	3	0	7	0

Semi-final

	GP	W	T	L	GF	GA	P
Switzerland	3	3	0	0	12	4	6
United States	3	2	0	1	9	3	4
Poland	3	1	0	2	5	11	2
Hungary	3	0	0	3	5	13	0

5-9 Placement Group

	GP	W	T	L	GF	GA	P
Germany	2	2	0	0	10	2	4
Poland	2	1	0	1	3	4	2
Hungary	2	0	0	2	2	9	0

*Great Britain withdrew

9-14 Placement Group A

	GP	W	T	L	GF	GA	P
Italy	2	2	0	0	4	2	4
Netherlands	2	1	0	1	3	3	2
Finland	2	0	0	2	2	4	0

9-14 Placement Group B

	GP	W	T	L	GF	GA	P
Latvia	2	2	0	0	9	1	4
Belgium	2	0	1	1	4	8	1
Yugoslavia	2	0	1	1	3	7	1

Final Group

	GP	W	T	L	GF	GA	P
Canada	3	3	0	0	15	0	6
United States	3	2	0	1	3	5	4
Switzerland	3	0	1	2	1	9	1
Czechoslovakia	3	0	1	2	0	5	1

Bronze Medal/European Champions Game
March 5   Switzerland 2   Czechoslovakia 0

14th WORLD CHAMPIONSHIP
February 15-23, 1947
Prague, Czechoslovakia

FINAL PLACING
1. Czechoslovakia   5. United States
2. Sweden   6. Poland
3. Austria   7. Romania
4. Switzerland   8. Belgium

FINAL STANDINGS

	GP	W	T	L	GF	GA	P
Czechoslovakia	7	6	0	1	85	10	12
Sweden	7	5	1	1	55	15	11
Austria	7	5	0	2	49	32	10
Switzerland	7	4	1	2	47	22	9
United States	7	4	0	3	42	26	8
Poland	7	2	0	5	27	40	4
Romania	7	1	0	6	17	88	2
Belgium	7	0	0	7	15	104	0

5th OLYMPIC WINTER GAMES & 15th WORLD HAMPIONSHIP
January 30-February 8, 1948
St. Moritz, Switzerland

FINAL PLACING
1. Canada   5. Great Britain
2. Czechoslovakia   6. Poland
3. Switzerland   7. Austria
4. Sweden   8. Italy

FINAL STANDINGS

	GP	W	T	L	GF	GA	P
Canada	8	7	1	0	69	5	15
Czechoslovakia	8	7	1	0	80	18	15
Switzerland	8	6	0	2	67	21	12
United States	8	5	0	3	86	33	10
Sweden	8	4	0	4	55	28	8
Great Britain	8	3	0	5	39	47	6
Poland	8	2	0	6	29	97	4
Austria	8	1	0	7	33	77	2
Italy	8	0	0	8	24	156	0

16th WORLD CHAMPIONSHIP
February 12-20, 1949
Stockholm, Sweden

FINAL PLACING
1. Czechoslovakia   6. Austria
2. Canada   7. Finland
3. United States   8. Norway
4. Sweden   9. Belgium
5. Switzerland   10. Denmark

FINAL STANDING
Group A

	GP	W	T	L	GF	GA	P
Canada	2	2	0	0	54	0	4
Austria	2	1	0	1	25	8	2
Denmark	2	0	0	2	1	72	0

Group B

	GP	W	T	L	GF	GA	P
Sweden	2	2	0	0	16	3	4
Czechoslovakia	2	1	0	1	21	6	2
Finland	2	0	0	2	3	31	0

Group C

	GP	W	T	L	GF	GA	P
United States	3	3	0	0	36	6	6
Switzerland	3	2	0	1	30	15	4
Norway	3	1	0	2	4	19	2
Belgium	3	0	0	3	2	32	0

7-10 Placement Group

	GP	W	T	L	GF	GA	P
Finland	3	3	0	0	26	5	6
Norway	3	2	0	1	22	8	4
Belgium	3	1	0	2	11	34	2
Denmark	3	0	0	3	3	18	0

Final Group

	GP	W	T	L	GF	GA	P
Czechoslovakia	5	4	0	1	21	6	8
Canada	5	2	2	1	20	10	6
United States	5	3	0	2	23	16	6
Sweden	5	2	1	2	26	12	5
Switzerland	5	2	1	2	18	17	5
Austria	5	0	0	5	5	52	0

17th WORLD CHAMPIONSHIP
February 13-22, 1950
London, Great Britain

FINAL PLACING
1. Canada   6. Norway
2. United States   7. Belgium
3. Switzerland   8. Netherlands
4. Great Britain   9. France
5. Sweden

FINAL STANDING
Group A

	GP	W	T	L	GF	GA	P
Canada	2	2	0	0	46	2	4
Switzerland	2	1	0	1	26	16	2
Belgium	2	0	0	2	3	57	0

Group B

	GP	W	T	L	GF	GA	P
Sweden	2	2	0	0	18	3	4
United States	2	1	0	1	20	9	2
Netherlands	2	0	0	2	1	27	0

Group C

	GP	W	T	L	GF	GA	P
Great Britain	2	2	0	0	11	0	4
Norway	2	1	0	1	11	2	2
France	2	0	0	2	0	20	0

Relegation Round

	GP	W	T	L	GF	GA	P
Belgium	2	2	0	0	11	3	4
Netherlands	2	1	0	1	6	6	2
France	2	0	0	2	3	11	0

Final Group

	GP	W	T	L	GF	GA	P
Canada	5	5	0	0	42	3	10
United States	5	4	0	1	29	20	8
Switzerland	5	3	0	2	31	30	6
Great Britain	5	2	0	3	14	32	4
Sweden	5	1	0	4	15	16	2
Norway	5	0	0	5	15	45	0

18th WORLD CHAMPIONSHIP
March 9-17, 1951
Paris, France

FINAL PLACING
1. Canada   5. Great Britain
2. Sweden   6. United States
3. Switzerland   7. Finland
4. Norway

FINAL STANDING

	GP	W	T	L	GF	GA	P
Canada	6	6	0	0	62	6	12
Sweden	6	4	1	1	33	14	9
Switzerland	6	4	1	1	28	12	9
Norway	6	2	0	4	10	27	4
Great Britain	6	1	1	4	18	42	3
United States	6	1	1	4	14	42	3
Finland	6	1	0	5	15	37	2

6th OLYMPIC WINTER GAMES & 19th WORLD CHAMPIONSHIP
February 15-25, 1952
Oslo, Norway

FINAL PLACING

1. Canada
2. United States
3. Sweden
4. Czechoslovakia
5. Switzerland
6. Poland
7. Finland
8. West Germany
9. Norway

FINAL STANDINGS

	GP	W	T	L	GF	GA	P
Canada	8	7	1	0	71	14	15
United States	8	6	1	1	43	21	13
Sweden	8	6	0	2	48	19	12
Czechoslovakia	8	6	0	2	47	18	12
Switzerland	8	4	0	4	40	40	8
Poland	8	2	1	5	21	56	5
Finland	8	2	0	6	21	60	4
Germany	8	1	1	6	21	53	3
Norway	8	0	0	8	15	46	0

20th WORLD CHAMPIONSHIP
March 6-15, 1953
Zurich/Basel, Switzerland

FINAL PLACING

1. Sweden
2. West Germany
3. Switzerland
Czechoslovakia (did not finish)

FINAL STANDINGS

	GP	W	T	L	GF	GA	P
Sweden	4	4	0	0	38	11	8
West Germany	4	1	0	3	17	26	2
Switzerland	4	1	0	3	9	27	2
Czechoslovakia*	4	3	0	1	32	15	6

*Czechoslovakia withdrew after 4 games because of the death of President Klement Gottwald. The standings omit all games involving Czechoslovakia.

21st WORLD CHAMPIONSHIP
February 26-March 7, 1954
Stockholm, Sweden

FINAL PLACING

1. Soviet Union
2. Canada
3. Sweden
4. Czechoslovakia
5. West Germany
6. Finland
7. Switzerland
8. Norway

FINAL STANDINGS

	GP	W	T	L	GF	GA	P
Soviet Union	7	6	1	0	37	10	13
Canada	7	6	0	1	59	12	12
Sweden	7	5	1	1	30	18	11
Czechoslovakia	7	4	0	3	41	21	8
West Germany	7	2	1	4	22	32	5
Finland	7	1	1	5	12	52	3
Switzerland	7	0	2	5	15	34	2
Norway	7	1	0	6	6	43	2

22nd WORLD CHAMPIONSHIP
February 25-March 6, 1955
Düsseldorf/Dortmund/Krefeld/Cologne,
West Germany

FINAL PLACING

1. Canada
2. Soviet Union
3. Czechoslovakia
4. United States
5. Sweden
6. West Germany
7. Poland
8. Swtizerland
9. Finland

FINAL STANDINGS

	GP	W	T	L	GF	GA	P
Canada	8	8	0	0	66	6	16
Soviet Union	8	7	0	1	39	13	14
Czechoslovakia	8	5	1	2	63	22	11
United States	8	4	2	2	33	29	10
Sweden	8	4	1	3	40	16	9
West Germany	8	2	0	6	28	43	4
Poland	8	2	0	6	19	59	4
Switzerland	8	1	0	7	15	59	2
Finland	8	1	0	7	16	72	2

7th OLYMPIC WINTER GAMES & 23rd WORLD CHAMPIONSHIP
January 26-February 4, 1956
Cortina d'Ampezzo, Italy

FINAL PLACING

1. Soviet Union
2. United States
3. Canada
4. Sweden
5. Czechoslovakia
6. Germany
7. Italy
8. Poland
9. Switzerland
10. Austria

FINAL STANDINGS

Pool A

	GP	W	T	L	GF	GA	P
Canada	3	3	0	0	30	1	6
Germany	3	1	1	1	9	6	3
Italy	3	0	2	1	5	7	2
Austria	3	0	1	2	2	32	1

Pool B

	GP	W	T	L	GF	GA	P
Czechoslovakia	2	2	0	0	12	6	4
United States	2	1	0	1	7	4	2
Poland	2	0	0	2	3	12	0

Pool C

	GP	W	T	L	GF	GA	P
Soviet Union	2	2	0	0	15	4	4
Sweden	2	1	0	1	7	10	2
Switzerland	2	0	0	2	8	16	0

Medal Round

	GP	W	T	L	GF	GA	P
Soviet Union	5	5	0	0	25	5	10
United States	5	4	0	1	26	12	8
Canada	5	3	0	2	23	11	6
Sweden	5	1	1	3	10	17	3
Czechoslovakia	5	1	0	4	20	30	2
Germany	5	0	1	4	6	35	1

24th WORLD CHAMPIONSHIP
February 24-March 5, 1957
Moscow, Soviet Union

FINAL PLACING

1. Sweden
2. Soviet Union
3. Czechoslovakia
4. Finland
5. East Germany
6. Poland
7. Austria
8. Japan

FINAL STANDINGS

	GP	W	T	L	GF	GA	P
Sweden	7	6	1	0	62	11	13
Soviet Union	7	5	2	0	77	9	12
Czechoslovakia	7	5	1	1	66	9	11
Finland	7	4	0	3	28	33	8
East Germany	7	3	0	4	23	48	6
Poland	7	2	0	5	25	45	4
Austria	7	0	1	6	8	61	1
Japan	7	0	1	6	11	84	1

25th WORLD CHAMPIONSHIP
February 25-March 9, 1958
Oslo, Norway

FINAL PLACING

1. Canada
2. Soviet Union
3. Sweden
4. Czechoslovakia
5. United States
6. Finland
7. Norway
8. Poland

FINAL STANDINGS

	GP	W	T	L	GF	GA	P
Canada	7	7	0	0	82	6	14
Soviet Union	7	5	1	1	44	15	11
Sweden	7	5	0	2	46	22	10
Czechoslovakia	7	3	2	2	21	21	8
United States	7	3	1	3	29	33	7
Finland	7	1	1	5	9	51	3
Norway	7	1	0	6	12	44	2
Poland	7	0	1	6	14	65	1

26th WORLD CHAMPIONSHIP
March 9-15, 1959
Bratislava/Brno/Ostrava/Kolin/Mlada
Boleslav/Kladno/Prague, Czechoslovakia

FINAL PLACING

1. Canada
2. Soviet Union
3. Czechoslovakia
4. United States
5. Sweden
6. Finland
7. East Germany
8. Norway
9. West Germany
10. Italy
11. Poland
12. Switzerland

FINAL STANDINGS

Group A

	GP	W	T	L	GF	GA	P
Canada	3	3	0	0	39	2	6
Czechoslovakia	3	2	0	1	24	8	4
Switzerland	3	1	0	2	8	35	2
Poland	3	0	0	3	4	30	0

Group B

	GP	W	T	L	GF	GA	P
Soviet Union	3	3	0	0	24	5	6
United States	3	2	0	1	22	10	4
Norway	3	1	0	2	10	26	2
East Germany	3	0	0	3	6	21	0

Group C

	GP	W	T	L	GF	GA	P
Sweden	3	2	1	0	21	8	5
Finland	3	1	1	1	13	12	3
West Germany	3	1	0	2	11	13	2
Italy	3	1	0	2	7	22	2

7-12 Placement Group

	GP	W	T	L	GF	GA	P
East Germany	5	4	1	0	30	9	9
Norway	5	3	1	1	20	20	7
West Germany	5	3	0	2	20	21	6
Italy	5	2	1	2	20	17	5
Poland	5	1	0	4	11	20	2
Switzerland	5	0	1	4	8	22	1

Medal Round

	GP	W	T	L	GF	GA	P
Canada	5	4	0	1	21	5	8
Soviet Union	5	4	0	1	20	10	8
Czechoslovakia	5	3	0	2	22	14	6
United States	5	3	0	2	23	15	6
Sweden	5	1	0	4	6	21	2
Finland	5	0	0	5	7	32	0

8th OLYMPIC WINTER GAMES & 27th WORLD CHAMPIONSHIP
February 19-28, 1960
Squaw Valley, United States

FINAL PLACING
1. United States
2. Canada
3. Soviet Union
4. Czechoslovakia
5. Sweden
6. Germany
7. Finland
8. Japan
9. Australia

FINAL STANDINGS
Pool A

	GP	W	T	L	GF	GA	P
Canada	2	2	0	0	24	3	4
Sweden	2	1	0	1	21	5	2
Japan	2	0	0	2	1	38	0

Pool B

	GP	W	T	L	GF	GA	P
Soviet Union	2	2	0	0	16	4	4
Germany	2	1	0	1	4	9	2
Finland	2	0	0	2	5	12	0

Pool C

	GP	W	T	L	GF	GA	P
United States	2	2	0	0	19	6	4
Czechoslovakia	2	1	1	0	23	8	2
Australia	2	0	0	2	2	30	0

Consolation Round

	GP	W	T	L	GF	GA	P
Finland	4	3	1	0	58	11	7
Japan	4	2	1	1	33	30	5
Australia	4	0	0	4	8	58	0

Medal Round

	GP	W	T	L	GF	GA	P
United States	5	5	0	0	29	11	10
Canada	5	4	0	1	31	12	8
Soviet Union	5	2	1	2	24	19	5
Czechoslovakia	5	2	0	3	21	23	4
Sweden	5	1	1	3	19	19	3
Germany	5	0	0	5	5	45	0

28th WORLD CHAMPIONSHIP
March 1-12, 1961
Geneva/Lausanne, Switzerland

FINAL PLACING
1. Canada
2. Czechoslovakia
3. Soviet Union
4. Sweden
5. East Germany
6. United States
7. Finland
8. West Germany

FINAL STANDINGS

	GP	W	T	L	GF	GA	P
Canada	7	6	1	0	45	11	13
Czechoslovakia	7	6	1	0	33	9	13
Soviet Union	7	5	0	2	51	20	10
Sweden	7	4	0	3	33	27	8
East Germany	7	2	0	5	21	33	4
United States	7	1	1	5	24	43	3
Finland	7	1	1	5	19	43	3
West Germany	7	0	2	5	10	50	2

29th WORLD CHAMPIONSHIP
March 8-18, 1962
Colorado Springs/Denver, United States

FINAL PLACING
1. Sweden
2. Canada
3. United States
4. Finland
5. Norway
6. West Germany
7. Switzerland
8. Great Britain

FINAL STANDINGS

	GP	W	T	L	GF	GA	P
Sweden	7	7	0	0	67	10	14
Canada	7	6	0	1	58	12	12
United States	7	5	0	2	54	23	10
Finland	7	3	0	4	32	42	6
Norway	7	3	0	4	32	54	6
West Germany	7	2	0	5	27	36	4
Switzerland	7	1	0	6	21	60	2
Great Britain	7	1	0	6	19	73	2

30th WORLD CHAMPIONSHIP
March 7-17, 1963
Stockholm, Sweden

FINAL PLACING
1. Soviet Union
2. Sweden
3. Czechoslovakia
4. Canada
5. Finland
6. East Germany
7. West Germany
8. United States

FINAL STANDINGS

	GP	W	T	L	GF	GA	P
Soviet Union	7	6	0	1	50	9	12
Sweden	7	6	0	1	44	10	12
Czechoslovakia	7	5	1	1	41	16	11
Canada	7	4	1	2	46	23	9
Finland	7	1	1	5	20	35	3
East Germany	7	1	1	5	16	43	3
West Germany	7	1	1	5	18	56	3
United States	7	1	1	5	21	64	3

9th OLYMPIC WINTER GAMES & 31st WORLD CHAMPIONSHIP
January 29-February 9, 1964
Innsbruck, Austria

FINAL PLACING
1. Soviet Union
2. Sweden
3. Czechoslovakia
4. Canada
5. United States
6. Finland
7. Germany
8. Switzerland
9. Poland
10. Norway
11. Japan
12. Romania
13. Austria
14. Yugoslavia
15. Italy
16. Hungary

FINAL STANDINGS

	GP	W	T	L	GF	GA	P
Soviet Union	7	7	0	0	54	10	14
Sweden	7	5	0	2	47	16	10
Czechoslovakia	7	5	0	2	38	19	10
Canada	7	5	0	2	32	17	10
United States	7	2	0	5	29	33	4
Finland	7	2	0	5	10	31	4
Germany	7	2	0	5	13	49	4
Switzerland	7	0	0	7	9	57	0

32nd WORLD CHAMPIONSHIP
March 3-14, 1965
Tampere, Finland

FINAL PLACING
1. Soviet Union
2. Czechoslovakia
3. Sweden
4. Canada
5. East Germany
6. United States
7. Finland
8. Norway

FINAL STANDINGS

	GP	W	T	L	GF	GA	P
Soviet Union	7	7	0	0	51	13	14
Czechoslovakia	7	6	0	1	43	10	12
Sweden	7	4	1	2	33	17	9
Canada	7	4	0	3	28	21	8
East Germany	7	3	0	4	18	33	6
United States	7	2	0	5	22	44	4
Finland	7	1	1	5	14	27	3
Norway	7	0	0	7	12	56	0

33rd WORLD CHAMPIONSHIP
March 3-14, 1966
Ljubljana, Yugoslavia

FINAL PLACING
1. Soviet Union
2. Czechoslovakia
3. Canada
4. Sweden
5. East Germany
6. United States
7. Finland
8. Poland

FINAL STANDINGS

	GP	W	T	L	GF	GA	P
Soviet Union	7	6	1	0	55	7	13
Czechoslovakia	7	6	0	1	32	15	12
Canada	7	5	0	2	33	10	10
Sweden	7	3	1	3	26	17	7
East Germany	7	3	0	4	12	30	6
United States	7	2	0	5	18	39	4
Finland	7	2	0	5	18	43	4
Poland	7	0	0	7	11	44	0

34th WORLD CHAMPIONSHIP
March 18-29, 1967
Vienna, Austria

FINAL PLACING

1. Soviet Union	5. United States
2. Sweden	6. Finland
3. Canada	7. East Germany
4. Czechoslovakia	8. West Germany

FINAL STANDINGS

	GP	W	T	L	GF	GA	P
Soviet Union	7	7	0	0	58	9	14
Sweden	7	4	1	2	31	22	9
Canada	7	4	1	2	28	15	9
Czechoslovakia	7	3	2	2	29	18	8
United States	7	3	1	3	20	23	7
Finland	7	2	1	4	14	24	5
East Germany	7	1	1	5	14	38	3
West Germany	7	0	1	6	11	56	1

10th OLYMPIC WINTER GAMES & 35th WORLD CHAMPIONSHIP
February 6-17, 1968
Grenoble, France

FINAL PLACING

1. Soviet Union	8. East Germany
2. Czechoslovakia	9. Yugoslavia
3. Canada	10. Japan
4. Sweden	11. Norway
5. Finland	12. Romania
6. United States	13. Austria
7. West Germany	14. France

FINAL STANDINGS

	GP	W	T	L	GF	GA	P
Soviet Union	7	6	0	1	48	10	12
Czechoslovakia	7	5	1	1	33	17	11
Canada	7	5	0	2	28	15	10
Sweden	7	4	1	2	23	18	9
Finland	7	3	1	3	17	23	7
United States	7	2	1	4	23	28	5
West Germany	7	1	0	6	13	39	2
East Germany	7	0	0	7	13	48	0

36th WORLD CHAMPIONSHIP
March 15-30, 1969
Stockholm, Sweden

FINAL PLACING

1. Soviet Union	4. Canada
2. Sweden	5. Finland
3. Czechoslovakia	6. United States

FINAL STANDINGS

	GP	W	T	L	GF	GA	P
Soviet Union	10	8	0	2	59	23	16
Sweden	10	8	0	2	45	19	16
Czechoslovakia	10	8	0	2	40	20	16
Canada	10	4	0	6	26	31	8
Finland	10	2	0	8	26	52	4
United States	10	0	0	10	23	74	0

37th WORLD CHAMPIONSHIP
March 14-30, 1970
Stockholm, Sweden

FINAL PLACING

1. Soviet Union	4. Finland
2. Sweden	5. East Germany
3. Czechoslovakia	6. Poland

FINAL STANDINGS

	GP	W	T	L	GF	GA	P
Soviet Union	10	9	0	1	68	11	18
Sweden	10	7	1	2	45	21	15
Czechoslovakia	10	5	1	4	47	30	11
Finland	10	5	0	5	31	40	10
East Germany	10	2	1	7	20	50	5
Poland	10	0	1	9	11	70	1

38th WORLD CHAMPIONSHIP
March 19-April 3, 1971
Bern/Geneva, Switzerland

FINAL PLACING

1. Soviet Union	4. Finland
2. Czechoslovakia	5. West Germany
3. Sweden	6. United States

FINAL STANDINGS

	GP	W	T	L	GF	GA	P
Soviet Union	10	8	1	1	77	24	17
Czechoslovakia	10	7	1	2	44	20	15
Sweden	10	5	1	4	29	33	11
Finland	10	4	1	5	31	42	9
West Germany	10	2	0	8	22	62	4
United States	10	2	0	8	31	53	4

11th OLYMPIC WINTER GAMES
February 5-13, 1972
Sapporo, Japan

FINAL PLACING

1. Soviet Union	7. West Germany
2. United States	8. Norway
3. Czechoslovakia	9. Japan
4. Sweden	10. Switzerland
5. Finland	11. Yugoslavia
6. Poland	

FINAL STANDINGS

	GP	W	T	L	GF	GA	P
Soviet Union	5	4	1	0	33	13	9
United States	5	3	0	2	18	15	6
Czechoslovakia	5	3	0	2	26	13	6
Sweden	5	2	1	2	17	13	5
Finland	5	2	0	3	14	24	4
Poland	5	0	0	5	9	39	0

39th WORLD CHAMPIONSHIP
April 7-22, 1972
Prague, Czechoslovakia

FINAL PLACING

1. Czechoslovakia	4. Finland
2. Soviet Union	5. West Germany
3. Sweden	6. Switzerland

	GP	W	T	L	GF	GA	P
Czechoslovakia	10	9	1	0	72	16	19
Soviet Union	10	7	2	1	78	19	16
Sweden	10	5	1	4	49	33	11
Finland	10	4	0	6	47	48	8
West Germany	10	2	0	8	23	76	4
Switzerland	10	1	0	9	19	96	2

40th WORLD CHAMPIONSHIP
March 31-April 15, 1973
Moscow, Soviet Union

FINAL PLACING

1. Soviet Union	4. Finland
2. Sweden	5. Poland
3. Czechoslovakia	6. West Germany

FINAL STANDINGS

	GP	W	T	L	GF	GA	P
Soviet Union	10	10	0	0	100	18	20
Sweden	10	7	1	2	53	23	15
Czechoslovakia	10	6	1	3	48	20	13
Finland	10	3	1	6	24	39	7
Poland	10	1	1	8	14	76	3
West Germany	10	1	0	9	19	82	2

41st WORLD CHAMPIONSHIP
April 5-20, 1974
Helsinki, Finland

FINAL PLACING

1. Soviet Union	4. Finland
2. Czechoslovakia	5. Poland
3. Sweden	6. East Germany

FINAL STANDINGS

	GP	W	T	L	GF	GA	P
Soviet Union	10	9	0	1	64	18	18
Czechoslovakia	10	7	0	3	57	20	14
Sweden	10	5	1	4	38	24	11
Finland	10	4	2	4	34	39	10
Poland	10	1	2	7	22	64	4
East Germany	10	1	1	8	21	71	3

42nd WORLD CHAMPIONSHIP
April 3-19, 1975
Munich/Düsseldorf, West Germany

FINAL PLACING

1. Soviet Union	4. Finland
2. Czechoslovakia	5. Poland
3. Sweden	6. United States

FINAL STANDINGS

	GP	W	T	L	GF	GA	P
Soviet Union	10	10	0	0	90	23	20
Czechoslovakia	10	8	0	2	55	19	16
Sweden	10	5	0	5	51	34	10
Finland	10	5	0	5	36	34	10
Poland	10	2	0	8	18	78	4
United States	10	0	0	10	22	84	0

12ᵗʰ OLYMPIC WINTER GAMES
February 5-14, 1976
Innsbruck, Austria

FINAL PLACING

1. Soviet Union
2. Czechoslovakia
3. West Germany
4. Finland
5. United States
6. Poland
7. Romania
8. Austria
9. Japan
10. Yugoslavia
11. Switzerland
11. Norway
13. Bulgaria

FINAL STANDINGS

	GP	W	T	L	GF	GA	P
Soviet Union	5	5	0	0	40	11	10
Czechoslovakia	5	3	0	2	24	10	6
West Germany	5	2	0	3	21	24	4
Finland	5	2	0	3	19	18	4
United States	5	2	0	3	15	21	4
Poland	5	1	0	4	9	44	2

43ʳᵈ WORLD CHAMPIONSHIP
April 8-25, 1976
Katowice, Poland

FINAL PLACING

1. Czechoslovakia
2. Soviet Union
3. Sweden
4. United States
5. Finland
6. West Germany
7. Poland
8. East Germany

FINAL STANDINGS

	GP	W	T	L	GF	GA	P
Czechoslovakia	7	7	0	0	54	7	14
Soviet Union	7	5	0	2	37	15	10
Sweden	7	4	0	3	22	18	8
United States	7	3	1	3	19	23	7
Poland	7	2	1	4	21	36	5
West Germany	7	2	0	5	19	35	4
Finland	7	1	2	4	17	29	4
East Germany	7	2	0	5	11	37	4

Relegation Round

	GP	W	T	L	GF	GA	P
Finland	10	2	4	4	35	41	8
West Germany	10	3	2	5	26	41	8
Poland	10	3	2	5	32	47	8
East Germany	10	2	1	7	19	52	5

Medal Round

	GP	W	T	L	GF	GA	P
Czechoslovakia	10	9	1	0	67	14	19
Soviet Union	10	6	1	3	50	23	13
Sweden	10	6	0	4	36	29	12
United States	10	3	1	6	24	42	7

44ᵗʰ WORLD CHAMPIONSHIP
April 21-May 8, 1977
Vienna, Austria

FINAL PLACING

1. Czechoslovakia
2. Sweden
3. Soviet Union
4. Canada
5. Finland
6. United States
7. West Germany
8. Romania

FINAL STANDINGS
Preliminary Round

	GP	W	T	L	GF	GA	P
Sweden	7	6	0	1	39	9	12
Soviet Union	7	6	0	1	65	16	12
Czechoslovakia	7	5	1	1	46	20	11
Canada	7	4	1	2	31	25	9
Finland	7	3	0	4	22	37	6
United States	7	1	1	5	18	35	3
West Germany	7	1	1	5	17	45	3
Romania	7	0	0	7	12	63	0

Relegation Round

	GP	W	T	L	GF	GA	P
Finland	10	5	0	5	45	43	10
United States	10	3	1	6	29	43	7
West Germany	10	2	1	7	23	58	5
Romania	10	1	0	9	20	84	2

Medal Round

	GP	W	T	L	GF	GA	P
Czechoslovakia	10	7	1	2	54	32	15
Sweden	10	7	0	3	43	19	14
Soviet Union	10	7	0	3	77	24	14
Canada	10	6	1	3	47	35	13

45ᵗʰ WORLD CHAMPIONSHIP
April 26-May 14, 1978
Prague, Czechoslovakia

FINAL PLACING

1. Soviet Union
2. Czechoslovakia
3. Canada
4. Sweden
5. West Germany
6. United States
7. Finland
8. East Germany

FINAL STANDINGS
Preliminary Round

	GP	W	T	L	GF	GA	P
Czechoslovakia	7	7	0	0	44	15	14
Soviet Union	7	6	0	1	46	23	12
Canada	7	4	0	3	32	26	8
Sweden	7	4	0	3	35	21	8
West Germany	7	2	1	4	23	35	5
United States	7	1	1	5	25	42	3
Finland	7	1	1	5	23	34	3
E.Germany	7	1	1	5	13	45	3

Relegation Round

	GP	W	T	L	GF	GA	P
West Germany	10	3	3	4	35	43	9
United States	10	2	2	6	38	58	6
Finland	10	2	2	6	37	44	6
East Germany	10	1	3	6	20	57	5

Medal Round

	GP	W	T	L	GF	GA	P
Soviet Union	10	9	0	1	61	26	18
Czechoslovakia	10	9	0	1	54	21	18
Canada	10	5	0	5	38	36	10
Sweden	10	4	0	6	39	37	8

46ᵗʰ WORLD CHAMPIONSHIP
April 14-27, 1979
Moscow, Soviet Union

FINAL PLACING

1. Soviet Union
2. Czechoslovakia
3. Sweden
4. Canada
5. Finland
6. West Germany
7. United States
8. Poland

FINAL STANDINGS
Group A

	GP	W	T	L	GF	GA	P
Soviet Union	3	3	0	0	19	5	6
Sweden	3	2	0	1	16	17	4
West Germany	3	0	1	2	8	13	1
Poland	3	0	1	2	8	16	1

Group B

	GP	W	T	L	GF	GA	P
Czechoslovakia	3	2	1	0	11	3	5
Canada	3	2	0	1	12	11	4
United States	3	0	2	1	6	9	2
Finland	3	0	1	2	5	11	1

Consolation Round

	GP	W	T	L	GF	GA	P
Finland	6	4	1	1	23	17	9
West Germany	6	3	1	2	27	21	7
United States	6	2	2	2	22	20	6
Poland	6	0	2	4	15	29	2

Final Group

	GP	W	T	L	GF	GA	P
Soviet Union	6	6	0	0	51	12	12
Czechoslovakia	6	3	1	2	25	30	7
Sweden	6	1	1	4	20	38	3
Canada	6	1	0	5	20	36	2

13ᵗʰ OLYMPIC WINTER GAMES
February 13-24, 1980
Lake Placid, United States

FINAL PLACING

1. United States
2. Soviet Union
3. Sweden
4. Finland
5. Czechoslovakia
6. Canada
7. Poland
8. Romania
9. Netherlands
9. Norway
11. West Germany
11. Yugoslavia
13. Japan

FINAL STANDINGS
Red Division

	GP	W	T	L	GF	GA	P
Soviet Union	5	5	0	0	51	11	10
Finland	5	3	0	2	26	18	6
Canada	5	3	0	2	28	12	6
Poland	5	2	0	3	15	23	4
Netherlands	5	1	1	3	16	43	3
Japan	5	0	1	4	7	36	1

Blue Division

	GP	W	T	L	GF	GA	P
Sweden	5	4	1	0	26	7	9
United States	5	4	1	0	25	10	9
Czechoslovakia	5	3	0	2	34	16	6
Romania	5	1	1	3	13	29	3
West Germany	5	1	0	4	21	30	2
Norway	5	0	1	4	9	36	1

Medal Round

	GP	W	T	L	GF	GA	P
United States	2	2	0	0	8	5	5
Soviet Union	2	1	0	1	12	6	4
Sweden	2	0	1	1	5	12	1
Finland	2	0	1	1	5	7	1

47th WORLD CHAMPIONSHIP
April 12-26, 1981
Gothenburg/Stockholm, Sweden

FINAL PLACING

1. Soviet Union
2. Sweden
3. Czechoslovakia
4. Canada
5. United States
6. Finland
7. West Germany
8. Netherlands

FINAL STANDINGS

Group A

	GP	W	T	L	GF	GA	P
Soviet Union	3	3	0	0	25	4	6
Canada	3	2	0	1	14	12	4
Finland	3	1	0	2	16	14	2
Netherlands	3	0	0	3	5	30	0

Group B

	GP	W	T	L	GF	GA	P
Czechoslovakia	3	2	1	0	20	7	5
Sweden	3	2	1	0	11	7	5
United States	3	1	0	2	14	21	2
West Germany	3	0	0	3	10	20	0

Relegation Round

	GP	W	T	L	GF	GA	P
United States	6	4	1	1	35	28	9
Finland	6	3	2	1	33	21	8
West Germany	6	3	1	2	40	30	7
Holland	6	0	0	6	22	51	0

Final Round

	GP	W	T	L	GF	GA	P
Soviet Union	6	4	2	0	38	12	10
Sweden	6	3	1	2	16	26	7
Czechoslovakia	6	2	2	2	20	22	6
Canada	6	0	1	5	16	30	1

48th WORLD CHAMPIONSHIP
April 15-29, 1982
Helsinki/Tampere, Finland

FINAL PLACING

1. Soviet Union
2. Czechoslovakia
3. Canada
4. Sweden
5. Finland
6. West Germany
7. Italy
8. United States

FINAL STANDINGS

Preliminary Round

	GP	W	T	L	GF	GA	P
Soviet Union	7	7	0	0	48	16	14
Czechoslovakia	7	4	1	2	33	14	9
Sweden	7	3	3	1	24	22	9
Canada	7	3	2	2	32	22	8
Finland	7	3	1	3	21	31	7
West Germany	7	2	1	4	19	30	5
Italy	7	1	1	5	20	44	3
United States	7	0	1	6	21	39	1

Medal Round

	GP	W	T	L	GF	GA	P
Soviet Union	10	9	1	0	58	20	19
Czechoslovakia	10	5	2	3	38	20	12
Canada	10	5	2	3	46	30	12
Sweden	10	3	3	4	26	35	9

49th WORLD CHAMPIONSHIP
April 16-May 2, 1983
Munich/Dortmund/Düsseldorf, West Germany

FINAL PLACING

1. Soviet Union
2. Czechoslovakia
3. Canada
4. Sweden
5. East Germany
6. West Germany
7. Finland
8. Italy

FINAL STANDINGS

Preliminary Round

	GP	W	T	L	GF	GA	P
Soviet Union	7	7	0	0	40	4	14
Canada	7	5	0	2	26	16	10
Czechoslovakia	7	4	1	2	30	15	9
Sweden	7	4	1	2	23	20	9
West Germany	7	3	1	3	17	23	7
East Germany	7	2	0	5	19	28	4
Finland	7	1	1	5	20	28	3
Italy	7	0	0	7	5	46	0

Relegation Round

	GP	W	T	L	GF	GA	P
East Germany	10	5	1	4	31	34	11
West Germany	10	3	0	7	29	40	6
Finland	10	2	2	6	30	40	6
Italy	10	1	1	8	16	56	3

Medal Round

	GP	W	T	L	GF	GA	P
Soviet Union	3	2	1	0	13	3	5
Czechoslovakia	3	2	1	0	10	6	5
Canada	3	1	0	2	9	14	2
Sweden	3	0	0	3	2	11	0

14th OLYMPIC WINTER GAMES
February 7-19, 1984
Sarajevo, Yugoslavia

FINAL PLACING

1. Soviet Union
2. Czechoslovakia
3. Sweden
4. Canada
5. West Germany
6. Finland
7. United States
8. Poland
9. Italy
10. Norway
11. Austria
11. Yugoslavia

FINAL STANDINGS

Group A

	GP	W	T	L	GF	GA	P
Soviet Union	5	5	0	0	42	5	10
Sweden	5	3	1	1	24	15	7
West Germany	5	3	1	1	27	17	7
Poland	5	1	0	4	16	37	2
Italy	5	1	0	4	15	21	2
Yugoslavia	5	1	0	4	8	37	2

Group B

	GP	W	T	L	GF	GA	P
Czechoslovakia	5	5	0	0	38	7	10
Canada	5	4	0	1	24	10	8
Finland	5	2	1	2	27	19	5
United States	5	1	2	2	16	17	4
Austria	5	1	0	4	13	37	2
Norway	5	0	1	4	15	43	1

Medal Round

	GP	W	L	T	GF	GA	P
Soviet Union	3	3	0	0	16	1	6
Czechoslovakia	3	2	1	0	6	2	4
Sweden	3	1	2	0	3	12	2
Canada	3	0	3	0	0	10	0

50th WORLD CHAMPIONSHIP
April 17-May 3, 1985
Prague, Czechoslovakia

FINAL PLACING

1. Czechoslovakia
2. Canada
3. Soviet Union
4. United States
5. Finland
6. Sweden
7. West Germany
8. East Germany

FINAL STANDINGS

Preliminary Round

	GP	W	T	L	GF	GA	P
Soviet Union	7	7	0	0	52	8	14
United States	7	4	1	2	24	34	9
Canada	7	4	1	2	33	23	9
Czechoslovakia	7	4	1	2	30	16	9
Finland	7	2	2	3	23	25	6
Sweden	7	2	0	5	24	30	4
West Germany	7	1	1	5	17	31	3
East Germany	7	0	2	5	11	47	2

Relegation Round

	GP	W	T	L	GF	GA	P
Finland	10	4	2	4	39	33	10
Sweden	10	4	0	6	37	40	8
West Germany	10	3	1	6	28	41	7
East Germany	10	0	2	8	16	64	2

Medal Round

	GP	W	T	L	GF	GA	P
Czechoslovakia	3	3	0	0	18	6	6
Canada	3	2	0	1	9	8	4
Soviet Union	3	1	0	2	12	8	2
United States	3	0	0	3	7	24	0

51st WORLD CHAMPIONSHIP
April 12-28, 1986
Moscow, Soviet Union

FINAL PLACING

1. Soviet Union
2. Sweden
3. Canada
4. Finland
5. Czechoslovakia
6. United States
7. West Germany
8. Poland

FINAL STANDINGS

Preliminary Round

	GP	W	T	L	GF	GA	P
Soviet Union	7	7	0	0	32	9	14
Sweden	7	5	1	1	34	18	11
Finland	7	4	2	1	28	18	10
Canada	7	3	0	4	24	22	6
Czechoslovakia	7	2	1	4	17	17	5
United States	7	2	0	5	27	28	4
West Germany	7	2	0	5	17	39	4
Poland	7	1	0	6	15	43	2

Relegation Round

	GP	W	T	L	GF	GA	P
Czechoslovakia	10	5	1	4	38	21	11
United States	10	4	0	6	41	43	8
West Germany	10	2	1	7	23	52	5
Poland	10	1	1	8	26	63	3

Final Round

	GP	W	T	L	GF	GA	P
Soviet Union	3	3	0	0	18	6	6
Sweden	3	1	1	1	12	12	3
Canada	3	1	0	2	13	16	2
Finland	3	0	1	2	7	16	1

52nd WORLD CHAMPIONSHIP
April 17-May 3, 1987
Vienna, Austria

FINAL PLACING

1. Sweden	5. Finland
2. Soviet Union	6. West Germany
3. Czechoslovakia	7. United States
4. Canada	8. Switzerland

FINAL STANDINGS
Preliminary Round

	GP	W	T	L	GF	GA	P
Soviet Union	7	7	0	0	48	12	14
Czechoslovakia	7	5	1	1	24	17	11
Sweden	7	4	0	3	30	17	8
Canada	7	3	1	3	25	17	7
West Germany	7	3	0	4	18	28	6
Finland	7	3	0	4	17	24	6
United States	7	2	0	5	21	36	4
Switzerland	7	0	0	7	17	49	0

Relegation Round

	GP	W	T	L	GF	GA	P
Finland	10	5	1	4	32	34	11
West Germany	10	4	1	5	31	37	9
United States	10	4	0	6	36	49	8
Switzerland	10	0	0	10	26	71	0

Medal Round

	GP	W	T	L	GF	GA	P
Sweden	3	1	2	0	14	5	4
Soviet Union	3	1	2	0	4	3	4
Czechoslovakia	3	1	1	1	8	7	3
Canada	3	0	1	2	2	13	1

15th OLYMPIC WINTER GAMES
February 13-28, 1988
Calgary, Canada

FINAL PLACING

1. Soviet Union	7. United States
2. Finland	8. Switzerland
3. Sweden	9. Austria
4. Canada	10. Poland
5. West Germany	11. France
6. Czechoslovakia	12. Norway

FINAL STANDINGS
Group A

	GP	W	T	L	GF	GA	P
Finland	5	3	1	1	22	8	7
Sweden	5	2	3	0	23	10	7
Canada	5	3	1	1	17	12	7
Switzerland	5	3	0	2	19	10	6
Poland	5	0	1	4	9	13	1
France	5	1	0	4	10	47	0

Group B

	GP	W	T	L	GF	GA	P
Soviet Union	5	5	0	0	32	10	10
West Germany	5	4	0	1	19	12	8
Czechoslovakia	5	3	0	2	23	14	6
United States	5	2	0	3	27	27	4
Austria	5	0	1	4	12	29	1
Norway	5	0	1	4	11	32	1

Medal Round

	GP	W	T	L	GF	GA	P
Soviet Union	5	4	0	1	25	7	8
Finland	5	3	1	1	18	10	7
Sweden	5	2	2	1	15	16	6
Canada	5	2	1	2	17	14	5
West Germany	5	1	0	4	8	26	2
Czechoslovakia	5	1	0	0	12	22	2

53rd WORLD CHAMPIONSHIP
April 15-May 1, 1989
Stockholm/Södertalje, Sweden

FINAL PLACING

1. Soviet Union	5. Finland
2. Canada	6. United States
3. Czechoslovakia	7. West Germany
4. Sweden	8. Poland

FINAL STANDINGS
Preliminary Round

	GP	W	T	L	GF	GA	P
Soviet Union	7	7	0	0	36	12	14
Sweden	7	4	2	1	29	20	10
Canada	7	5	0	2	45	18	10
Czechoslovakia	7	3	2	2	33	15	8
Finland	7	2	1	4	22	25	5
United States	7	2	1	4	20	29	5
Poland	7	1	0	6	10	59	2
West Germany	7	0	2	5	17	34	2

Relegation Round

	GP	W	T	L	GF	GA	P
Finland	10	5	1	4	35	27	11
United States	10	4	1	5	37	40	9
West Germany	10	1	2	7	22	41	4
Poland	10	1	0	9	12	76	2

Medal Round

	GP	W	T	L	GF	GA	P
Soviet Union	3	3	0	0	11	4	6
Canada	3	2	0	1	12	11	4
Czechoslovakia	3	1	0	2	5	6	2
Sweden	3	0	0	3	5	12	0

54th WORLD CHAMPIONSHIP
April 16-May 2, 1990
Bern/Fribourg, Switzerland

FINAL PLACING

1. Soviet Union	5. United States
2. Sweden	6. Finland
3. Czechoslovakia	7. West Germany
4. Canada	8. Norway

FINAL STANDINGS
Preliminary Round

	GP	W	T	L	GF	GA	P
Canada	7	6	1	0	36	16	13
Sweden	7	6	0	1	29	11	12
Soviet Union	7	5	1	1	38	12	11
Czechoslovakia	7	4	0	3	28	18	8
United States	7	3	0	4	23	37	6
Finland	7	1	1	5	18	27	3
Norway	7	1	1	5	19	45	3
West Germany	7	0	0	7	11	36	0

Relegation Round

	GP	W	T	L	GF	GA	P
United States	10	6	0	4	35	43	12
Finland	10	2	2	7	24	32	6
West Germany	10	1	1	8	19	42	3
Norway	10	1	1	8	21	61	3

Medal Round

	GP	W	T	L	GF	GA	P
Soviet Union	3	3	0	0	15	1	6
Sweden	3	1	1	1	11	12	3
Czechoslovakia	3	1	1	1	8	12	3
Canada	3	0	0	3	7	16	0

55th WORLD CHAMPIONSHIP
April 14-May 5, 1991
Helsinki/Turku/Tampere, Finland

FINAL PLACING

1. Sweden	5. Finland
2. Canada	6. Czechoslovakia
3. Soviet Union	7. Switzerland
4. United States	8. Germany

FINAL STANDINGS
Preliminary Round

	GP	W	T	L	GF	GA	P
Soviet Union	7	6	1	0	41	16	13
Sweden	7	3	4	0	30	21	10
Canada	7	4	1	2	24	20	9
United States	7	3	2	2	23	28	8
Finland	7	3	1	3	22	15	7
Czechoslovakia	7	3	0	4	19	19	6
Switzerland	7	1	0	6	13	26	2
West Germany	7	0	1	6	13	40	1

Relegation Round

	GP	W	T	L	GF	GA	P
Finland	10	6	1	3	35	21	13
Czechoslovakia	10	4	0	6	28	27	8
Switzerland	10	2	1	7	22	38	5
West Germany	10	0	2	8	19	51	2

Medal Round

	GP	W	T	L	GF	GA	P
Sweden	3	2	1	0	13	8	5
Canada	3	1	2	0	15	10	4
Soviet Union	3	1	1	1	10	9	3
United States	3	0	0	3	12	23	0

16th OLYMPIC WINTER GAMES
February 8-23, 1992
Albertville, France

FINAL PLACING

1. Russia	7. Finland
2. Canada	8. France
3. Czechoslovakia	9. Norway
4. United States	10. Switzerland
5. Sweden	11. Poland
6. Germany	12. Italy

FINAL STANDINGS
Pool A

	GP	W	T	L	GF	GA	P
United States	5	4	1	0	18	7	9
Sweden	5	3	2	0	22	11	8
Finland	5	3	1	1	22	11	7
Germany	5	2	0	3	11	12	4
Italy	5	1	0	4	18	24	2
Poland	5	0	0	5	4	30	0

Pool B

	GP	W	T	L	GF	GA	P
Canada	5	4	0	1	28	9	8
Russia	5	4	0	1	32	10	8
Czechoslovakia	5	4	0	1	25	15	8
France	5	2	0	3	14	22	4
Switzerland	5	1	0	4	13	25	2
Norway	5	0	0	5	7	38	0

Quarter-finals
February 18	Canada 4	Germany 3 (OT/SO)
February 18	United States 4	France 1
February 19	Czechoslovakia 3	Sweden 1
February 19	Russia 6	Finland 1

Semi-finals
February 21	Canada 4	Czechoslovakia 2
February 21	Russia 5	United States 2

Bronze Medal Game
February 22	Czechoslovakia 6	United States 1

Gold Medal Game
February 23	Russia 3	Canada 1

56th WORLD CHAMPIONSHIP
April 28-May 10, 1992
Prague/Bratislava, Czechoslovakia

FINAL PLACING
1. Sweden
2. Finland
3. Czechoslovakia
4. Switzerland
5. Russia
6. Germany
7. United States
8. Canada
9. Italy
10. Norway
11. France
12. Poland

FINAL STANDINGS
Group A
	GP	W	T	L	GF	GA	P
Finland	5	5	0	0	32	8	10
Germany	5	4	0	1	30	14	8
United States	5	2	1	2	14	15	5
Sweden	5	1	2	2	14	12	4
Italy	5	1	1	3	10	18	3
Poland	5	0	0	5	8	41	0

Group B
	GP	W	T	L	GF	GA	P
Russia	5	4	1	0	23	10	9
Czechoslovakia	5	4	0	1	18	7	8
Switzerland	5	2	2	1	12	11	6
Canada	5	2	1	2	15	18	5
Norway	5	1	0	4	8	16	2
France	5	0	0	5	8	22	0

Quarter-finals
May 6	Finland 4	Canada 3
May 6	Sweden 2	Russia 0
May 7	Switzerland 3	Germany 1
May 7	Czechoslovakia 8	United States 1

Semi-finals
May 9	Finland 3	Czechoslovakia 2 (OT/SO)
May 9	Sweden 4	Switzerland 1

Bronze Medal Game
May 10	Czechoslovakia 5	Switzerland 2

Gold Medal Game
May 10	Sweden 5	Finland 2

EISHOCKEY WM 93
München · Dortmund
18. April · 2. Mai '93

57th WORLD CHAMPIONSHIP
April 18-May 2, 1993
Munich/Dortmund, Germany

FINAL PLACING
1. Russia
2. Sweden
3. Czech Republic
4. Canada
5. Germany
6. United States
7. Finland
8. Italy
9. Austria
10. France
11. Norway
12. Switzerland

FINAL STANDINGS
Group A
	GP	W	T	L	GF	GA	P
Czech Republic	5	4	1	0	17	4	9
Germany	5	4	0	1	20	12	8
United States	5	2	2	1	14	10	6
Finland	5	2	1	2	7	7	5
Norway	5	1	0	4	6	17	2
France	5	0	0	5	10	24	0

Group B
	GP	W	T	L	GF	GA	P
Canada	5	5	0	0	31	4	10
Sweden	5	3	0	2	17	14	6
Russia	5	2	1	2	15	12	5
Italy	5	1	2	2	8	20	4
Switzerland	5	2	0	3	11	14	4
Austria	5	0	1	4	4	22	1

Quarter-finals
April 27	Sweden 5	United States 2
April 27	Russia 5	Germany 1
April 28	Canada 5	Finland 1
April 28	Czech Republic 8	Italy 1

Semi-finals
April 30	Sweden 4	Czech Republic 3 (OT)
April 30	Russia 7	Canada 4

Bronze Medal Game
May 1	Czech Republic 5	Canada 1

Gold Medal Game
May 2	Russia 3	Sweden 1

17th OLYMPIC WINTER GAMES
February 13-27, 1994
Lillehammer, Norway

FINAL PLACING
1. Sweden
2. Canada
3. Finland
4. Russia
5. Czech Republic
6. Slovakia
7. Germany
8. United States
9. Italy
10. France
11. Norway
12. Austria

FINAL STANDINGS
Pool A
	GP	W	T	L	GF	GA	P
Finland	5	5	0	0	25	4	10
Germany	5	3	0	2	11	14	6
Czech Republic	5	3	0	2	16	11	6
Russia	5	3	0	2	20	14	6
Austria	5	1	0	4	13	28	2
Norway	5	0	0	5	5	19	0

Pool B
	GP	W	T	L	GF	GA	P
Slovakia	5	3	2	0	26	14	8
Canada	5	3	1	1	17	11	7
Sweden	5	3	1	1	23	13	7
United States	5	1	3	1	21	17	5
Italy	5	1	0	4	15	31	2
France	5	0	1	4	11	27	1

Quarter-finals
February 23	Canada 3	Czech Republic 2 (OT)
February 23	Sweden 3	Germany 0
February 23	Russia 3	Slovakia 2 (OT)
February 23	Finland 6	United States 1

Semi-finals
February 25	Canada 5	Finland 3
February 25	Sweden 4	Russia 3

Bronze Medal Game
February 26	Finland 4	Russia 0

Gold Medal Game
February 27	Sweden 3	Canada 2 (OT/SO)

58th WORLD CHAMPIONSHIP
April 25-May 8, 1994
Bolzano/Canazei/Milan, Italy

FINAL PLACING
1. Canada
2. Finland
3. Sweden
4. United States
5. Russia
6. Italy
7. Czech Republic
8. Austria
9. Germany
10. France
11. Norway
12. Great Britain

FINAL STANDINGS
Group A
	GP	W	T	L	GF	GA	P
Canada	5	5	0	0	24	7	10
Russia	5	4	0	1	30	7	8
Italy	5	3	0	2	17	15	6
Austria	5	1	1	3	15	15	3
Germany	5	1	1	3	9	14	3
Great Britain	5	0	0	5	7	44	0

Group B
	GP	W	T	L	GF	GA	P
Finland	5	4	1	0	29	11	9
Sweden	5	3	1	1	22	11	7
United States	5	3	0	2	21	19	6
Czech Republic	5	1	2	2	15	17	4
France	5	1	0	4	8	25	2
Norway	5	0	2	3	9	21	2

Quarter-finals
May 4	United States 3	Russia 1
May 4	Sweden 7	Italy 2
May 5	Canada 3	Czech Republic 2
May 5	Finland 10	Austria 0

Semi-finals
May 7	Canada 6	Sweden 0
May 7	Finland 8	United States 0

Bronze Medal Game
May 8   Sweden 7   United States 2

Gold Medal Game
May 8   Canada 2   Finland 1 (OT/SO)

59th WORLD CHAMPIONSHIP
April 23-May 7, 1995
Stockholm/Gavle, Sweden

FINAL PLACING
1. Finland	7. Italy
2. Sweden	8. France
3. Canada	9. Germany
4. Czech Republic	10. Norway
5. Russia	11. Austria
6. United States	12. Switzerland

FINAL STANDINGS
Group A

	GP	W	T	L	GF	GA	P
Russia	5	5	0	0	26	10	10
Italy	5	3	1	1	14	11	7
France	5	3	0	2	14	11	6
Canada	5	2	1	2	17	16	5
Germany	5	1	0	4	11	20	2
Switzerland	5	0	0	5	10	24	0

Group B

	GP	W	T	L	GF	GA	P
United States	5	3	2	0	17	11	8
Finland	5	3	1	1	22	14	7
Sweden	5	3	1	1	17	9	7
Czech Republic	5	3	0	2	14	9	6
Norway	5	1	0	4	9	18	2
Austria	5	0	0	5	9	27	0

Quarter-finals
May 2	Sweden 7	Italy 0
May 2	Finland 5	France 0
May 3	Czech Republic 2	Russia 0
May 3	Canada 4	United States 1

Semi-finals
May 5	Sweden 3	Canada 2 (OT)
May 5	Finland 3	Czech Republic 0

Bronze Medal Game
May 6   Canada 4   Czech Republic 1

Gold Medal Game
May 7   Finland 4   Sweden 1

60th WORLD CHAMPIONSHIP
April 21-May 5, 1996
Vienna, Austria

FINAL PLACING
1. Czech Republic	7. Italy
2. Canada	8. Germany
3. United States	9. Norway
4. Russia	10. Slovakia
5. Finland	11. France
6. Sweden	12. Austria

FINAL STANDINGS
Group A

	GP	W	T	L	GF	GA	P
Russia	5	5	0	0	23	8	10
United States	5	3	0	2	15	14	6
Canada	5	2	1	2	17	15	5
Germany	5	2	0	3	12	11	4
Slovakia	5	1	1	3	13	16	3
Austria	5	1	0	4	3	19	2

Group B

	GP	W	T	L	GF	GA	P
Czech Republic	5	4	1	0	27	12	9
Finland	5	2	2	1	23	15	6
Sweden	5	2	2	1	14	12	6
Italy	5	2	1	2	20	26	5
Norway	5	1	2	2	6	11	4
France	5	0	0	5	12	26	0

Quarter-finals
April 30	United States 3	Sweden 2
April 30	Canada 3	Finland 1
May 1	Russia 5	Italy 2
May 1	Czech Republic 6	Germany 1

Semi-finals
May 3	Czech Republic 5	United States 0
May 3	Canada 3	Russia 2 (SO)

Bronze Medal Game
May 4   United States 4   Russia 3 (OT)

Gold Medal Game
May 5   Czech Republic 4   Canada 2

61st WORLD CHAMPIONSHIP
April 26-May 14, 1997
Helsinki/Tampere/Turku, Finland

FINAL PLACING
1. Canada	7. Latvia
2. Sweden	8. Italy
3. Czech Republic	9. Slovakia
4. Russia	10. France
5. Finland	11. Germany
6. United States	12. Norway

FINAL STANDINGS
Group A

	GP	W	T	L	GF	GA	P
Czech Republic	5	4	0	1	18	9	8
Finland	5	4	0	1	25	9	8
Russia	5	3	1	1	19	16	7
Slovakia	5	1	1	3	10	14	3
France	5	1	0	4	13	26	2
Germany	5	1	0	4	4	15	2

Group B

	GP	W	T	L	GF	GA	P
Sweden	5	4	1	0	20	8	9
Canada	5	3	1	1	23	11	7
United States	5	3	0	2	14	15	6
Latvia	5	1	2	2	18	17	4
Italy	5	1	1	3	12	21	3
Norway	5	0	1	4	7	22	1

Relegation Round

	GP	W	T	L	GF	GA	P
Latvia	5	4	0	1	29	14	8
Italy	5	3	1	1	23	13	7
Slovakia	5	3	0	2	15	13	6
France	5	2	0	3	12	23	4
Germany	5	2	0	3	8	17	4
Norway	5	0	1	4	11	18	1

Final Round

	GP	W	T	L	GF	GA	P
Sweden	5	4	0	1	17	9	8
Canada	5	3	0	2	13	14	6
Russia	5	2	1	2	13	13	5
Czech Republic	5	2	0	3	12	12	4
Finland	5	2	0	3	12	12	4
United States	5	1	1	3	7	14	3

Bronze Medal Game
May 10   Czech Republic 4   Russia 3

Gold Medal Games (best-of-three)
May 11	Sweden 3	Canada 2
May 13	Canada 3	Sweden 1
May 14	Canada 2	Sweden 1

18th OLYMPIC WINTER GAMES
February 7-22, 1998
Nagano, Japan

FINAL PLACING
1. Czech Republic	8. Kazakstan
2. Russia	9. Germany
3. Finland	10. Slovakia
4. Canada	11. France
5. Sweden	12. Italy
6. United States	13. Japan
7. Belarus	14. Austria

FINAL STANDINGS
Preliminary Round
Group A

	GP	W	T	L	GF	GA	P
Kazakhstan	3	2	1	0	14	11	5
Slovakia	3	1	1	1	9	9	3
Italy	3	1	0	2	11	11	2
Austria	3	0	2	1	9	12	2

Group B

	GP	W	T	L	GF	GA	P
Belarus	3	2	1	0	14	4	5
Germany	3	2	0	1	7	9	4
France	3	1	0	2	5	8	2
Japan	3	0	1	2	5	10	1

Final Round
Group C

	GP	W	T	L	GF	GA	P
Russia	3	3	0	0	15	6	6
Czech Republic	3	2	0	1	12	4	4
Finland	3	1	0	2	11	9	2
Kazakhstan	3	0	0	3	6	25	0

Group D

	GP	W	T	L	GF	GA	P
Canada	3	3	0	0	12	3	6
Sweden	3	2	0	1	11	7	4
United States	3	1	0	2	8	10	2
Belarus	3	0	0	3	4	15	0

Quarter-finals
February 18	Czech Republic 4	United States 1
February 18	Russia 4	Belarus 1
February 18	Canada 4	Kazakhstan 1
February 18	Finland 2	Sweden 1

Semi-finals
February 20	Czech Republic 2	Canada 1 (OT/SO)
	Russia 7	Finland 4

Bronze Medal Game

| February 21 | Finland 3 | Canada 2 |

Gold Medal Game

| February 22 | Czech Republic 1 | Russia 0 |

62ⁿᵈ WORLD CHAMPIONSHIP
May 1-17, 1998
Zurich/Basel, Switzerland

FINAL PLACING
1. Sweden
2. Finland
3. Czech Republic
4. Switzerland
5. Russia
6. Canada
7. Slovakia
8. Belarus
9. Latvia
10. Italy
11. Germany
12. United States
13. France
14. Japan
15. Austria
16. Kazakhstan

FINAL STANDINGS
Group A

	GP	W	T	L	GF	GA	P
Czech Republic	3	3	0	0	20	5	6
Belarus	3	2	0	1	12	10	4
Germany	3	1	0	2	8	13	2
Japan	3	0	0	3	7	19	0

Group B

	GP	W	T	L	GF	GA	P
Canada	3	2	1	0	12	5	5
Slovakia	3	2	1	0	9	4	5
Italy	3	1	0	2	8	8	2
Austria	3	0	0	3	3	15	0

Group C

	GP	W	T	L	GF	GA	P
Sweden	3	3	0	0	16	4	6
Switzerland	3	1	0	2	9	10	2
United States	3	1	0	2	7	11	2
France	3	1	0	2	5	12	2

Group D

	GP	W	T	L	GF	GA	P
Russia	3	3	0	0	19	11	6
Finland	3	2	0	1	12	4	4
Latvia	3	1	0	2	12	15	2
Kazakhstan	3	0	0	3	6	19	0

Qualifying Round
Group E

	GP	W	T	L	GF	GA	P
Sweden	3	3	0	0	16	2	6
Finland	3	1	1	1	8	6	3
Canada	3	1	1	1	10	12	3
Belarus	3	0	0	3	5	13	0

Group F

	GP	W	T	L	GF	GA	P
CzechRepublic	3	2	1	0	6	3	5
Switzerland	3	1	1	1	6	6	3
Russia	3	1	1	1	10	7	3
Slovakia	3	0	1	2	2	8	1

Placement Round
Group G

	GP	W	T	L	GF	GA	P
Latvia	3	2	1	0	9	3	5
Italy	3	1	2	0	9	5	4
Germany	3	0	2	1	5	10	2
United States	3	0	1	2	3	8	1

Semi-finals (best-of-two)

May 12	Sweden 4	Switzerland 1
May 12	Finland 4	Czech Republic 1
May 14	Sweden 7	Switzerland 2
May 14	Finland 2	Czech Republic 2

Bronze Medal Game

| May 15 | Czech Republic 4 | Switzerland 0 |

Gold Medal Games (best-of-two)

| May 16 | Sweden 1 | Finland 0 |
| May 17 | Sweden 0 | Finland 0 |

ISHOCKEY VM '99
LILLEHAMMER - HAMAR - OSLO
1. Mai - 16. Mai

63ʳᵈ WORLD CHAMPIONSHIP
May 1-16, 1999
Oslo/Hamar/Lillehammer, Norway

FINAL PLACING
1. Czech Republic
2. Finland
3. Sweden
4. Canada
5. Russia
6. United States
7. Slovakia
8. Switzerland
9. Belarus
10. Austria
11. Latvia
12. Norway
13. Italy
14. Ukraine
15. France
16. Japan

FINAL STANDINGS
Group A

	GP	W	T	L	GF	GA	P
Canada	3	3	0	0	12	6	6
Slovakia	3	2	0	1	17	9	4
Norway	3	1	0	2	9	14	2
Italy	3	0	0	3	8	17	0

Group B

	GP	W	T	L	GF	GA	P
Sweden	3	3	0	0	14	5	6
Switzerland	3	2	0	1	12	9	4
Latvia	3	1	0	2	14	14	2
France	3	0	0	3	6	18	0

Group C

	GP	W	T	L	GF	GA	P
Czech Republic	3	3	0	0	23	5	6
United States	3	2	0	1	15	7	4
Austria	3	1	0	2	6	14	2
Japan	3	0	0	3	5	23	0

Group D

	GP	W	T	L	GF	GA	P
Finland	3	2	1	0	10	5	5
Russia	3	1	2	0	9	6	4
Belarus	3	1	1	1	9	7	3
Ukraine	3	0	0	3	3	13	0

Relegation Round
Group G

	GP	W	T	L	GF	GA	P
Belarus	3	3	0	0	7	3	6
Austria	3	2	0	1	10	5	4
Latvia	3	1	0	2	10	8	2
Norway	3	0	0	3	1	12	0

Final Round
Group E

	GP	W	T	L	GF	GA	P
Finland	3	3	0	0	13	6	6
Canada	3	2	0	1	14	7	4
United States	3	1	0	2	7	8	2
Switzerland	3	0	0	3	3	16	0

Group F

	GP	W	T	L	GF	GA	P
Czech Republic	3	2	0	1	11	8	4
Sweden	3	2	0	1	6	4	4
Russia	3	1	1	1	9	7	3
Slovakia	3	0	1	2	5	12	1

Semi-finals (best-of-two)

May 12	Canada 2	Czech Republic 1
May 13	Czech Republic 6*	Canada 4 (SO)
May 12	Finland 3	Sweden 1
May 13	Sweden 2**	Finland 1 (OT)

*Czech Republic won game two, forcing overtime. No goal was scored, resulting in a shootout which the Czechs won.
**Sweden won game two to force overtime, which Finland won

Bronze Medal Game

| May 15 | Sweden 3 | Canada 2 |

Gold Medal Games (best-of-two)

| May 15 | Czech Republic 3 | Finland 1 |
| May 16 | Finland 4* | Czech Republic 1 (OT) |

*Finland won game two to force overtime, which Czech Republic won.

64ᵗʰ WORLD CHAMPIONSHIP
April 29-May 14, 2000
St. Petersburg, Russia

FINAL PLACING
1. Czech Republic
2. Slovakia
3. Finland
4. Canada
5. United States
6. Switzerland
7. Sweden
8. Latvia
9. Belarus
10. Norway
11. Russia
12. Italy
13. Austria
14. Ukraine
15. France
16. Japan

FINAL STANDINGS
Group A

	GP	W	T	L	GF	GA	P
Sweden	3	3	0	0	17	3	6
Latvia	3	2	0	1	9	7	4
Belarus	3	1	0	2	10	16	2
Ukraine	3	0	0	3	6	16	0

Group B

	GP	W	T	L	GF	GA	P
Slovakia	3	2	1	0	10	4	5
Finland	3	1	2	0	11	5	4
Italy	3	1	0	2	5	12	2
Austria	3	0	1	2	3	8	1

Group C

	GP	W	T	L	GF	GA	P
Czech Republic	3	3	0	0	12	4	6
Norway	3	2	0	1	13	7	4
Canada	3	1	0	2	10	6	2
Japan	3	0	0	3	3	21	0

Group D

	GP	W	T	L	GF	GA	P
United States	3	2	1	0	9	5	5
Switzerland	3	1	1	1	8	9	3
Russia	3	1	0	2	10	7	2
France	3	1	0	2	7	13	2

Relegation Round
Group G

	GP	W	T	L	GF	GA	P
Austria	3	2	1	0	11	8	5
Ukraine	3	2	0	1	9	5	4
France	3	1	1	1	12	8	3
Japan	3	0	0	3	5	16	0

Qualifying Round
Group E

	GP	W	T	L	GF	GA	P
United States	5	3	2	0	13	7	8
Switzerland	5	2	2	1	14	12	6
Sweden	5	2	1	2	16	11	5
Latvia	5	2	1	2	12	13	5
Belarus	5	2	0	3	9	17	4
Russia	5	1	0	4	8	12	2

Group F

	GP	W	T	L	GF	GA	P
Czech Republic	5	4	0	1	25	11	8
Finland	5	3	1	1	22	15	7
Canada	5	3	0	2	19	10	6
Slovakia	5	2	1	2	22	15	5
Norway	5	1	1	3	10	24	3
Italy	5	0	1	4	5	28	1

Quarter-finals

May 11	Canada 5	Switzerland 3
May 11	Finland 2	Sweden 1
May 11	Czech Republic 3	Latvia 1
May 11	Slovakia 4	United States 1

Semi-finals

May 12	Czech Republic 2	Canada 1
May 12	Slovakia 3	Finland 1

Bronze Medal Game

May 14	Finland 2	Canada 1

Gold Medal Game

May 14	Czech Republic 5	Slovakia 3

WM 2001 GERMANY
HANNOVER · COLOGNE · NUREMBERG

65th WORLD CHAMPIONSHIP
April 28-May 13, 2001
Hanover/Cologne/Nuremburg, Germany

FINAL PLACING

1. Czech Republic	9. Switzerland
2. Finland	10. Ukraine
3. Sweden	11. Austria
4. United States	12. Italy
5. Canada	13. Latvia
6. Russia	14. Belarus
7. Slovakia	15. Norway
8. Germany	16. Japan

FINAL STANDINGS
Group A

	GP	W	T	L	GF	GA	P
Czech Republic	3	2	1	0	10	4	5
Germany	3	1	1	1	5	5	3
Switzerland	3	1	0	2	7	8	2
Belarus	3	1	0	2	5	10	2

Group B

	GP	W	T	L	GF	GA	P
Finland	3	3	0	0	18	3	6
Slovakia	3	2	0	1	15	9	4
Austria	3	1	0	2	4	12	2
Japan	3	0	0	3	6	19	0

Group C

	GP	W	T	L	GF	GA	P
Sweden	3	2	1	0	12	4	5
United States	3	1	1	1	8	7	3
Ukraine	3	1	0	2	7	13	2
Latvia	3	1	0	2	6	9	2

Group D

	GP	W	T	L	GF	GA	P
Canada	3	3	0	0	13	2	6
Russia	3	2	0	1	12	5	4
Italy	3	0	1	2	5	14	1
Norway	3	0	1	2	4	13	1

Relegation Round
Group G

	GP	W	T	L	GF	GA	P
Latvia	3	2	1	0	13	4	5
Belarus	3	2	1	0	9	5	5
Norway	3	0	1	2	5	9	1
Japan	3	0	1	2	6	15	1

Qualifying Round
Group E

	GP	W	T	L	GF	GA	P
Czech Republic	5	4	1	0	24	8	9
Canada	5	3	1	1	19	11	7
Russia	5	3	0	2	16	11	6
Germany	5	1	2	2	10	12	4
Switzerland	5	1	0	4	13	15	2
Italy	5	1	0	4	5	30	2

Group F

	GP	W	T	L	GF	GA	P
Finland	5	4	0	1	23	12	8
Sweden	5	3	1	1	25	8	7
United States	5	3	1	1	15	10	7
Slovakia	5	2	0	3	12	12	4
Ukraine	5	1	0	4	7	21	2
Austria	5	1	0	4	4	23	2

Quarter-finals

May 10	United States 4	Canada 3 (OT)
May 10	Czech Republic 2	Slovakia 0
May 10	Finland 4	Germany 1
May 10	Sweden 4	Russia 3 (OT)

Semi-finals

May 12	Czech Republic 3	Sweden 2 (OT/SO)
May 12	Finland 3	United States 1

Bronze Medal Game

May 13	Sweden 3	United States 2

Gold Medal Game

May 13	Czech Republic 3	Finland 2 (OT)

19th OLYMPIC WINTER GAMES
February 9-24, 2002
Salt Lake City, United States

FINAL PLACING

1. Canada	8. Germany
2. United States	9. Latvia
3. Russia	10. Ukraine
4. Belarus	11. Switzerland
5. Sweden	12. Austria
6. Finland	13. Slovakia
7. Czech Republic	14. France

FINAL STANDINGS
Preliminary Round
Group A

	GP	W	T	L	GF	GA	P
Germany	3	3	0	0	10	3	6
Latvia	3	1	1	1	11	12	3
Austria	3	1	0	2	7	9	2
Slovakia	3	0	1	2	8	12	1

Group B

	GP	W	T	L	GF	GA	P
Belarus	3	2	1	0	5	3	4
Ukraine	3	2	0	1	9	5	4
Switzerland	3	1	1	1	7	9	3
France	3	0	1	2	6	10	1

Final Round
Group C

	GP	W	T	L	GF	GA	P
Sweden	3	3	0	0	14	4	6
Czech Republic	3	1	1	1	12	7	3
Canada	3	1	1	1	8	10	3
Germany	3	0	0	3	5	18	0

Group D

	GP	W	T	L	GF	GA	P
Canada	3	2	1	0	16	3	5
Sweden	3	2	0	1	11	8	4
United States	3	1	1	1	9	9	3
Belarus	3	0	0	3	6	22	0

Quarter-finals

February 20	Belarus 4	Sweden 3
February 20	Russia 1	Czech Republic 0
February 20	United States 5	Germany 0
February 20	Canada 2	Finland 1

Semi-finals

February 22	Canada 7	Belarus 1
February 22	United States 3	Russia 2

Bronze Medal Game

February 23	Russia 7	Belarus 2

Gold Medal Game

February 24	Canada 5	United States 2

66th WORLD CHAMPIONSHIP
April 26-May 11, 2002
Gothenburg/Karlstad/Jonkoping, Sweden

FINAL PLACING

1. Slovakia	9. Ukraine
2. Russia	10. Switzerland
3. Sweden	11. Latvia
4. Finland	12. Austria
5. Czech Republic	13. Slovenia
6. Canada	14. Poland
7. United States	15. Italy
8. Germany	16. Japan

FINAL STANDINGS

Group A

	GP	W	T	L	GF	GA	P
Czech Republic	3	3	0	0	17	8	6
Germany	3	2	0	1	17	9	4
Switzerland	3	1	0	2	5	9	2
Japan	3	0	0	3	6	19	0

Group B

	GP	W	T	L	GF	GA	P
Finland	3	3	0	0	14	1	6
Slovakia	3	2	0	1	13	7	4
Ukraine	3	1	0	2	7	8	2
Poland	3	0	0	3	0	18	0

Group C

	GP	W	T	L	GF	GA	P
Sweden	3	3	0	0	15	5	6
Russia	3	2	0	1	14	6	4
Austria	3	1	0	2	11	14	2
Slovenia	3	0	0	3	6	21	0

Group D

	GP	W	T	L	GF	GA	P
Canada	3	3	0	0	11	2	6
United States	3	2	0	1	9	6	4
Latvia	3	1	0	2	7	8	2
Italy	3	0	0	3	3	14	0

Qualification Round
Group E

	GP	W	T	L	GF	GA	P
Czech Republic	5	5	0	0	25	11	10
Canada	5	4	0	1	13	10	8
United States	5	2	1	2	13	11	5
Germany	5	2	1	2	14	14	5
Switzerland	5	1	0	4	8	18	2
Latvia	5	0	0	5	10	19	0

Group F

	GP	W	T	L	GF	GA	P
Sweden	5	4	0	1	19	7	8
Finland	5	4	0	1	12	6	8
Slovakia	5	4	0	1	20	15	8
Russia	5	1	1	3	13	15	3
Ukraine	5	1	1	3	10	20	3
Austria	5	0	0	5	12	23	0

Relegation Round
Group G

	GP	W	T	L	GF	GA	P
Slovenia	3	3	0	0	12	5	6
Poland	3	2	0	1	12	7	4
Italy	3	1	0	2	7	11	2
Japan	3	0	0	3	7	15	0

Quarter-finals
May 7	Slovakia 3	Canada 2
May 7	Sweden 6	Germany 2
May 7	Russia 3	Czech Republic 1
May 7	Finland 3	United States 1

Semi-finals
May 9	Russia 3	Finland 2 (OT/SO)
May 9	Slovakia 3	Sweden 2 (OT/SO)

Bronze Medal Game
May 10	Sweden 5	Finland 3

Gold Medal Game
May 11	Slovakia 4	Russia 3

67th WORLD CHAMPIONSHIP
April 27-May 11, 2003
Helsinki/Tampere/Turku, Finland

FINAL PLACING
1. Canada
2. Sweden
3. Slovakia
4. Czech Republic
5. Finland
6. Germany
7. Russia
8. Switzerland
9. Latvia
10. Austria
11. Denmark
12. Ukraine
13. United States
14. Belarus
15. Slovenia
16. Japan

FINAL STANDINGS
Group A

	GP	W	T	L	GF	GA	P
Slovakia	3	3	0	0	22	5	6
Germany	3	2	0	1	9	8	4
Ukraine	3	1	0	2	9	13	2
Japan	3	0	0	3	6	20	0

Group B

	GP	W	T	L	GF	GA	P
Russia	3	3	0	0	14	5	6
Switzerland	3	2	0	1	9	7	4
Denmark	3	1	0	2	8	14	2
United States	3	0	0	3	4	9	0

Group C

	GP	W	T	L	GF	GA	P
Canada	3	3	0	0	12	2	6
Sweden	3	2	0	1	6	5	4
Latvia	3	1	0	2	6	9	2
Belarus	3	0	0	3	1	9	0

Group D

	GP	W	T	L	GF	GA	P
Czech Republic	3	3	0	0	15	4	6
Finland	3	2	0	1	18	3	4
Austria	3	1	0	2	8	15	2
Slovenia	3	0	0	3	4	23	0

Relegation Round
Group G

	GP	W	T	L	GF	GA	P
United States	3	3	0	0	19	5	6
Belarus	3	2	0	1	9	8	4
Slovenia	3	0	1	2	8	14	1
Japan	3	0	1	2	5	14	1

Qualification Round
Group E

	GP	W	T	L	GF	GA	P
Slovakia	5	4	1	0	27	9	9
Czech Republic	5	4	1	0	22	7	9
Finland	5	2	1	2	18	10	5
Germany	5	2	1	2	11	11	5
Austria	5	1	0	4	9	27	2
Ukraine	5	0	0	5	8	31	0

Group F

	GP	W	T	L	GF	GA	P
Canada	5	4	1	0	18	6	9
Sweden	5	4	0	1	20	9	8
Russia	5	2	0	3	16	14	4
Switzerland	5	2	0	3	14	16	4
Latvia	5	2	0	3	10	16	4
Denmark	5	0	1	4	8	25	1

Quarter-finals
May 7	Canada 3	Germany 2 (OT)
May 7	Slovakia 3	Switzerland 1
May 7	Czech Republic 3	Russia 0
May 7	Sweden 6	Finland 5

Semi-finals
May 9	Canada 8	Czech Republic 4
May 9	Sweden 4	Slovakia 1

Bronze Medal Game
May 10	Slovakia 4	Czech Republic 2

Gold Medal Game
May 11	Canada 3	Sweden 2 (OT)

68th WORLD CHAMPIONSHIP
April 24-May 9, 2004
Prague/Ostrava, Czech Republic

FINAL PLACING
1. Canada
2. Sweden
3. United States
4. Slovakia
5. Czech Republic
6. Finland
7. Latvia
8. Switzerland
9. Germany
10. Russia
11. Austria
12. Denmark
13. Kazakhstan
14. Ukraine
15. Japan
16. France

FINAL STANDINGS
Group A

	GP	W	T	L	GF	GA	P
Czech Republic	3	3	0	0	15	2	6
Latvia	3	1	1	1	5	5	3
Germany	3	1	1	1	6	8	3
Kazakhstan	3	0	0	3	3	14	0

Group B

	GP	W	T	L	GF	GA	P
Slovakia	3	2	1	0	10	5	5
Finland	3	2	0	1	11	8	4
United States	3	1	1	1	12	8	3
Ukraine	3	0	0	3	2	14	0

Group C

	GP	W	T	L	GF	GA	P
Sweden	3	3	0	0	13	4	6
Russia	3	2	0	1	14	6	4
Denmark	3	1	0	2	7	14	2
Japan	3	0	0	3	5	15	0

Group D

	GP	W	T	L	GF	GA	P
Canada	3	2	1	0	8	3	5
Austria	3	1	2	0	12	6	4
Switzerland	3	1	1	1	11	7	3
France	3	0	0	3	0	15	0

Relegation Round

	GP	W	T	L	GF	GA	P
Kazakhstan	3	2	1	0	12	5	5
Ukraine	3	1	2	0	10	6	4
Japan	3	0	2	1	7	9	2
France	3	0	1	2	4	13	1

Qualifying Round
Group E

	GP	W	T	L	GF	GA	P
Czech Republic	5	5	0	0	19	5	10
Canada	5	3	1	1	15	10	7
Latvia	5	1	2	2	8	9	4
Switzerland	5	1	2	2	8	11	4
Germany	5	1	1	3	6	14	3
Austria	5	0	2	3	9	16	2

Group F

	GP	W	T	L	GF	GA	P
Slovakia	5	3	2	0	18	5	8
Sweden	5	3	2	0	12	5	8
Finland	5	3	1	1	17	8	7
United States	5	2	1	2	17	15	5
Russia	5	1	0	4	10	14	2
Denmark	5	0	0	5	6	33	0

Quarter-finals
May 5	Sweden 4	Latvia 1	
May 5	United States 3	Czech Republic 2 (OT/SO)	
May 6	Canada 5	Finland 4 (OT)	
May 6	Slovakia 3	Switzerland 1	

Semi-finals
May 8	Canada 2	Slovakia 1	
May 8	Sweden 3	United States 2	

Bronze Medal Game
May 9	United States 1	Slovakia 0 (OT/SO)

Gold Medal Game
May 9	Canada 5	Sweden 3

69th WORLD CHAMPIONSHIP
April 30-May 15, 2005
Vienna/Innsbruck, Austria

FINAL PLACING
1. Czech Republic	9. Latvia
2. Canada	10. Belarus
3. Russia	11. Ukraine
4. Sweden	12. Kazakhstan
5. Slovakia	13. Slovenia
6. United States	14. Denmark
7. Finland	15. Germany
8. Switzerland	16. Austria

FINAL STANDINGS
Group A
	GP	W	T	L	GF	GA	P
Slovakia	3	2	1	0	13	5	5
Russia	3	2	1	0	9	5	5
Belarus	3	1	0	2	6	4	2
Austria	3	0	0	3	3	17	0

Group B
	GP	W	T	L	GF	GA	P
Canada	3	3	0	0	17	5	6
United States	3	2	0	1	11	4	4
Latvia	3	1	0	2	8	10	2
Slovenia	3	0	0	3	1	18	0

Group C
	GP	W	T	L	GF	GA	P
Sweden	3	3	0	0	15	3	6
Finland	3	2	0	1	7	7	4
Ukraine	3	1	0	2	5	8	2
Denmark	3	0	0	3	2	11	0

Group D
	GP	W	T	L	GF	GA	P
Czech Republic	3	3	0	0	6	1	6
Switzerland	3	2	0	1	8	5	4
Kazakhstan	3	1	0	2	3	4	2
Germany	3	0	0	3	2	9	0

Relegation Round
	GP	W	T	L	GF	GA	P
Slovenia	3	2	0	1	11	14	4
Denmark	3	2	0	1	10	9	4
Germany	3	1	1	1	13	6	3
Austria	3	0	1	2	7	12	1

Qualifying Round
Group E
	GP	W	T	L	GF	GA	P
Russia	5	3	2	0	13	8	8
Czech Republic	5	4	0	1	15	5	8
Slovakia	5	3	1	1	12	11	7
Switzerland	5	2	1	2	9	10	5
Belarus	5	1	0	4	4	11	2
Kazakhstan	5	0	0	5	3	11	0

Group F
	GP	W	T	L	GF	GA	P
Sweden	5	4	0	1	23	13	8
Canada	5	3	1	1	18	14	7
United States	5	2	2	1	14	10	6
Finland	5	1	3	1	12	13	5
Latvia	5	1	1	3	9	18	3
Ukraine	5	0	1	4	5	13	1

Quarter-finals
May 12	Czech Republic 3	United States 2 (OT/SO)	
May 12	Canada 5	Slovakia 4	
May 12	Russia 4	Finland 3 (OT/SO)	
May 12	Sweden 2	Switzerland 1	

Semi-finals
May 14	Canada 4	Russia 3	
May 14	Czech Republic 3	Sweden 2 (OT)	

Bronze Medal Game
May 15	Russia 6	Sweden 3

Gold Medal Game
May 15	Czech Republic 3	Canada 0

20th OLYMPIC WINTER GAMES
February 15-26, 2006
Turin, Italy

FINAL PLACING
1. Sweden	7. Canada
2. Finland	8. United States
3. Czech Republic	9. Kazakhstan
4. Russia	10. Germany
5. Slovakia	11. Italy
6. Switzerland	12. Latvia

FINAL STANDINGS
Group A
	GP	W	T	L	GF	GA	P
Finland	5	5	0	0	19	2	10
Switzerland	5	2	2	1	10	12	6
Canada	5	3	0	2	15	9	6
Czech Republic	5	2	0	3	14	12	4
Germany	5	0	2	3	7	16	2
Italy	5	0	2	3	9	23	2

Group B
	GP	W	T	L	GF	GA	P
Slovakia	5	5	0	0	18	8	10
Russia	5	4	0	1	23	11	8
Sweden	5	3	0	2	15	12	6
United States	5	1	1	3	13	13	3
Kazakhstan	5	1	0	4	9	16	2
Latvia	5	0	1	4	11	29	1

Quarter-finals
February 22	Sweden 6	Switzerland 2	
February 22	Finland 4	United States 3	
February 22	Russia 2	Canada 0	
February 22	Czech Republic 3	Slovakia 1	

Semi-finals
February 24	Sweden 7	Czech Republic 3	
February 22	Finland 4	Russia 0	

Bronze Medal Game
February 25	Czech Republic 3	Russia 0

Gold Medal Game
February 26	Sweden 3	Finland 2

70th WORLD CHAMPIONSHIP
May 5-21, 2006
Riga, Latvia

FINAL PLACING
1. Sweden	9. Switzerland
2. Czech Republic	10. Latvia
3. Finland	11. Norway
4. Canada	12. Ukraine
5. Russia	13. Denmark
6. Belarus	14. Italy
7. United States	15. Kazakhstan
8. Slovakia	16. Slovenia

FINAL STANDINGS
Preliminary Round
Group A
	GP	W	T	L	GF	GA	P
Finland	3	2	1	0	13	6	5
Czech Republic	3	1	2	0	9	8	4
Latvia	3	1	1	1	6	7	3
Slovenia	3	0	0	3	8	15	0

Group B
	GP	W	T	L	GF	GA	P
Sweden	3	2	1	0	12	6	5
Switzerland	3	2	1	0	9	6	5
Ukraine	3	1	0	2	7	8	2
Italy	3	0	0	3	3	11	0

Group C
	GP	W	T	L	GF	GA	P
Russia	3	3	0	0	17	6	6
Belarus	3	2	0	1	11	5	4
Slovakia	3	1	0	2	10	6	2
Kazakhstan	3	0	0	3	2	23	0

Group D
	GP	W	T	L	GF	GA	P
Canada	3	3	0	0	14	5	6
United States	3	2	0	1	7	3	4
Norway	3	1	0	2	8	13	2
Denmark	3	0	0	3	6	14	0

Qualifying Round
Group E
	GP	W	T	L	GF	GA	P
Canada	5	4	0	1	28	10	8
Finland	5	3	1	1	17	7	7
United States	5	3	0	2	11	10	6
Czech Republic	5	2	2	1	14	12	6
Latvia	5	1	1	3	7	23	3
Norway	5	0	0	5	5	20	0

Group F
	GP	W	T	L	GF	GA	P
Russia	5	4	1	0	22	11	9
Sweden	5	2	2	1	17	15	6
Belarus	5	3	0	2	16	10	6
Slovakia	5	2	1	2	19	10	5
Switzerland	5	1	2	2	12	15	4
Ukraine	5	0	0	5	4	29	0

Relegation Round

	GP	W	T	L	GF	GA	P
Denmark	3	2	1	0	11	5	5
Italy	3	1	1	1	6	10	3
Kazakhstan	3	1	0	2	9	6	2
Slovenia	3	0	2	1	6	11	2

Quarter-finals
May 17	Sweden 6	United States 0
May 17	Canada 4	Slovakia 1
May 18	Russia 4	Czech Republic 3 (OT)
May 18	Finland 4	Belarus 0

Semi-finals
May 20	Czech Republic 3	Finland 1
May 20	Sweden 5	Canada 4

Bronze Medal Game
May 21	Canada 0	Finland 5

Gold Medal Game
May 21	Sweden 4	Czech Republic 0

71st WORLD CHAMPIONSHIP
April 24-May 10, 2007
Moscow/Mytischi, Russia

FINAL PLACING

1. Canada	9. Germany
2. Finland	10. Denmark
3. Russia	11. Belarus
4. Sweden	12. Italy
5. United States	13. Latvia
6. Slovakia	14. Norway
7. Czech Republic	15. Austria
8. Switzerland	16. Ukraine

FINAL STANDINGS
Preliminary Round
Group A

	GP	W	OTW	OTL	L	GF	GA	P
Sweden	3	3	0	0	0	21	3	9
Switzerland	3	2	0	0	1	4	8	6
Italy	3	0	1	0	2	6	12	2
Latvia	3	0	0	1	2	6	14	1

Group B

	GP	W	OTW	OTL	L	GF	GA	P
Czech Republic	3	3	0	0	0	18	6	9
USA	3	2	0	0	1	14	7	6
Belarus	3	1	0	0	2	8	15	3
Austria	3	0	0	0	3	5	17	0

Group C

	GP	W	OTW	OTL	L	GF	GA	P
Canada	3	3	0	0	0	12	8	9
Slovakia	3	2	0	0	1	12	6	6
Germany	3	1	0	0	2	8	11	3
Norway	3	0	0	0	3	5	12	0

Group D

	GP	W	OTW	OTL	L	GF	GA	P
Russia	3	3	0	0	0	22	6	9
Finland	3	2	0	0	0	15	7	6
Denmark	3	1	0	0	0	7	18	3
Ukraine	3	0	0	0	0	4	17	0

Group E

	GP	W	OTW	OTL	L	GF	GA	P
Russia	5	5	0	0	0	27	10	15
Sweden	5	4	0	0	1	21	7	12
Finland	5	3	0	0	2	15	8	9
Switzerland	5	2	0	0	3	9	16	6
Denmark	5	1	0	0	4	11	26	3
Italy	5	0	0	0	5	4	20	0

Group F

	GP	W	OTW	OTL	L	GF	GA	P
Canada	5	4	1	0	0	24	15	14
USA	5	3	0	0	2	18	13	9
Slovakia	5	3	0	0	2	18	15	9
Czech Republic	5	2	0	1	2	17	14	7
Germany	5	2	0	0	3	11	16	6
Belarus	5	0	0	0	5	14	29	0

Group G

	GP	W	OTW	OTL	L	GF	GA	P
Latvia	3	2	0	0	1	14	8	6
Norway	3	1	1	0	1	12	9	5
Austria	3	1	0	1	1	11	12	4
Ukraine	3	1	0	0	2	7	15	3

Quarter-finals
May 9	Russia 4	Czech Republic 0
May 9	Sweden 7	Slovakia 4
May 10	Canada 5	Switzerland 1
May 10	Finland 5	USA 4 (OT/SO)

Semi-finals
May 12	Finland 2	Russia 1 (OT)
May 12	Canada 4	Sweden 1

Bronze Medal Game
May 13	Russia 3	Sweden 1

Gold Medal Game
May 13	Canada 4	Finland 2

ALL-TIME
WORLD WOMEN'S CHAMPIONSHIP RESULTS
1st WORLD WOMEN'S CHAMPIONSHIP
March 19-25, 1990
Ottawa, Canada

FINAL PLACING

1. Canada	5. Switzerland
2. United States	6. Norway
3. Finland	7. Germany
4. Sweden	8. Japan

FINAL STANDINGS
Group A

	GP	W	T	L	GF	GA	P
Canada	3	3	0	0	50	1	6
Sweden	3	2	0	1	19	19	4
Germany	3	1	0	2	4	25	2
Japan	3	0	0	3	5	33	0

Group B

	GP	W	T	L	GF	GA	P
United States	3	3	0	0	38	7	6
Finland	3	2	0	1	24	6	4
Switzerland	3	1	0	2	11	29	2
Norway	3	0	0	3	4	35	0

Semi-finals
March 24	United States 10	Sweden 3
March 24	Canada 6	Finland 5

Bronze Medal Game
March 25	Finland 6	Sweden 3

Gold Medal Game
March 25	Canada 5	United States 2

2nd WORLD WOMEN'S CHAMPIONSHIP
April 20-26, 1992
Tampere, Finland

FINAL PLACING

1. Canada	5. China
2. United States	6. Norway
3. Finland	7. Denmark
4. Sweden	8. Switzerland

FINAL STANDINGS
Group A

	GP	W	T	L	GF	GA	P
Canada	3	3	0	0	24	1	6
Sweden	3	2	0	1	11	9	4
China	3	1	0	2	7	16	2
Denmark	3	0	0	3	3	19	0

Group B

	GP	W	T	L	GF	GA	P
United States	3	3	0	0	31	4	6
Finland	3	2	0	1	27	9	4
Norway	3	1	0	2	8	21	2
Switzerland	3	0	0	3	2	34	0

Semi-finals
April 25	Canada 6	Finland 2
April 25	United States 6	Sweden 4

Bronze Medal Game
April 26	Finland 5	Sweden 4 (OT)

Gold Medal Game
April 26	Canada 8	United States 0

3rd WORLD WOMEN'S CHAMPIONSHIP
April 11-17, 1994
Lake Placid, United States

FINAL PLACING

1. Canada	5. Sweden
2. United States	6. Norway
3. Finland	7. Switzerland
4. China	8. Germany

FINAL STANDINGS
Group A

	GP	W	T	L	GF	GA	P
Canada	3	3	0	0	27	3	6
China	3	1	1	1	13	12	3
Sweden	3	1	1	1	9	13	3
Norway	3	0	0	3	2	23	0

Group B

	GP	W	T	L	GF	GA	P
United States	3	3	0	0	24	1	6
Finland	3	2	0	1	31	3	4
Switzerland	3	1	0	2	2	20	2
Germany	3	0	0	3	2	35	0

Semi-finals

| April 15 | Canada 4 | Finland 1 |
| April 15 | United States 14 | China 3 |

Bronze Medal Game

| April 17 | Finland 8 | China 1 |

Gold Medal Game

| April 17 | Canada 6 | United States 3 |

4th WORLD WOMEN'S CHAMPIONSHIP
March 31-April 6, 1997
Kitchener, Canada

FINAL PLACING

1. Canada
2. United States
3. Finland
4. China
5. Sweden
6. Russia
7. Switzerland
8. Norway

FINAL STANDINGS

Group A

	GP	W	T	L	GF	GA	P
Canada	3	3	0	0	22	2	6
China	3	2	0	1	18	12	4
Russia	3	0	1	2	6	18	1
Switzerland	3	0	1	2	6	20	1

Group B

	GP	W	T	L	GF	GA	P
United States	3	2	1	0	20	3	5
Finland	3	2	1	0	18	3	5
Sweden	3	0	1	2	2	17	1
Norway	3	0	1	2	2	19	1

Semi-finals

| April 5 | Canada 2 | Finland 1 |
| April 5 | United States 6 | China 0 |

Bronze Medal Game

| April 6 | Finland 3 | China 0 |

Gold Medal Game

| April 6 | Canada 4 | United States 3 (OT) |

18th OLYMPIC WINTER GAMES
February 7-22, 1998
Nagano, Japan

FINAL PLACING

1. United States
2. Canada
3. Finland
4. China
5. Sweden
6. Japan

FINAL STANDINGS

	GP	W	T	L	GF	GA	P
United States	5	5	0	0	33	7	10
Canada	5	4	0	1	28	12	8
Finland	5	3	0	2	27	10	6
China	5	2	0	3	10	15	4
Sweden	5	1	0	4	10	21	2
Japan	5	0	0	5	2	45	0

Bronze Medal Game

| February 17 | Finland 4 | China 1 |

Gold Medal Game

| February 17 | United States 3 | Canada 1 |

5th WORLD WOMEN'S CHAMPIONSHIP
March 8-14, 1999
Espoo, Finland

FINAL PLACING

1. Canada
2. United States
3. Finland
4. Sweden
5. China
6. Russia
7. Germany
8. Switzerland

FINAL STANDINGS

Group A

	GP	W	T	L	GF	GA	P
United States	3	3	0	0	27	2	6
Sweden	3	2	0	1	10	12	4
China	3	1	0	2	4	11	2
Russia	3	0	0	3	4	20	0

Group B

	GP	W	T	L	GF	GA	P
Canada	3	3	0	0	24	0	6
Finland	3	2	0	1	16	1	4
Germany	3	1	0	2	5	26	2
Switzerland	3	0	0	3	4	22	0

Semi-finals

| March 13 | Canada 4 | Sweden 1 |
| March 13 | United States 3 | Finland 1 |

Bronze Medal Game

| March 14 | Finland 8 | Sweden 2 |

Gold Medal Game

| March 14 | Canada 3 | United States 1 |

6th WORLD WOMEN'S CHAMPIONSHIP
April 3-9, 2000
Mississauga, Canada

FINAL PLACING

1. Canada
2. United States
3. Finland
4. Sweden
5. Russia
6. China
7. Germany
8. Japan

FINAL STANDINGS

Group A

	GP	W	T	L	GF	GA	P
Canada	3	3	0	0	21	1	6
Sweden	3	1	1	1	11	5	3
China	3	1	1	1	5	9	3
Japan	3	0	0	3	0	22	0

Group B

	GP	W	T	L	GF	GA	P
United States	3	3	0	0	35	4	6
Finland	3	2	0	1	14	6	4
Russia	3	1	0	2	8	24	2
Germany	3	0	0	3	4	27	0

Semi Finals

| April 8 | Canada 3 | Finland 2 |
| April 8 | United States 7 | Sweden 1 |

Bronze Medal Game

| April 9 | Finland 7 | Sweden 1 |

Gold Medal Game

| April 9 | Canada 3 | United States 2 (OT) |

7th WORLD WOMEN'S CHAMPIONSHIP
April 2-8, 2001
Minneapolis, United States

FINAL PLACING

1. Canada
2. United States
3. Russia
4. Finland
5. Sweden
6. Germany
7. China
8. Kazakhstan

FINAL STANDINGS

Group A

	GP	W	T	L	GF	GA	P
Canada	3	3	0	0	29	1	6
Russia	3	2	0	1	12	7	4
Sweden	3	1	0	2	3	17	2
Kazakhstan	3	0	0	3	3	22	0

Group B

	GP	W	T	L	GF	GA	P
United States	3	3	0	0	35	0	6
Finland	3	2	0	1	12	17	4
China	3	0	1	2	6	20	1
Germany	3	0	1	2	2	18	1

Semi Finals

| April 7 | Canada 8 | Finland 0 |
| April 7 | United States 6 | Russia 1 |

Bronze Medal Game

| April 8 | Russia 2 | Finland 1 |

Gold Medal Game

| April 8 | Canada 3 | United States 2 |

19th OLYMPIC WINTER GAMES
February 9-24, 2002
Salt Lake City, United States

FINAL PLACING

1. Canada
2. United States
3. Sweden
4. Finland
5. Russia
6. Germany
7. China
8. Kazakhstan

FINAL STANDINGS

Group A

	GP	W	T	L	GF	GA	P
Canada	3	3	0	0	25	0	6
Sweden	3	2	0	1	10	13	4
Russia	3	1	0	2	6	11	2
Kazakhstan	3	0	0	3	1	18	0

Group B

	GP	W	T	L	GF	GA	P
United States	3	3	0	0	27	1	6
Finland	3	2	0	1	7	6	4
Germany	3	0	1	2	6	18	1
China	3	0	1	2	6	21	1

Semi-finals

| February 19 | Canada 7 | Finland 3 |
| February 19 | United States 4 | Sweden 0 |

Bronze Medal Game

| February 21 | Sweden 2 | Finland 1 |

Gold Medal Game

| February 21 | Canada 3 | United States 2 |

8ᵗʰ WORLD WOMEN'S CHAMPIONSHIP
April 3-9, 2003
Beijing, China

CANCELLED BECAUSE OF SARS

8ᵗʰ WORLD WOMEN'S CHAMPIONSHIP
March 30-April 6, 2004
Halifax, Canada

FINAL PLACING
1. Canada
2. United States
3. Finland
4. Sweden
5. Russia
6. Germany
7. China
8. Switzerland
9. Japan

FINAL STANDINGS
Group A

	GP	W	T	L	GF	GA	P
Canada	2	2	0	0	24	0	4
Germany	2	1	0	1	4	15	2
China	2	0	0	2	2	15	0

Group B

	GP	W	T	L	GF	GA	P
United States	2	2	0	0	17	1	4
Russia	2	1	0	1	2	9	2
Switzerland	2	0	0	2	2	11	0

Group C

	GP	W	T	L	GF	GA	P
Sweden	2	1	1	0	10	4	3
Finland	2	1	1	0	3	2	3
Japan	2	0	0	2	2	9	0

Group D

	GP	W	T	L	GF	GA	P
United States	2	2	0	0	12	3	4
Canada	2	1	0	1	8	4	2
Sweden	2	0	0	2	3	16	0

Group E

	GP	W	T	L	GF	GA	P
Finland	2	2	0	0	6	1	4
Russia	2	1	0	1	5	4	2
Germany	2	0	0	2	2	8	0

Group F

	GP	W	T	L	GF	GA	P
China	2	2	0	0	11	5	4
Switzerland	2	1	0	1	7	6	2
Japan	2	0	0	2	2	9	0

Bronze Medal Game
April 6 Halifax	Finland 3	Sweden 2

Gold Medal Game
April 6 Halifax	Canada 2	United States 0

9ᵗʰ WORLD WOMEN'S CHAMPIONSHIP
April 2-9, 2005
Linköping/Norrköping, Sweden

FINAL PLACING
1. United States
2. Canada
3. Sweden
4. Finland
5. Germany
6. China
7. Kazakhstan
8. Russia

FINAL STANDINGS
Group A

	GP	W	T	L	GF	GA	P
Canada	3	3	0	0	35	0	6
Sweden	3	2	0	1	8	12	4
Russia	3	0	1	2	3	17	1
Kazakhstan	3	0	1	2	3	20	1

Group B

	GP	W	T	L	GF	GA	P
United States	3	3	0	0	23	3	6
Finland	3	2	0	1	11	10	4
China	3	0	1	2	6	16	1
Germany	3	0	1	2	4	15	1

Semi-finals
April 8	Canada 3	Finland 0
April 8	United States 4	Sweden 1

Bronze Medal Game
April 9	Sweden 5	Finland 2

Gold Medal Game
April 9	United States 1	Canada 0 (OT/SO)

20ᵗʰ OLYMPIC WINTER GAMES
February 10-26, 2006
Turin, Italy

FINAL PLACING
1. Canada
2. Sweden
3. United States
4. Finland
5. Germany
6. Russia
7. Switzerland
8. Italy

Final Standings
Group A

	GP	W	T	L	GF	GA	P
Canada	3	3	0	0	36	1	6
Sweden	3	2	0	1	15	9	4
Russia	3	1	0	2	6	16	2
Italy	3	0	0	3	1	32	0

Group B

	GP	W	T	L	GF	GA	P
United States	3	3	0	0	18	3	6
Finland	3	2	0	1	10	7	4
Germany	3	1	0	2	2	9	2
Switzerland	3	0	0	3	1	12	0

Semi-finals
February 17	Canada 6	Finland 0
February 17	Sweden 3	United States 2 (OT/SO)

Bronze Medal Game
February 20	United States 4	Finland 0

Gold Medal Game
February 20	Canada 4	Sweden 1

10ᵗʰ WORLD WOMEN'S CHAMPIONSHIP
April 3-10, 2007
Winnipeg/Selkirk, Canada

FINAL PLACINGS
1. Canada
2. United States
3. Sweden
4. Finland
5. Switzerland
6. China
7. Russia
8. Germany
9. Kazakhstan

RESULTS & FINAL STANDINGS
Group A

	GP	W	OTW	OTL	L	GF	GA	P
USA	2	2	0	0	0	18	1	6
China	2	1	0	0	1	8	9	3
Kazakhstan	2	0	0	0	2	0	16	0

Group B

	GP	W	OTW	OTL	L	GF	GA	P
Canada	2	2	0	0	0	17	0	6
Switzerland	2	1	0	0	1	9	3	3
Germany	2	0	0	0	2	0	9	0

Group C

	GP	W	OTW	OTL	L	GF	GA	P
Finland	2	1	1	0	0	5	0	5
Sweden	2	1	0	1	0	3	3	4
Russia	2	0	0	0	2	2	7	0

Group D

	GP	W	OTW	OTL	L	GF	GA	P
Canada	2	1	1	0	0	10	4	5
USA	2	1	0	1	0	8	5	4
Finland	2	0	0	0	2	0	9	0

Group E

	GP	W	OTW	OTL	L	GF	GA	P
Sweden	2	2	0	0	0	16	2	6
Switzerland	2	1	0	0	1	5	5	3
China	2	0	0	0	2	3	17	0

Group F

	GP	W	OTW	OTL	L	GF	GA	P
Russia	2	2	0	0	0	11	1	6
Germany	2	1	0	0	1	4	4	3
Kazakhstan	2	0	0	0	2	0	10	0

Bronze Medal Game
April 10	Sweden 1	Finland 0

Gold Medal Game
April 10	Canada 5	USA 1

NON-IIHF INTERNATIONAL EVENTS
1972 SUMMIT SERIES
September 2-28, 1972
Canada/Soviet Union

FINAL STANDINGS

	GP	W	T	L	GF	GA
Canada	8	4	1	3	31	32
Soviet Union	8	3	1	4	32	31

Game 1 Montreal
September 2	Soviet Union 7	Canada 3

Game 2 Toronto
September 4	Canada 4	Soviet Union 1

Game 3 Winnipeg
September 6	Canada 4	Soviet Union 4

Game 4 Vancouver
September 8	Soviet Union 5	Canada 3

Game 5 Moscow
September 22	Soviet Union 5	Canada 4

Game 6 Moscow
September 24   Canada 3   Soviet Union 2

Game 7 Moscow
September 26   Canada 4   Soviet Union 3

Game 8 Moscow
September 28   Canada 6   Soviet Union 5

1976 CANADA CUP
September 2-15, 1976
Canada

FINAL STANDINGS

	GP	W	T	L	GF	GA	P
Canada	5	4	0	1	22	6	8
Czechoslovakia	5	3	1	1	19	9	7
Soviet Union	5	2	1	2	23	14	5
Sweden	5	2	1	2	16	18	5
United States	5	1	1	3	14	21	3
Finland	5	1	0	4	16	42	2

Finals (best two-of-three)
September 13   Canada 6   Czechoslovakia 0
September 15   Canada 5   Czechoslovakia 4 (OT)

1981 CANADA CUP
September 1-13, 1981
Canada

FINAL STANDINGS

	GP	W	T	L	GF	GA	P
Canada	5	4	1	0	32	13	9
Soviet Union	5	3	1	1	20	13	7
Czechoslovakia	5	2	2	1	21	13	6
United States	5	2	1	2	17	19	5
Sweden	5	1	0	4	13	20	2
Finland	5	0	1	4	6	31	1

Semi-finals
September 11   Canada 4   United States 1
September 11   Soviet Union 4   Czechoslovakia 1

Finals
September 13   Soviet Union 8   Canada 1

1984 CANADA CUP
September 1-18, 1984
Canada

FINAL STANDINGS

	GP	W	T	L	GF	GA	P
Soviet Union	5	5	0	0	22	7	10
United States	5	3	1	1	21	13	7
Sweden	5	3	0	2	15	16	6
Canada	5	2	1	2	23	18	5
West Germany	5	0	1	4	13	29	1
Czechoslovakia	5	0	1	4	10	21	1

Semi-finals
September 12   Sweden 9   United States 2
September 13   Canada 3   Soviet Union 2 (OT)

Finals (best two-of-three)
September 16   Canada 5   Sweden 2
September 18   Canada 6   Sweden 5

1987 CANADA CUP
August 28-September 15, 1987
Canada

FINAL STANDINGS

	GP	W	T	L	GF	GA	P
Canada	5	3	2	0	19	13	8
Soviet Union	5	3	1	1	22	13	7
Sweden	5	3	0	2	17	14	6
Czechoslovakia	5	2	1	2	12	15	5
United States	5	2	0	3	13	14	4
Finland	5	0	0	5	9	23	0

Semi-finals
September 8   Soviet Union 4   Sweden 2
September 9   Canada 5   Czechoslovakia 3

Finals (best two-of-three)
September 11   Soviet Union 6   Canada 5 (OT)
September 13   Canada 6   Soviet Union 5 (OT)
September 15   Canada 6   Soviet Union 5

1991 CANADA CUP
August 31-September 16, 1991
Canada

FINAL STANDINGS

	GP	W	T	L	GF	GA	P
Canada	5	3	2	0	21	11	8
United States	5	4	0	1	19	15	8
Finland	5	2	1	2	10	13	5
Sweden	5	2	0	3	13	17	4
Soviet Union	5	1	1	3	14	14	3
Czechoslovakia	5	1	0	4	11	18	2

Semi-finals
September 11   United States 7   Finland 3
September 12   Canada 4   Sweden 0

Finals (best two-of-three)
September 14   Canada 4   United States 1
September 16   Canada 4   United States 2

1996 WORLD CUP OF HOCKEY
August 26-September 14, 1996
Canada/Europe/United States

FINAL STANDINGS
North American Pool

	GP	W	T	L	GF	GA	P
United States	3	3	0	0	19	8	6
Canada	3	2	0	1	11	10	4
Russia	3	1	0	2	12	14	2
Slovakia	3	0	0	3	9	19	0

European Pool

	GP	W	L	T	GF	GA	P
Sweden	3	3	0	0	14	3	6
Finland	3	2	0	1	17	11	4
Germany	3	1	0	2	11	15	2
Czech Republic	3	0	0	3	4	17	0

Quarter-finals
September 5   Canada 4   Germany 1
September 6   Russia 5   Finland 0

Semi-finals
September 7   Canada 3   Sweden 2 (OT)
September 8   United States 5   Russia 2

Finals (best two-of-three)
September 10   Canada 4   United States 3 (OT)
September 12   United States 5   Canada 2
September 14   United States 5   Canada 2

2004 WORLD CUP OF HOCKEY
August 30-September 14, 2004
Canada/Europe/United States

PRELIMINARY ROUND STANDINGS
European Pool

	GP	W	T	L	GF	GA	P
Finland	3	2	1	0	11	4	5
Sweden	3	2	1	0	13	9	5
Czech Republic	3	1	0	2	10	10	2
Germany	3	0	0	3	4	15	0

North American Pool

	GP	W	T	L	GF	GA	P
Canada	3	3	0	0	10	3	6
Russia	3	2	0	1	9	6	4
United States	3	1	0	2	5	6	2
Slovakia	3	0	0	3	4	13	0

Quarter-finals
September 6   Finland 2   Germany 1
September 7   Czech Republic 6 Sweden 1
September 7   United States 5   Russia 2
September 8   Canada 5   Slovakia 1

Semi-finals
September 11   Finland 2   United States 1
September 12   Canada 4   Czech Republic 3 (OT)

Finals
September 14   Canada 3   Finland 2

Photo Credits

Contributor's Biographies

EDITORS

Szymon Szemberg is the Director of Communications of the IIHF. He previously covered hockey for the Swedish daily, *Göteborgs-Posten* and has followed the international game since 1968.

Andrew Podnieks is the author of more than 40 books on hockey. He has also produced several media guides for the IIHF and has worked for www.IHWC.net at the World Championships since 2002. (www.andrewpodnieks.com).

Craig Campbell is the Manager, Resource Centre at the Hockey Hall of Fame in Toronto and responsible for maintaining the photo archives from which many photographs in this book are culled.

WRITERS

Lucas Aykroyd has written on the IIHF World Championship since 2000 as the editor of IHWC.NET, and his NHL articles have appeared in various publications in North America and Europe.

Pavel Barta is a Czech hockey writer and historian who has worked both in journalism as well as with media relations for the Czech Ice Hockey Association.

Patrick Houda is a Swedish hockey historian, specializing in the roots of the game and international hockey for the period between the world wars.

Vsevolod Kukushkin is a veteran Russian sportswriter, currently working for the sports daily Sport-Express. He has covered international hockey since the 1960s.

Igor Kuperman is a former hockey journalist from Moscow who later went on to work for the Winnipeg Jets and the Phoenix Coyotes. He is one of the most recognized hockey historians and experts on the international game.

Birger Nordmark is a Swedish hockey historian whose extensive research has shed light on how the game developed from the early 1900s. His particular expertise is the game in small hockey nations.

John Sanful is a freelance writer in New York City who has covered all IIHF World Championships since 2000. He is the author of *Russian Revolution — Exodus to the NHL*.

Klaus Zaugg is the hockey editor of the Swiss newspaper *Blick*. He writes about the game on a daily basis and has covered international hockey since the early 1980s.

For the IIHF

COUNCIL MEMBERS

René Fasel (President)
Miro Subrt (Life-President)
Shoichi Tomita (Vice-President)
Walter Bush (Vice-President)
Kalervo Kummola (Vice-President)
Hans Dobida (Treasurer)
Frederick Meredith
Murray Costello
Alexander Steblin
Ernest Aljancic
Frank Gonzalez
Juraj Siroky
Doris Hogne-Rydheim
Beate Grupp

STAFF as of 2006-2007 season

Horst Lichtner (General Secretary)
Hannes Ederer (Deputy General Secretary)
Dave Fitzpatrick (Sport Director)
Rob van Rijswijk (Director of Event Management)
Kimmo Leinonen (PR & Marketing Director)
Federico Saviozzi (Director of Special Projects)
Konstantin Komissarov (Sport Development Manager, Officiating)
Darryl Easson (Sport Development Manager, Youth Hockey)
Andy Ecker (Event Manager)
Darren Boyko (Hockey Hall of Fame & International Relations)
Szymon Szemberg (Information & Media Relations Manager)
Thomas Freyer (Marketing Manager)
Gion Veraguth (Financial Manager)
Martin Zoellner (IT Manager)
Konstantin Gasilin (IT System Support)
Johanna May (Secretary to the President)
Eslie Dall'Oglio (Assistant)
Veronika Muhlhofer (Assistant)
Jenny Wiedeke (Assistant)
Simone Micheletti (Assistant)
Anna Eskola (Assistant)
Sofia Chatzis (Assistant)
Claire Robinson (Assistant)
Stephanie Kallai (Receptionist)
Slavko Bartulovic (Facility Manager)
Hervé Buttin (Facility Manager)